BUSINESS COMMUNICATION

Business Communication

Shailendra Singh
PhD., M.T.M, DHMCTAN,
Fellow of International Educationist Society

AMAN PUBLICATIONS
NEW DELHI

Published by
Rajiv Jain for Aman Publications
LG-4A, Ganpati Bhawan,
4675-B/21, Ansari Road,
Darya Ganj, Delhi - 110002
PH: 23255012, 23282127
E-mail: sshjbs@yahoo.com

First Published – 2010

ISBN-81-8204-061-2
ISBN-978-81-8204-061-8

SOLE DISTRIBUTOR
JINDAL BOOK SERVICES
LG-4A, Ganpati Bhawan,
4675-B/21, Ansari Road,
Darya Ganj, Delhi - 110002

Jacket Designed by :
S.M. Graphics

Printed by:
Balaji Offset, Delhi, India

Preface

Communications are fundamental to business - some form of communication is at the heart of every business process whether internal or external. How do you communicate? Technology has added to the possibilities of travel by horse or the quill pen, and fuelled an expectation of speed of communication which a century ago would have been unthinkable.

At its most general and abstract, the party line is often declared publicly in the company's mission statement. As you might expect, however, not everyone interprets it in the spirit that head office intends: When three large engineering firms – two from Northern Europe and one from the USA – merged, they invested a lot of time, money and resources in producing the new company's mission statement. At a seminar designed to bring middle management together, the top directors invited delegates to explain how they had disseminated the new core values among their local employees.

Corporate communication is the communication issued by a corporate/organization/body/institute to all its public(s). Publics here can be both internal (employees, stakeholders, i.e. share and stock holders) and external (agencies, channel partners, media, government, industry bodies and institutes, educational institutes and general public). An organization needs to talk the same message to all of its stakeholders, in order to transmit coherence, credibility and ethic. If one of these points is broken, the whole community can make this organization disappear. The Corporate Communication area will help this organization to build its message, combining its vision, mission and values and will also support the organization by communicating its message, activities and practices to all of its stakeholders.

—*Author*

Contents

1

Business Communication: Introduction, Concept and Types

Introduction

Business Communication used to promote a product, service, or organization; relay information within the business; or deal with legal and similar issues. It is also a means of relying between a supply chain, for example the consumer and manufacturer. Business Communication is known simply as "Communications." It encompasses a variety of topics, including Marketing, Branding, Customer relations, Consumer behaviour, Advertising, Public relations, Corporate communication, Community engagement, Research and Measurement, Reputation management, Interpersonal communication, Employee engagement, Online communication, and Event management.

It is closely related to the fields of professional communication and technical communication. In business, the term communications encompasses various channels of communication, including the Internet, Print (Publications), Radio, Television, Ambient media, Outdoor, and Word of mouth. Business Communication can also refer to internal communication. A communications director will typically manage internal communication and craft messages sent to employees.

It is vital that internal communications are managed properly because a poorly crafted or managed message could foster distrust or hostility from employees. Business Communication is a common topic included in the curricula of Masters of Business

Administration (MBA) programmes of many universities. AS well, many community colleges and universities offer degrees in Communications.

Types of Communication

Writing in the business arena is critical. Often times a well-written document can make or break an assignment. It can be the difference between getting an account and not getting it. A customer often makes a decision about an entire company's competence, based on the competence of one letter. This is even more important in the world of electronic communications. A well-written email, even a short one, can say a lot about a company. This is why no matter what field you are thinking of going into; this may be the most important section of the course. A technical writer in a corporation may wear many different hats. They may be expected to produce internal and external memos, as well as corporate publications. They may produce financial papers and human resource documents. They may be in charge of marketing. This could entail a variety of things from copywriting and editing to writing promotions and assisting in external and internal publications.

A technical writer may also produce the technical publications for a corporation. They may produce the manuals for a company's software and other products. A technical writer may also be a corporation's trainer and produce the documents needed to help instruct new employees on how to do their jobs; as well as produce training demonstrations. In most companies a technical writer would only provide some of the above services; however in a small company they may be called on to do most, if not all of them.

As an entry level technical writer you will most likely only be called upon to create written or perhaps web-based communications; or perhaps simply edit the work of others. As times goes on you may find yourself creating pamphlets, newsletters, websites, external reports, internal reports, software documentation etc. Eventually, you may find yourself in charge of a whole myriad of publications. It is important to understand the role of each of the various publications. This will help you determine if this is something you might be interested in, or if you have an aptitude for it. Internal communications are those between people in a corporation, while external communications are those that they put out to the general population etc.

Internal communications have two functions: one can be to inform employees about changes in the corporation's business and another can be to serve as a reminder of that company's purpose. It may also serve a human resources function - to let the employees know of changes to their benefits, etc. Many entry level writers begin by doing internal communications. They will write company newsletters, training materials, report on meetings, and report on happenings outside the corporation that affect the corporation's employees. They may even do Human Resources projects such as reporting on marriages, births, retirement etc. They may also report on business changes such as buy outs or new purchases. External communications are those aimed at people outside the company. These people may be anywhere in the world. A writer will often have to determine what to give his audience by where they are located. What a company reports to a local audience may be quite different than what they report to an international one.

External communications are incredibly important from a public relations point of view. These communications are often the calling card for a corporation; even the littlest detail may effect how the public views the company. A writer has to constantly take into account what image their company wants to put out into the public when they write an external communication. With these two differences in mind. Think of a company that you know intimately and write both an internal memo and an internal technical report. It will help you to read the definitions on pages five and six.

There are three important types of communications a scientific or technical communicator will use, they are written, oral, and visual. It is important to understand the differences and how they compliment each other. There are courses that can help to prepare you to communicate better in each of these styles.

Written communication is obviously that which is recorded either on paper or more than likely a computer drive somewhere. It is important to be able to produce great written communications.

There are many types of courses that can assist in preparing you to get more proficient and confident in your written communications.

Oral Communications are the spoken forms of communication. These are most likely to include interpersonal and public speaking. This is a form of communication that often goes hand in hand...or hand and mouth . . . with written communications. In many jobs as a technical writer you will be expected to give presentations on your communications. Courses to assist you with these skills are listed on page nineteen and include, public speaking, interpersonal communication, intercultural communications, persuasion, forensics and debate.

Visual Communications are being integrated more and more into business every day. These courses are more than likely the ones to use computers and Internet applications.

Information Systems Management

All organisations using ICT, whether in the private or public sector, need someone to oversee their systems. The information systems manager is the person who provides the overall 'vision' as to how ICT is used within the organisation, and also plans the work of other ICT specialists. Many companies contract out this work to a specialist computer consultancy. Job titles vary – information systems manager, network administrator, data processing manager or service delivery manager. The work of information systems managers can involve:

- ensuring the organisation has the right hardware and software
- setting the policy for back-up systems, security and anti-virus protection
- making sure that staff are properly trained
- managing the ICT budget
- keeping up to date with new computing developments
- overseeing the development and maintenance of the organisation's website
- managing how major problems in the ICT systems should be dealt with

- identifying any need for change to the systems, as the organisation itself changes
- setting quality standards
- planning for future ICT developments.

In large organisations, information systems managers may lead a team of staff who each have responsibility for a particular aspect of ICT – such as technical support, security, the organisation's website etc. Security includes making sure that data held electronically is not vulnerable to interference from within or outside the organisation. It also involves making sure that confidential information (about the organisation or personal details of members of the public or staff, for example) is kept securely and can only be accessed by authorised users.

It is an increasingly important area, and opportunities for working in this field are expected to grow. Although there are no set entry requirements, most information systems managers have a degree, or equivalent qualification. Generally a lot of computing experience is required – such as several years in systems analysis work. Time spent as a team leader or supervisor is usually necessary. Managers also need a good understanding of the requirements of the business or organisation.

Database Controller/administrator

Organisations store vast amounts of information on their computers – about their customers or clients, about accounts or stock. The growing amount of stored information means that database controllers are always in demand to manage the storage and retrieval of information. Information can be collected in many different ways; for example, supermarkets use loyalty cards to electronically collect details of their customers' shopping habits. Creating a central database, which can provide the information that the user needs, is a complex matter. The database controller, administrator or manager looks after the database, and:

- ensures the database is accurate and up to date
- makes sure security systems are operating correctly
- supports users of the system – to make sure the systems are easy to access

- makes sure back-up systems are working effectively
- helps to make decisions about long-term storage and archiving
- works closely with the information systems manager.

Opportunities exist in all areas of business and industry and in public services. Database controllers can work for insurers, government departments, catalogue companies, hospitals, banks and telecommunications companies.

Although there are no set entry requirements for a career as a database administrator, new ICT/computing graduates may be sought. For information on qualifications and entry requirements for degree courses etc, see leaflet D 01 in this series. People may enter this area from a business career, but generally a good technical background in systems programming or systems analysis and design is required.

What it Takes

Managing ICT systems calls for:

- a high level of technical knowledge
- a keen business sense
- good communication skills
- problem-solving skills
- excellent management ability
- teamworking skills.

Pay and Prospects

There are no set pay scales. An information systems manager or database administrator may earn anything from Rs. 80,000 on entry to Rs. 2,25,000+ with experience. Salaries depend on the nature and size of the organisation and the individual's experience. It may be necessary to move from one employer to another in order to progress. Systems managers and database administrators may go into other areas of computing, general management, training, journalism or technical writing.

Written Business Communication

Business Communication involves exchange of information within an organizational setup. It is a continuous process. The more the business expands, the greater is the pressure on the business to find more effective means of communication both with the employees and with the society at large. Business communication is both written as well as oral. But written communication is very important aspect of business communication. It is important to fix accountability and responsibility of people in organization. This requires more of written communication (much of paper work). Everything should be communicated in written by the manager to the people in the organization. Written messages can be saved for future references and cannot be denied.

Business Communication is a permanent means of communication and is much easier understanding then oral means of communication. Good written communication contributes to success of an organization. It helps in building goodwill of an organization. Written business communication includes - letters, memoranda, agenda, manuals, reports etc.

1. **Business Letters**: It must have a good appealing layout. The content of the letter should be clear in mind of the writer. The letter must be divided into paragraphs. It must have subject written and should be enclosed in an envelope. It should be surely used for future reference. It should be carefully written as it has an impact on goodwill of the organization. Examples of Business letters are - sales letters, information letters, problem letters etc.
2. Memoranda: Memos are generally short means of written communication within an organization. They are used to convey specific information to the people within an organization.
3. **Reports**: A report is prepared after lot of investigation. Whatever observations are made, an account of them is written in the report. Reports are important for analyzing the performance of the organization. It helps in taking important decisions within an organization.

4. **Agenda**: Agenda is an outline about all the contents of the meeting. It tells what is the purpose of the meeting and where are the participants heading. While designing an agenda one should be very specific. Designing an agenda beforehand helps the people to come prepared for the meeting.

The Globalization of Internal Communication

Translation (or lack thereof) throws a huge wrench into the corporate communications cog. If you don't have people on staff who can do their own translations, it can be trick and quite expensive. And for those who have tried to globalize their communications, you know how challenging it is. Intranets were supposed to be a big help and are in most cases. But if you've ever been part of developing a global intranet. It's a brutal, brutal undertaking. Many are never the same afterward.

Some companies attempt to put out a global newsletter but it's all handled at the top. Very rarely is their local input or authority on content. The corporate messages are key, but so are the local messages. And the integration of the two will determine success. Unfortunately, print is one of the "easy cuts" that companies make when budgets get attacked. We've seen companies have success with using digital signage as a global tool. Not only can the corporate contribute the wide-reaching messages, but the local communicators can also add in their own unique messaging. This helps employees tie what they do to the larger corporate objectives - a challenge for those troubled with employee engagement.

If you're a global communicator, ask yourself if your tools and messages are truly representative of your audience. If you're a local communicator, are your messages reaching "the top" and can you customize the big picture? You're at a prime point to make a huge impact globally. Employees are hungry for information and need to trust the information source. Become the trust adviser to your business and deliver value across borders.

Communication in the Modern Business World

Whatever industry you work in, talk of communication or more importantly a lack of communication is never far away from the mouths of management and workers. This article looks at how modern Two-way Radio is being used to enhance communication at work. Communication takes many forms from face to face to more advanced methods like modern mobile and cell phone technology. The key to successful communication within many businesses is having a good mix of communication methods including team briefings and meetings, emails, teleconferencing and more.

So with the need for businesses to find the best methods of communication for their company Two-way Radios are now being used to further enhance their communication mix. Two-way Radio gives business a reliable, robust and portable way for their staff to stay in touch in many different circumstances. These radios can be used over a wide area and benefit from no call charges which often makes them far more appealing than other portable communication equipment like mobile or cell phones.

Some examples include security staff at licensed premises or sporting venues being able to keep in touch and alert colleagues to disturbances, queues and potential problems. They, therefore, aid not just communication but health and safety as well. Schools, colleges, nurseries and universities are also using Two-way Radios for various members of staff to stay in touch. Teachers on field trips, caretakers, ground workers and teaching assistants whilst organizing sporting events can all now take advantage of the benefits that portable radios can bring. With features including long battery lives, panic alarms and license free communication.

Other businesses where the use of Two-way Radio has greatly enhanced their performance and ability to stay in touch include factories and retailers. The retail sector in particular find the radio technology extremely useful as it allows workers on the shop floor to easily communicate with the distribution team to check stock levels, deliveries and again as in other industries to report accidents and therefore enhance their health and safety practices. The retail sector like many others is now extremely competitive so shops and retail outlets who want to enhance the service they provide customers can use two way radios to further differentiate them from their competitors.

Picture the scenario, you go into a shop and ask a member of staff if they have a particular item in stock. The member of staff disappears what seems like forever only to return with the news that the item is or is not in stock. Compare this to another retailer whose staff carry 2 way radios. You approach them and ask if an item is in stock. They immediately connect the stock room using their 2 way radio and within seconds you find out if the item you are after is available. This is just one of the ways that the retail industry is using two way radio but there are many others. Communication in the business world is vital and modern 2 way radio can now be used by businesses of all types to make sure their staff and customers benefit.

International Business Communication

At its most general and abstract, the party line is often declared publicly in the company's mission statement. As you might expect, however, not everyone interprets it in the spirit that head office intends: When three large engineering firms – two from Northern Europe and one from the USA – merged, they invested a lot of time, money and resources in producing the new company's mission statement. At a seminar designed to bring middle management together, the top directors invited delegates to explain how they had disseminated the new core values among their local employees.

Each of the Northern European countries involved (Germany, Finland, Sweden) had presented the statement to their teams at a series of short meetings held during working hours. The teams had discussed the core values briefly, and that was that. To their embarrassment, very few of the managers on the seminar could remember them in any detail. The Americans, on the other hand, had met regularly, outside working hours, to discuss what the new core values meant to each of them. They had translated the abstract aims into concrete guidelines which they could relate to their daily work. Everyone carried a copy of the statement with them at all times and consulted it regularly.

Each side had been very surprised to hear the other's approach. After a few beers in the bar at the end of the day, one of the Finns leaned across to one of the Americans and said: 'What you said about the mission statement – that was just bullshit for the board, wasn't it?' The American was astonished. 'No', he replied, 'why would you think that?'

It was unthinkable to the Northern Europeans that the Americans could take the mission statement so seriously. Equally, it was unthinkable to the Americans that the Northern Europeans could dismiss it so casually. Of course, the two firms had only recently merged; so these two groups of managers *were bound to be* (couldn't avoid being) influenced by their premerger ways of doing things. But that doesn't explain why there was such a wide gap in their perceptions on this particular issue. It's highly likely that cultural conditioning was also playing a major part here.

Mission statements often say things like:

We believe that the Zoetica brand must represent a positive force in the world. We will act in line with this belief at all times.

or

We believe in the integrity of human beings, and will treat our employees, customers and anyone coming into contact with Zoetica accordingly, inviting them all to be part of the Zoetica family.

These are, of course, honourable sentiments that no reasonable person could object to. The trouble is, they're framed in very abstract terms. But then, of course, they have to be. A company can't make a concrete and meaningful statement of intent and values without losing flexibility. And flexibility is what businesses need if they are to survive. They've got to be able to take decisions quickly, and act upon them right away. They've got to retain absolute flexibility to diversify, downsize, grow, and so on.

The American managers in this situation would probably lean towards the theoretical end of the scale. They took the abstract values expressed in the mission statement very seriously and were prepared to spend their own time discussing them in depth. They had no trouble translating these general theories into concrete, practical guidelines that they could relate to their daily work. If you like using abstract concepts to solve problems, you may well respond to your company's mission statement as positively as these American managers did.

If, on the other hand, you lean towards the empirical end of the scale, you may find it hard to take this kind of abstract theorizing seriously. The Northern European managers here discussed the core values briefly and dismissed them as meaningless. What possible relevance could they have to their daily working lives? We recently asked the German HR manager of a large multinational how she felt about her company's mission statement. She said: 'Well, we have to have one. It's good PR. But, in practical terms, it isn't worth the paper it's written on.' The Northern Europeans would probably share her view. That's why they couldn't even remember in any detail what the mission statement said; and why the Finnish manager was convinced that the American managers' explanation of how they had disseminated the new core values was *just bullshit for the board.*

We're not trying to suggest that all Americans would lean to the left of this scale; nor that all Northern Europeans would fall to the right. But there's no denying that attitudes towards mission statements do vary considerably from culture to culture. And when an empiricist meets a theorist there's considerable scope for misunderstanding. The idea that anyone could take all this abstract theorizing seriously didn't even occur to the Finn, while his American colleague was astonished to learn that there were people in the world who didn't take it seriously.

Working Rhythms

The need to present a united front makes life difficult for everyone: the people like Harvey who are trying to disseminate a party line; and the people like Luc who are on the receiving end. If you work in a subsidiary, you may end up regarding the people from HQ as *corporate seagulls*: they fly in, shit on you from on high, and fly out again. It's hard enough to resist HQ diktats when they are imposed from afar. It's even harder when the corporate seagull builds a nest in your workplace. This is exactly what happened at the Irish production facility of a Swiss multinational:

When the head of the Irish plant resigned, the Swiss decided to parachute in one of their own people. The new Swiss manager's office was very close to the canteen and he was disturbed to note that the Irish employees were going for frequent and extensive coffee breaks. Instead of taking just one 10-minute break in the morning, and one in the afternoon – which was what happened in Switzerland – they seemed to go to the canteen whenever they felt like it, and to sit around laughing and joking with their friends for 20 minutes at a time. The new Swiss manager decided that something would have to be done to stop all this time-wasting. So he made a unilateral decision to install coffee-making equipment in every department; and announced that, in future, the canteen would only open at lunchtime.

The Irish employees were not impressed by the new party line. Far from wasting time under the old regime, they had spent their coffee breaks sharing departmental news, asking advice and generally networking. When this forum was closed down, interdepartmental communication started to deteriorate. It wasn't long before productivity at this, the company's biggest plant, started to go down. The Swiss, of course, are famous for their attachment to time. If you're from a monochronic culture too, you may find that you instinctively do one thing after another, in a linear fashion. And you probably feel that unless each moment is used for a specific purpose, it's wasted. If, on the other hand, you lean towards the polychronic end of the scale, you may well regard time as more elastic, and you could even find yourself doing several things at the same time.

The Swiss Germans (and, indeed, the Germans) tend to plan their time in a very structured and ordered way – and, in this respect, it's their master. As they work out *Die Tagesordnung* (the Daily Order), they will often allot a specific and precise amount of time to each task – including their coffee breaks. So, while the Irish are not particularly polychronic, they certainly lie to the right of the Swiss on this scale. As a result, their working rhythms are more relaxed. That's not to say they get less done than their Swiss counterparts. They just use their time in a different way. And that was probably the underlying cause of this misunderstanding.

But there is a puzzling aspect to this situation. Business hierarchies in both Ireland and Switzerland are relatively flat. And in flat business cultures, bosses tend to consult widely, and subordinates generally feel free to express their own views fairly openly. So why didn't that happen here? Why did the new Swiss manager behave in such an autocratic way? And why didn't his Irish subordinates challenge his decision? Maybe the Swiss guy simply panicked. It's not easy taking over as manager of a foreign subsidiary. When you first arrive in a new country, everything strikes you as very strange. The way people do things seems completely different from the way you do things back home. You can feel so dislocated that you fail to notice the many similarities between where you are and where you come from. What the Swiss manager saw was an undisciplined workforce who seemed to be *blatantly* (very openly) taking advantage of the management's goodwill. While he wouldn't have behaved so autocratically back home, he probably felt it was the only thing he could do under these strange new circumstances.

But what about the Irish? Why didn't someone try to explain how useful the coffee breaks were? Well, perhaps they regarded HQ with suspicion and resentment. People in an overseas subsidiary often do, as you will know if you have ever worked in one. Complaints like: *They have no idea of the conditions over here, and they're not interested; all they ever do is issue instructions; they never ask us what we think* are commonplace. If this was how the Irish employees felt, they would have seen no point in challenging the new boss's diktat. He was just doing what people from HQ had always done: shitting on them from on high.

The lack of communication in this situation had a damaging effect on all concerned: the Irish, the Swiss boss and the company. The moral to this tale is clear: if you are being asked to accept a party line that conflicts with the way you do things in your part of the world, don't just assume that HQ's motives are sinister, or that the sole purpose of the directive is to make your life difficult. Try to find out what's behind it. Ask some questions, and listen to the answers with an open mind. However hard it may be, try for a moment to put yourself in HQ's position. And then, as clearly, calmly and objectively as you can, explain your own position and the impact that the new directive will have on you and your colleagues. This won't guarantee success, of course. But it has to be more productive than keeping quiet and letting things go from bad to worse.

Communication Styles

It's a problem that confronts the corporate seagull all too often. You arrive at the subsidiary, issue your instructions, and then later discover that everyone has completely ignored them: A large French company decided to introduce a new global purchasing policy.

In the past, subsidiaries had sourced many of their supplies locally. In future, they would be expected, where possible, to use the same suppliers as the French parent company. The French purchasing manager visited the subsidiaries one by one to explain the new arrangements. In each case, she presented the facts and figures very clearly, and made sure the purchasing teams were fully aware of the considerable cost savings that would be achieved. She had been expecting a certain amount of resistance from the Japanese subsidiary.

So she wasn't particularly worried by the surprised glances and exhalations of breath that greeted her announcement. Nor was she unduly concerned when one of the team said: 'This will be very difficult for us.' After all, they were bound to say that. The important thing was that no one rejected the proposals. She went home feeling relatively pleased with herself. Six months later, she was surprised to see that the Japanese had not made one single purchase through the new system. She phoned Tokyo to find out what was going on. Her colleague said: 'We made it very clear, when you were here, that we couldn't use this new system.'

It's hard to believe that they were all present at the same meeting, isn't it? So what went wrong here? Were the Japanese being deliberately two-faced and underhand? Did they think that if they pretended to go along with the joint purchasing project to the French woman's face, they could simply ignore it once she had gone back to France? And what about the French woman? Was she being arrogant, or just incredibly obtuse? Well, in all probability, both sides were behaving in what they regarded as a professional and straightforward way. The Japanese thought they had made it perfectly clear that they couldn't source their supplies from France. The French woman was equally sure that the Japanese had no serious objections to the new arrangements. It was just that their understanding of the word *difficult* was not the same.

The Japanese impulse is to preserve harmony. For them, consensus rather than open disagreement or conflict is the name of the game, and their communication style reflects this. In this cultural context the word *difficult*, accompanied by eye and body language that every other Japanese would immediately understand, means: *This is absolutely out of the question. There's no way we can agree to this.* But when the French say *difficult* they mean: *Not easy, but not impossible either.*

Have a look at this pair of statements:

Edward T Hall (the American anthropologist) divides the cultures of the world into low context and high context communicators and a number of cross-cultural experts have adopted his terminology. Low context communicators tend to express themselves in explicit, concrete, unequivocal terms. There's little cultural baggage or 'context' attached to the words they use and you can usually take what they say at face value. If you are, for example, American, German, Scandinavian or Finnish, you will probably fall into this category. And when you're doing business with other low context communicators, you will probably find their communication style reassuringly straightforward and comprehensible. High context communicators, on the other hand, tend to communicate more implicitly. They expect you to be able to interpret what they mean from your knowledge of the cultural values that lie behind the words, what they're actually talking about at the time, their tone of voice and, of course, their eye and body language. Interestingly enough, both the French and the Japanese would fall well to the right of this scale. But, of course, their cultural contexts are different. You may be a high context communicator yourself, but that won't necessarily make it any easier for you to understand a high context communicator from another culture.

It didn't occur to the French woman to check that she had understood her Japanese colleagues correctly. As a result, a lot of time and money was wasted and HQ's relations with their subsidiary were disrupted. If you're a corporate seagull, you can learn from her mistake. Don't take what the people in your subsidiaries say at face value. Watch their body language too. If she had taken notice of those surprised glances and exhalations of breath, the French woman would have realized that her Japanese colleagues weren't prepared to accept her proposals. Making sure you understand exactly what the other person means won't guarantee success. But at least you will know where you stand. In this situation, for example, the Japanese refused to accept the party line because they were worried about quality. If this concern had been brought out into the open, the French could have discussed it objectively with their Japanese partners, and tried to find ways to overcome their concerns.

In *Working rhythms* above, we looked at the difficulties a Swiss manager had when he banned coffee breaks in an Irish plant. The Irish clearly have a more relaxed attitude towards time than the Swiss. And this may well have been one of the reasons the problem arose. But the misunderstanding was most probably compounded by their differing communication styles. The Swiss are low context communicators. In fact, they generally fall to the far left of this scale, while the Irish (along with the British) would lean towards the right. And when a low context communicator meets a higher context communicator, they may both misinterpret the signals the other is sending. When the Swiss guy gave the Irish the bad news about coffee breaks, he probably did so in very frank and explicit terms:

> You are wasting too much time laughing and joking in the canteen when you should be working at your desks. This is completely unacceptable. In future, the canteen will only open at lunchtime. You will find coffee-making equipment in your department. Please remember that you are allowed one 10-minute break in the morning and one in the afternoon.

But this approach would have come across to the Irish as autocratic, impersonal and cold. When we described this situation to Padraig, an Irish business acquaintance of ours from Dublin, he told us that if the Irish have bad news to give, they generally try to *sugar the pill* (sweeten the medicine). He illustrated his point by telling us the following joke:

A tourist approaches two fellows and ask them how far it is to the town. The first fellow assures the tourist it's just two miles down the road. The tourist thanks them and goes off. The second fellow then says: 'Why did you tell him that? Don't you know that it's four miles?' To which his friend replies: 'Sure I know, but the poor man is walking.'

Modern Communications

Communications are fundamental to business - some form of communication is at the heart of every business process whether internal or external. How do you communicate? Technology has added to the possibilities of travel by horse or the quill pen, and fuelled an expectation of speed of communication which a century ago would have been unthinkable.

In this section, we look at the pros and cons of different ways of communicating and give some ideas for finding out more.

- *Face-to-face* is still a valuable tool for imparting and building trust, negotiating, enthusing.
- *Video-conferencing* allows some of the benefits of meeting in person without the travel - especially if the purpose of the meeting is transactional
- *Telephone* - personal but loses the nuance of body expressions - a major part of communication. Voicemail and 'call waiting' have generated enormous revenues although their effectiveness is debatable.
- *Mobile phone* - if a conventional call is to a location, a call to a mobile is to a person. Some people think that the major use of this is as a tool for making calls...
- *Letter* - still an excellent tool for contractual and complex communications, also for drawings.
- *E-mail* - quicker and cheaper than a letter, the biggest danger here is that too few people re-read what has been written before hitting the 'send' button. Also a point of danger for systems - you won't get anthrax but some e-

mails will be as terminal to your office systems if you aren't careful.

- *Fax* - the last 'big thing' before e-mail usurped it; is still an excellent tool for getting pictures sent quickly.
- *Text* - For the worst of all worlds, SMS ("Texting") to a mobile 'phone is high on impact but often low on clarity and personalisation.
- *Computer systems* can talk directly to each other - settling invoices direct between company accounts for instance.
- *Websites* - largely aimed at one-way communications, the Internet has transformed the way that we can get hold of information.
- *WAP phones* - the internet on the move.

It is worth while examining the way your company communicates - are you using the appropriate tool every time? Even if it is the right tool - could you do it more cheaply? As an example - look at telephone bills. Our Sussex Telecom service might help you to find a cheaper tariff - but how many of your calls are between your offices? Can you piggy-back them on your data links?

2

Business Strategy Theory

Strategic Management

Much of what is practised as Strategic Management is based upon an (often implicit) foundation of micro-economics. Indeed a distinct 'new' sub-discipline called 'Business Economics' is steadily evolving where the aim of its contributors is to produce useful insights into the nature of the firm and its competitive environment which in turn inform the practice of Strategic Management. Inevitably it has been the practice thus far to base this Business Economics upon neoclassical thinking rather than the newly emerging evolutionary models of economic systems. Evolutionary economics is essentially concerned with dynamic systems and with behavioural trajectories within such systems.

This is in strong contrast with the neo-classical fixation upon stasis, equilibrium and global rationality (i.e. all-seeing, all-knowing decision makers). Such an approach renders difficult (*inter alia*) the examination of bounded rationality and the development of competitive advantage in an ever changing environment. In this chapter we argue that the emerging evolutionary perspective on the competitive structures in which strategic management is practised has a pivotal role to play in the practice of strategy. In particular we identify specific approaches to strategic management (and particularly competitive strategy) which result from an acceptance of the evolutionary nature of the strategic environment. Further, we identify a number normative Strategic Management responses (complementary to conventional strategic thinking), drawing upon the three essential elements of evolutionary systems (variety generation, fitness testing and retention) to characterise these responses. Today much of what is practised under the rubric of Strategic Management is based upon an (often implicit) foundation of micro-economics.

Inevitably it has been the practice thus far to build this foundation on the received wisdom that is distilled in mainstream/ textbook economic theory. This mainstream economics mimics, partly because of contemporaneity of development and partly through an essential mathematical homology, the methodology of Newtonian mechanics and in consequence much emphasis is placed upon equilibrium configurations of socioeconomic phenomena. Newtonian mechanics is, of course, one of the significant paradigms of modern science and it is fitting that its principles be applied outside of the sphere of physics. However, one may question just how relevant to the world of business such a mechanistic framework of analysis can be; by describing individual agents as being subject to certain immutable laws 'of nature' this approach trivialises the role of human agency in the economic system. Yet business is an activity pursued by human beings and even casual observation suggests that we are not homogeneous automatons; in fact we are a heterogeneous lot and our idiosyncrasies do much to shape business activity in a variety of ways. Economists have recognised this problem for some time and as a result have begun to develop seriously the evolutionary theory of economic systems.

General evolutionary theory is another example of a significant paradigm of modern science. The natural and original domain for evolutionary discussion is in the field of biology where popular writers have brought some of its complex ideas and debates into the public domain. A reading of these two popular authors will reveal that there is more to evolutionary theorising than is captured by the oft used epithet 'the survival of the fittest'. In this chapter we explain the fundamental principles that underpin the evolutionary theory of economics to date and we explore some of the implications of this perspective for what might be called 'business economics', being the nascent branch of economic theory that both informs and is informed by strategic management. Our approach is not exhaustive, but it is unlike other research in the field in the sense that we do not call upon evolutionary theory to explain historical observations but, instead, ask how a firm might best go about creating and nurturing competitive advantage in an explicitly evolutionary world.

The normative rationale of our approach is not something with which economists are entirely comfortable outside of the public policy arena. Indeed, the somewhat staid view of traditional economists is illustrated by the much respected and forthright Fritz Machlup who describes what does and what does not constitute topics of legitimate interest for economics, "We are not primarily interested in businessmen, business decisions, business routine and business reactions; we are interested in firms only because of the effects of their actions and reactions upon production, resource use, incomes, and prices". Opinions in the economics profession towards business policy seem to have softened somewhat and John Kay has done much to push forward the role of economics as a framework for business policy decisions, "Microeconomics has potentially the same role to play in relation to management issues that macroeconomics currently has for political issues."

Because of the ways in which the subject has evolved over the past 100 years, it has conspicuously failed to play that role . . . ". It is appropriate from the points of view both of an economist working in a business environment and of a strategic manager expecting a contribution from economics as a discipline, that we should address how this type of economics might be developed. Here, we take as our point of departure the critique of neoclassical economics and its relevance to management education. In essence, neoclassical approaches to the analysis of firms and industries present problems for business strategists; in particular, the concentration upon the equilibrium positions of economic systems leads to a paucity of advice to strategists in respect of the means of progression to those equilibria. We take as a given that the activity of directing a business is at least as much a matter of determining a development path as it is of judging the desirability of the end-point of that path. In this chapter we work to the definition of business economics as being the study of business activity through the eyes of the economist in order to offer prescriptions and advice to business managers. Given this remit it is obvious that business economics shares common concerns with strategic management and later in this paper we see that the approaches of evolutionary economics raise issues of policy in each of the convenient sub-divisions of strategy into product-based, market-based, industry-based and horizontal strategies. In that all four of these (almost arbitrarily distinguished) sub-divisions are inextricably bound together in their effect, a unified business economics approach is a necessary foundation for the most basic of business decisions about the strategic policy of the firm.

Evolutionary Economics as a Framework for Business Economics

In this section we explore two questions: (1) what are the fundamental features of general evolutionary theory?; (2) what might an evolutionary theory of business economics consist of? We leave the important topic of the manner in which such a theory might inform strategic management until a later section.

Basic Features of Evolutionary Theory

Although the term 'evolutionary' is perhaps best known for its association with Darwinian and Lamarckian biology:

> ". . . much of the appeal of evolutionary language in economics is connected with the broader use of the term, as contrasted with its specific use in biology . . . it seems more fruitful to start with a general notion of evolution, and then examine applications in specific areas - like biology or economics - as special cases."

Evolutionary economics is the application of general evolutionary concepts to economic phenomena. Thus, the broad definition is a useful starting point for the discussion to follow, ". . . evolutionary economics [is] . . . that body of economic theory in which the transformation of already existing structures and the emergence and possible spread of novelties are investigated . . . evolutionary economics is occupied with the "becoming" rather than the "being" aspects of the economy. . . ."

General evolutionary theory is often characterised as being based upon the principles of 'variety', 'selection' and 'heredity' and the focus of attention is upon explaining the process of observed change in a system in terms of the interaction of these three characteristics. In simple terms, if a system is subject to variety or novelty among its elements then only those elements which best fit the environment will survive; the idea being that they are 'selected' according to some criteria of 'fitness' peculiar to that environment. The notion of heredity applies in the sense that those elements which survive continue to display their positive attributes in the following time period (while those attributes which belonged to non-surviving elements die out with them). The use of the term 'heredity' is, perhaps, too overtly biological, since it implies that attributes are passed on from parents to offspring and, in the general economic case where no offspring are produced, there is clearly plenty of scope for confusion. It may be better to think in terms of transmission of attributes through time from one 'incarnation' of the system element to the next 'incarnation'; that is, 'retention'.

Taking the three principles outlined above, evolutionary economists are beginning to articulate insights into several phenomena. In particular, a seminal application and expression of the stated ideas to the context of an evolving industry. Another particularly well worked out and explicit application of the evolutionary principles is in the field of technology policy. Typically, in work of this kind, the basic principles are used to help explain observed phenomena or work out logical consequences in a contextspecific manner. It is a notable feature of these exercises that the principles are applied at several levels of analysis or aggregation. While evolutionary theory is generally perceived to be a theory about the evolution of populations (phylogenetics)1, any population can only evolve if it is made up of heterogeneous units, since it is variety between these units which drives change at the population level. Consequently, the aggregate or population level theory is itself built upon:

> ". . . phylogeny is the complete and ongoing evolution of a population, including changes in its composition and that of the gene pool."

Similarly, we can disaggregate further and explain how individuals evolve by examining the forces which change their individual characteristics. With no obvious guidelines as to which level of analysis we should adopt it will be apparent that there is much scope for confusion here. It may be more helpful to recognise that the fundamental unit of analysis is not the population, nor the individual, but what might broadly be described as 'information' in some form or another. Common to any evolutionary system is the idea that 'information' is retained through time and it is the nature, management and, above all, the propagation of this information which forms the basis of success (life) or failure (death).

Towards an Evolutionary Theory of Business Economics

Our aim in this section is to suggest how we might construct an evolutionary-led approach to business economics. A useful point of departure is to ask how any economic theory of business should be expected to contribute to the understanding of practising managers and those people who formulate business policy within firms.

While some economists may call upon the 'as if' defence of neoclassical methodology. It should be clear that any plausible theory of business will not have much prescriptive power if its conclusions and recommendations are not based upon thinking that attempts to incorporate many of the salient features of the 'real world' of business. This is not a call for highly detailed (conceptual and formal) models which are descriptively accurate in every way; the point about the utility of abstraction as an aid to understanding a more complex reality is well taken, instead it is a point based upon the strong contention that a useful theory of business must incorporate a representation of the processes which the 'real world' counterparts of the model elements follow - only then can useful insights be communicated to management since they are themselves the moulders and shapers of the process being studied. In other words, at the extreme, while a neoclassical maximising equilibrium model may derive a result which is reflected in the 'real world', the fact remains that all it can generate is the result alone.

That is, it does not provide a plausible account of the 'real world' mechanism(s) which generated the result which means that this type of economics is of quite limited utility with respect to helping management understand how their actions and those of others influence the success or otherwise of their firm; a theory which generates a correspondence between modelled outcomes and observed outcomes alone may prove to be a useful tool for predicting outcomes, but it almost certainly little of relevance to say about the essential strategic management agenda items of flexibility, resource and competence husbandry and adaptive competitive strategy under uncertainty. A necessary prerequisite for the development of an evolutionary theory of business economics is an acceptance of the contention that capitalism (more specifically economic competition) is an example of evolutionary struggle. That is, the three features of general evolutionary theory are present in some form and allow us to both describe the system and understand better the detailed workings of the system. This is a key point and it follows, therefore, that the ultimate aim of evolutionary business economics must be to identify systemically derived sources of competitive advantage to a firm in this evolutionary struggle. Importantly, it should be noted that unlike the biological theory of evolution, the focus of attention (in any theory of business) is not upon factors which lead to continued survival of the general species as a collective whole (i.e. the population), but instead it is upon continued survival of one member of the species, namely the firm. That is to say, the theory does not focus upon the continued survival of the industry to which the firm belongs but rather suggests how a firm might best survive given the presence of rivals who are seeking also the patronage of the available 'pool' of consumers. This fundamental difference in focus must be recognised to help avoid confusion.

It should be recognised also, that focusing upon the individual and formulating 'survival strategies' does not necessarily imply that all of these strategies will be based in competitive behaviour. In many instances industry-based strategies having a component of co-operation with rivals and with powerful suppliers may offer the best hope of survival. How might we describe the activity of business? On the face of it 'business' is such a diverse activity that the task seems to be impossibly large, but if we ignore the social externalities created by firms (e.g. status of managers, organisations as a repository of the individual's legacy etc.) then we may note that the economic result of firm activity is the residual profit.

We may take this to mean that the aim of the firm is to make a positive profit, but this is an unnecessarily narrow view (perpetuated by neoclassical economics) which limits the contexts to which the evolutionary theory of business economics can be applied. Consequently, it is preferable to postulate that the aim of a firm is simply to survive the passage of time and note that positive profit generation is one way of achieving this (particularly in the competitive market context). In evolutionary terminology positive profits are an indication that the firm has passed the selection test imposed by the market. The important issue for the firm, therefore, becomes how to go about generating a sustainable source of profits.

At a general level we can state that survival for the firm depends crucially upon owning and developing physical and intangible assets which are of use in the selection environment. For most firms this means owning assets which can be used to meet demands created in the market. By itself, however, ownership of relevant assets is not a sufficient condition to ensure survival because these assets must be employed in such a way that their potential for profit generation is actually realised and, consequently, the size of a firm's profits depends upon how effectively these assets are managed. Theory suggests, then, that one crucial element of successful business activity involves ensuring that the assets of the firm are matched to the selection environment which best suits those assets. In other words, it is crucial to be clear about the type of business the firm is going to be engaged in (as defined by of norm-setting in differentiated markets.

Direct Implications for Strategic Thinking

We now turn our attention to the specifics of the strategic management of the firm and the likely way in which an all-embracing evolutionary theory may be able to assist strategic managers in establishing well-founded policies. We shall do this by examining the ways in which the three components of the evolutionary model (variety, selection and heredity/retention) can contribute to four convenient subdivisions of strategy, namely product-based strategy, market-based strategy, industry-based strategy and horizontal strategy. Two preliminary points need to be made. First, it is accepted that these convenient divisions in no way characterise the product of strategic thinking. Because the extent of a company's strategy is to be viewed as one interconnected whole, it is dangerous in practice to isolate falsely, let us say, actions taken with the aim of developing product differentiation or cost effectiveness without considering the likely effects on market considerations. Perhaps more obviously, the connection between product development and the industry component of strategy (through changed relations with suppliers and partner companies) is clear.

The sub-divisions of strategy adopted here serve merely as convenient ways of beginning to think about the strategic policy of a company. To the extent that they limit our conception of strategy they are bad masters of our decision making process. Second, we observe that just as in biology survival mechanisms are insufficient on their own to explain the actions of an organism, so evolutionary economics alone will not be sufficient to provide all the normative framework for a strategic manager. It is not the aim of this section to sketch the limits of a complete normative framework, but rather to identify likely testable normative issues arising from the acceptance and postulation of an overarching evolutionary economic theory.

Product Strategy Implications

The conception that the firm is a single organism in a population of adapting competing organisms in product strategic terms is a fertile one. The vast and fecund literature on innovation within the firm can then be seen in terms of the need for the individual firm to explore the fitness of mutated replications of its products. This need for replication is distinct from the evolutionary mechanism at the population level. Industry-wide innovation is good for the industry as a whole, and therefore contributory to our strategic context,, but we as strategists are concerned at heart with the future fitness of our company. Coupled with this is the recognition that under an evolutionary model, demand cannot be accurately predicted.

The comfortable rubric of 'matching opportunity and competence, ". . . once each has been accurately identified and its future significance established, [it being] this combination which establishes a company's economic mission and its position in the environment." . . . is an unachievable dream made real only to the extent that the evolutionary characteristics of environment can be suspended or simplified into a predictable and temporary surety. We observe that conventional approaches of core competence and resource-based analysis, while remaining essentially correct as a unifying normative theory require amendment to cope with the need to define these competences not at the core competence- core product level of operationalisation alone, but also at a higher conceptual level, where core competences are to do with management of the (conventional) core competences. Analogous with Argyris's polemic for double loop learning we should seek for a core competence theory which includes the operationalised core competence theory of as a limiting case, adding adaptive competences as a superstructure aimed at ensuring rapid adaptation to the changing economic environment.

Attempting to fit our core competences to existing and conjectured opportunities is insufficient. We need also to appreciate that the husbandry itself of the core competences under assumptions of uncertain demand becomes a core competence at a higher level, since, if we rely on our ability to husband our core competences in the direction of a dimly-seen market opportunity we will reach that opportunity only to find that it has been moved on by the complex interaction of the actors in the evolutionary surroundings. How then are we to approach product strategy? We need a stream of replications of our offerings each with incremental mutations to our existing product position. On that basis we seek a series of trials of the fitness of a variety of products in the market. Some types of companies are in the position of achieving such trialling easily and at low cost.

The symbiosis, for example, between a haute couture house and its prêt-à-porter arm, from the viewpoint of the haute couturier is simply that of conventional innovative theory. Tacit bundles of routines are invoked to generate new highly differentiated products for its localised high ticket market. From the point of view of the prêt-à-porter arm, however, we see the haute couturier almost as a random design generator, producing each season a series of embryonic offerings only loosely related to our previous season's high street fashions. On the basis of the publicity that these haute couture offerings receive we can judge the market reaction of potential customers. While they may not be entirely happy with a completely transparent dress for the office, they may well be prepared to accept the innovation of a lingerie-based outer garment of less extreme characteristics. We see the mechanism of variety, selection in a market and retention of the fitness trial through the routines of the prêt-à-porter arm of the company.

Haute couture is an extreme case. We could also invoke the relationship between a large motor company and its racing division, where the innovative act is perhaps less unfettered, more purposive in nature, but which is nevertheless, from an evolutionary perspective, seen as presenting mutated replications for market trial. Similarly, in an innovative aircraft firm the design process can be interpreted as a response to both predicted demand and unpredicted demand. The difficult management decision here is to determine the balance of effort to be placed in 'blue skies' design as against incremental design development. Expenditure on the latter is posited upon an assumption that the future demand is closely coupled to present demand, an assumption itself closely coupled to neo-classical assumptions of equilibrium. Expenditure on the former is not justified by such assumptions, but provides for the firm a kind of insurance against the uncertainties of the market. To the extent then that evolutionary assumptions are valid in demand prediction there should be an appropriate allocation of resources to blue skies design, but the management dilemma is that the neo-classical models allow only for the prediction of incremental demand, while no encompassing business theory allows the mobilisation of evolutionary theory to the strategic risk assessment.

A further example is presented by entrepreneurial decision making in market entry. Let us consider the decision whether to start a new restaurant in a city. In part the decision as to the style of offering will be determined by customers' expectations based on existing offerings and in part upon the demands of fashion and the search for the new. In the first respect the neo-classical assumptions present an excellent basis on which a business case can be drawn together: demand can be predicted by examination of existing customer behaviour; revenue can be extrapolated from existing market share information. The investment risk can be clearly identified, both by the entrepreneur and by her bankers. In respect of the fashion-led component of demand, however, there is a more complicated, dynamic problem, since the arrival of new offerings (perhaps a new cuisine) will itself alter demand.

Expectations well be alerted. Moreover the existing restaurants are not isolated from the information gained in the local market in terms of which offerings were successful and which went to the wall. The fashion-led component is seen to be ineluctably an evolutionary process. Critically, while there may be appropriate models of such adaptive economic systems on a market basis there is no business theory which allow the entrepreneurial restaurateur to mobilise understanding about the general market behaviour into a set of product and service strategies for the proposed new restaurant.

The internal processes of the firm themselves represent an opportunity to discover and implement new ways of functioning in various respects. One way is to attempt to implement new production practices which reduce waste and inventory holdings such as Total Quality Management (TQM) and Just in Time (JIT), although such strategies would appear to have a finite limit to their benefits. A more fundamental source of advantage is to discover new production processes which reveal more efficient techniques that lead to either cheaper or improved products (e.g. Pilkington and its float glass production process). The appropriate organisation of the firm's management hierarchies represents yet another potential source of efficiency gain. A feature common to all of the internal processes is that they present the potential for efficiency improvements in some way, so in order to realise an advantage in the selection environment these efficiencies will have to be transferred to customers in some degree. In both these cases the limited ability of the firm to predict long term the appropriate processes and structures to meet an evolved demand militates for a level of experimentation which is not demanded by a neo-classical economic model.

Market-based Strategy

Much of the product strategy thinking of the previous section will find an echo but when attention is turned to the implications of evolutionary assumptions on market strategy the possible normative conclusions are less conventional. Just as products demand mutated replication so too do market postures. In pursuit of this we can conceive of setting up small market penetration activities - market trialling by the usage of small scale agents in a new market, for example, might represent a feasible pattern of replication at the market.

Such approaches are already common in market development activities, of course; it is normal market research practice to offer (at least conjecturally) a series of products to a targeted new market, seeking the responses of consumer samples to predict demand. An acceptance of the reality of an evolutionary context for the firm would militate for a more randomised approach to the trialled markets or products, as opposed to the more controlled, predictive, purposive and incremental approach emerging from a neo-classical model. Additionally, and specifically, a unified evolutionary based business economics would provide a sound basis for the riskinvestment decisions made by the firm in respect of these micro-trials of markets and products. It is to be noted here that these micro-trials are not an innovation emerging in some unsupported way from a theoretical basis of evolutionary adaptive systems but an existing heuristic response of managers to uncertainty inherent in their businesses. The strategic management problem is then that this replicative activity is driven by decisions unsupported by a theory linking the general market models with a model of appropriate risk-taking and developmental behaviour by the individual firm. A second consequence of an evolutionary assumption is that we can expect the competitors, too, to learn from the selection processes of the market. To the extent that we cannot respond in a predictive fashion to their learning we must seek to husband not only our markets as such, but our ability to change market focus flexibly.

Industry-based Strategy

The firm will inevitably have to enter into external relationships with various parties. In effect, markets in the faceless neoclassical sense of the phenomenon rarely exist in many goods and services and, consequently, firms have to seek out suppliers and ensure that customers can be reached through various channels. With respect to suppliers, firms may wish to contract with several sources for identical inputs or they may choose to deal with a single supplier or even work through intermediaries.

The route to customers may be via intermediaries or be direct, in the form of dedicated outlets or mail-order, for example. Each of the relationships a firm enters into reflects a balance of advantages and disadvantages and will influence costs incurred and quality, but the nature of any external structural organisation is not easily understood without reference to the risk exposure inherent in it and the relationship which the firm has cultivated with the other party. Clearly, the development and maintenance of socioeconomic relationships can provide a source of continued advantage to the firm by helping it to create its own 'identity' which is distinct from those of its rivals - scholar calls such activity 'relational exchange'. Again, without a theory linking overall industry behaviour with normative structures for the individual firm no sound basis exists for what could be costly experimentation necessary to react to an evolutionary context.

The important point here, is that by viewing transactions with external parties as a form of reciprocal relationship, rather than a one-off transaction, the firm may be able to cultivate longer term benefits for itself (and indeed the other party) which are a valuable aid to survival in an uncertain world. The concept of adaptiveness as a response to the limited predictability of the industry and market applies here as much as in product and market-based strategy. As partners, suppliers and buyers change their own contexts, say through changes in ownership or through their own reactions to selection pressures, so must our own relationships change.

A failure to recognise the inappropriateness of trust in a purely instrumental trading relationship, or the importance of integrity in a evolutionary trading system such as that of Axelrod (1984.) would be unwise. The lesson for industry strategy then is that the continued observation of the appropriateness of such postures is an essential part of the strategic plan. The replicative stance advocated in market and product strategy is more difficult to achieve in terms of industry strategy, but one can interpret the activities of firms such as SAIC Inc, a company composed of a federation of 'intrapreneurs' in the US R&D sector as an example of replication at the industry level. SAIC operates by encouraging groups of individuals within their existing employees to present business cases to the SAIC board on which basis pump-priming money may be made available to them to start up ventures under the umbrella of SAIC Inc. Competition between these intrapreneurial groups is frequent and information is made available thereby as to the fitness or otherwise of relationship postures as well as the fitness of products and market positions.

Horizontal Strategy

SAIC Inc also offers a model for the horizontal strategy of the company. A wide variety of technological innovation takes place within the spread of the intrapreneurial groups, some of which will succeed in their chosen market and some of which will fail. The structure of the company insulates SAIC as a whole from any wider consequences of failure. Technology is transferred between groups on the basis of arm's length trading with the corporate centre engendering rather than demanding co-operation. Groups are brought together to bid on large contracts and the existence of important information and know-how is thereby shared between groups. We can see here the practical application of some very clear consequences of the acceptance of the economic environment as evolutionary.

First is the need for resource allocation to engender duplication of response, in contrast to the obvious efficiency arguments of reducing duplication.

Second, the replication of structures within the firm can be interpreted as a search for the maintenance of multiple development paths towards uncertain futures. To the extent that the future cannot be predicted, planning consists not of choosing so much as maintaining valid progression paths towards the set of futures which remain feasible and which must therefore be comprehended in planning. As the future unfolds this originally perceived set of futures becomes smaller in extent. The connection with scenario planning, and in particular the concept of transition-based planning, (where the future of the firm is seen as a set of states of nature among which it seeks to move towards futures it prefers but which is subject to the vagaries of chance and the activities of competitors) is relevant here. Third, the knowledge retention issues are seen as driven not just by a desire to produce innovative offerings matched to a predicted market demand, but also by the need to retain within the firm the products of the replicative trialling, an activity carried out often at significant opportunity cost to the firm. Fourth and last, the evolutionary approach informs and strengthens the resource-based approach to strategy by bolstering the arguments that the objective of core-competence husbandry is to strengthen the position of the firm relative to other companies and not in any absolute sense. Unthinking altruism may raise the fitness of the firm, but if it raises the fitness of a competitor more, say by altering market conditions in our favour, but more so in the favour of the competitor, the ultimate result will be the demise of our relatively less fit firm.

Corporate Communication

Corporate communication is the communication issued by a corporate/organization/body/institute to all its public(s). Publics here can be both internal (employees, stakeholders, i.e. share and stock holders) and external (agencies, channel partners, media, government, industry bodies and institutes, educational institutes and general public). An organization needs to talk the same message to all of its stakeholders, in order to transmit coherence, credibility and ethic.

If one of these points is broken, the whole community can make this organization disappear. The Corporate Communication area will help this organization to build its message, combining its vision, mission and values and will also support the organization by communicating its message, activities and practices to all of its stakeholders.

According to the book *Essentials of Corporate Communication* by Cees van Riel and Charles Fombrun the term *Corporate*

Communication can be defined as the set of activities involved in managing and orchestrating all internal and external communications aimed at creating favorable starting points with stakeholders on which the company depends. Corporate communication consists of the dissemination of information by a variety of specialists and generalists in an organization, with the common goal of enhancing the organization's ability to retain its license to operate.

Tired of being called on to fix the company switchboard, recommend an answering machine or meet a computer salesman, I long ago adopted this form as being more accurate and left communications to the telecommunications specialists. It's a small point but another attempt to bring clarity out of confusion. Corporate communication serves as the liaison between an organization and its publics.

Organizations can strategically communicate to their audiences through public relations and advertising. This may involve an employee newsletter or video, crisis management with the news media, special events planning, building product value and communicating with stockholders, clients or donors.

What Corporate Communication Encodes and Promotes

- Strong corporate culture
- Coherent corporate identity
- Reasonable corporate philosophy
- Genuine sense of corporate citizenship
- An appropriate and professional relationship with the press, including quick, responsible ways of communicating in a crisis
- Understanding of communication tools and technologies
- Sophisticated approaches to global communications.

How an organization communicates with its employees, its extended audiences, the press and its customers brings its values to life. Corporate communications is all about managing perceptions and ensuring:

- Effective and timely dissemination of information

- Positive corporate image
- Smooth and affirmative relationship with all stakeholders.

Be it a corporate body, company, organization, institution, non-governmental organization, governmental body, all of them need to have a respectable image and reputation. In today's day and age of increasing competition, easy access to information and the media explosion, reputation management has gained even more importance. Therefore, corporate communications as a role has become significant and professional in nature. Gone are the days when corporate communication merely meant 'wining and dining the client' - it has now emerged as a science and art of perception management.

Key Tasks of Corporate Communication

The responsibilities of corporate communication are therefore:

- to flesh out the profile of the "company behind the brand" (corporate branding);
- to develop initiatives that minimize discrepancies between the company's desired identity and brand features;
- to indicate who should perform which tasks in the field of communication;
- to formulate and execute effective procedures in order to facilitate decision making about matters concerning communication;
- to mobilize internal and external support behind corporate objectives.
- to co ordinate with international business firms.

Tools of Corporate Communication

Integrated communication can be achieved in various ways. The main four practices are:

1. application of visual identity systems (sometimes referred to as "house style")
2. use of integrated marketing communications;
3. reliance on coordinating teams;
4. adoption of a centralized planning system.

The Communication Agenda: to Build Reputation

Corporate communication helps an organization to create distictive and appealing images with its stakeholder groups, build a strong corporate brand, and develop reputation capital. To achieve those ends, all forms of communication must be orchestrated into a coherent whole, and success criteria developed that enable measuring the effects of the organization's communication on its reputation and value.

External Communication

This involves building and maintaining a positive relationship with the media (television, print, web, etc.). This includes, but is not limited to, drafting and dissemination of press releases, organizing press conferences and meeting with media professionals and organizing events for the media as a group.

External Events

Could involve vendor/supplier/distributor meets, channel partner meetings, events related to product launches, important initiatives, etc.

Company/spokesperson Profiling

Ensuring that the company/organization spokesperson is in the public limelight, is well-known and considered as an authority in the respective sector/field.

- Managing content of corporate websites and/or other external touch points
- Managing corporate publications - for the external world
- Managing print media.

Brand Management

- Development and upkeep of the corporate identity to ensure adherence to corporate brand guidelines

To improve overall business communications so as to clearly and effectively communicate the essence of the company.

Corporate Identity/organizational Identity

There are two approaches for Identity, respectively Corporate Identity and Organizational Identity.

- "Corporate identity is the reality and uniqueness of an organization, which is integrally related to its external and internal image and reputation through corporate communication".
- "Organizational Identity comprises those characteristics of an organization that its members believe are central, distinctive and enduring. That is, organizational identity consists of those attributes that members feel are fundamental to (central) and uniquely descriptive of (distinctive) the organization and that persist within the organization over time (enduring)".

Corporate Reputation

Reputations are overall assessments of organizations by their stakeholders. They are aggregate perceptions by stakeholders of an organizaitons's ability to fulfil their expectations, whether these stakeholders are interested in buying the company's products, working for the company, or investing in the company's shares.

In 2000, the US based Council of PR Firms identified seven programmes that were developed by either media organizations or market research firms, and that were being used by companies to assess or benchmark their corporate reputations. Of these only three are conducted regularly and have broad visibility:

- "America's Most Admired Companies" by *Fortune Magazine;*
- The "Brand Asset Valuator" by Young & Rubicam;
- "RepTrak" by Reputation Institute.

Crisis Communications

- Sharing information with employees, building employer pride, managing employee issues, et cetera.
- Manage the Intranet and other internal web portals.

Organisational Communication

Encourage and enable the employees to plan for new ideas and effectively implement them.

Internal Communication

- Managing corporate publications for employees and partners
- Organising internal events for staff.

Corporate Communication Officers

Recent research on the corporate communication function reports that corporate communication officers (CCOs) in Global Fortune 500 companies tend to have average tenures of about 4.5 years and that nearly one-half (48 per cent) report to the Chief Executive Officer. CCOs say that approximately 42 per cent of their job is strategic and 58 per cent is tactical. Over the next year, they will be focusing more on social responsibility, social media and reputation. In a research it is found distinct differences between CCOs in Most Admired companies versus Contender companies.

Interpersonal Communication

Interpersonal communication is usually defined by communication scholars in numerous ways, usually describing participants who are dependent upon one another and have a shared history. Communication channels, the conceptualization of mediums that carry messages from sender to receiver, take two distinct forms: direct and indirect. Direct channels are obvious and easily recognized by the receiver. Both verbal and non-verbal information is completely controlled by the sender. *Verbal* channels rely on words, as in written or spoken communication. *Non-verbal* channels encompass facial expressions, controlled body movements (police present hand gestures to control traffic), color (red signals 'stop', green signals 'go'), and sound (warning sirens).

Indirect channels are usually recognized subconsciously by the receiver, and are not always under direct control of the sender. Body language, comprising most of the indirect channel, may inadvertently reveal one's true emotions, and thereby either unintentionally taint or bolster the believability of any intended verbal message. Subconscious reception and interpretation of these signals is often described with arbitrary terms like gut-feeling, hunch, or premonition.

Context refers to the conditions that precede or surround the communication. It consists of present or past events from which the meaning of the message is derived, though it may also, in the case of written communications, depend upon the statements preceding and following the quotation in question. Immediate surroundings may also color the perceived meaning of words; normally safe discourse may easily become contextually ambiguous or offensive in a restroom or shower hall. These influences do not constitute the message by themselves, but rather these extraneous nuances subtly change the message's effective meaning. Ultimately, context includes the entire world, but usually refers to salient factors such as the following:

- Physical milieu: the season or weather, current physical location and environment
- Situational milieu: classroom, military conflict, supermarket checkout
- Cultural and linguistic backgrounds
- Developmental progress (maturity) or emotional state
- Complementary or contrasting roles: boss and employee; teacher and student; parent, child, and spouse; friend or enemy; partner or competitor.

Interpersonal Communication

What do we mean when we talk about interpersonal communication? Read how researchers define interpersonal communication and then complete the interactive activity and quiz at the end of this section.

The Contextual View

One way of defining interpersonal communication is to compare it to other forms of communication. In so doing, we would examine how many people are involved, how physically close they are to one another, how many sensory channels are used, and the feedback provided. Interpersonal communication differs from other forms of communication in that there are few participants involved, the interactants are in close physical proximity to each other, there are many sensory channels used, and feedback is immediate. An important point to note about the contextual definition is that it does not take into account the relationship between the interactants.

The Developmental View

We have many different relationships with people. Some researchers say that our definition of interpersonal communication must account for these differences. These researchers say that interacting with a sales clerk in a store is different than the relationship we have with our friends and family members. Thus, some researchers have proposed an alternative way of defining interpersonal communication. This is called the developmental view. From this view, interpersonal communication is defined as communication that occurs between people who have known each other for some time. Importantly, these people view each other as unique individuals, not as people who are simply acting out social situations.

Functions of Interpersonal Communication

Interpersonal communication is important because of the functions its achieves. Whenever we engage in communication with another person, we seek to gain information about them. We also give off information through a wide variety of verbal and nonverbal cues. Read more about the various functions of interpersonal communication and then complete the interactive activity and the quiz at the end of this unit.

Gaining Information

One reason we engage in interpersonal communication is so that we can gain knowledge about another individual. Social Penetration Theory says that we attempt to gain information about others so that we can interact with them more effectively. We can better predict how they will think, feel, and act if we know who they are. We gain this information passively, by observing them; actively, by having others engage them; or interactively, by engaging them ourselves. Self-disclosure is often used to get information from another person.

Building a Context of Understanding

We also engage in interpersonal communication to help us better understand what someone says in a given context. The words we say can mean very different things depending on how they are said or in what context. Content Messages refer to the surface level meaning of a message. Relationship Messages refer to how a message is said. The two are sent simultaneously, but each affects the meaning assigned to the communication. Interpersonal communication helps us understand each other better.

Establishing Identity

Another reason we engage in interpersonal communication is to establish an identity. The roles we play in our relationships help us establish identity. So too does the face, the public self-image we present to others. Both roles and face are constructed based on how we interact with others.

Interpersonal Needs

Finally, we engage in interpersonal communication because we need to express and receive interpersonal needs. William Schutz has identified three such needs: inclusion, control, and affection.

- Inclusion is the need to establish identity with others.
- Control is the need to exercise leadership and prove one's abilities. Groups provide outlets for this need. Some individuals do not want to be a leader. For them, groups provide the necessary control over aspects of their lives.
- Affection is the need to develop relationships with people. Groups are an excellent way to make friends and establish relationships.

Your Managers and Employees

If you were a school teacher at report card time, what kind of communication grades would you give the members of your team? How important are interpersonal skills in your business?

Most organizations do a great job in training their managers and employees in on-the-job skills, but completely overlook interpersonal skills training. How important is communication training? What is the value of an interpersonal communication workshop? No other single investment you can make will give you the kind of ROI you'll receive from training your team in the art and science of *effective interpersonal communication*. The way your managers and employees communicate dramatically affects morale, teamwork, productivity, employee retention, customer relations and your bottom line. If your team could achieve a 10%, 20% or 30% improvement in their communication skills, what would it mean to your business?

Effective Interpersonal Communication

Interpersonal communication is an art. Some people are naturally good at it, and they can't really tell you why. They are just great communicators. They get along with most people and know how to build strong working relationships. They know how to listen. They know how to get their point across. They know how to collaborate and negotiate. When they need to confront, they don't hesitate, but they don't erode the relationship in the process. In fact, the clarity they bring to difficult situations strengthens the respect that underlies their working relationships. These people are artists. Some communication artists have an amazing in-born talent for effective interpersonal communication. Others have developed their skills through study, practice and a lot of trial and error. Regardless of how they aquired their interpersonal skills, effective communicators stand head and shoulders above their peers.

Interpersonal communication is truly an art, but it's also a science. The science of clear communication, active listening, persuasion and collaboration is easy to teach, but hard to learn. Effective communication is situational. The "right" thing to say or do in one situation may backfire in another. What works with one person doesn't work with another. Effective communicators have mastered both the science and the art of interpersonal communication, applying the principles of emotional intelligence to each situation they encounter.

Training Workshops

In our interpersonal communication workshops and seminars, we teach the art and the science of effective communication. Each participant typically completes an assessment prior to the workshop and receives a 20-page personal profile outlining her/his communication style. During the workshop participants get to know themselves, how they act (or react) in various situations, and where they are effective or ineffective as communicators. We teach them the science of interpersonal communication, and we coach them on becoming more effective as communication artists. Our interpersonal communication workshops are fun, entertaining, practical, challenging and highly effective in bringing about a change in behaviour. Roger Reece conducts each workshop, and teaches the principles of interpersonal communication through a wealth of personal stories and illustrations. As an expert facilitator, he uses role play, group discussions and interactive dialogues to actively involve every participant in the learning process. If you want to expand your manager/employee training programme to include effective interpersonal skills training, all you have to do is contact us to learn more about our communication workshops. Don't wait. Schedule an in-house interpersonal communication workshop for your team today!

3

The Organization of International Business

Introduction

The theme of this chapter is that in order to succeed an international business must have the appropriate formal and informal organizational structure and control mechanisms.

Organizational architecture

This term refers to the totality of firm's organization including the formal organization structure, control systems and incentives, organizational culture, process and people.

What is appropriate depends upon the strategy of the firm, which as we saw in the last chapter is inter-related with the demands of the industry environment. The organization structure means three things: the formal division of the organization into sub units such as product divisions, national operations and functions. (Organizational charts), the location of decision making responsibilities within that structure (e.g., centralized or decentralized etc) and the establishment of integrating mechanisms to coordinate the activities of sub units including cross functional terms or regional committees.

Control systems

Control systems are the metrics used to measure the performance of sub units and make judgments about how will the mangers are running the sub units. Unilever measured the performance of its subsidiary companies according to profitability. Profitability was the control systems.

Incentives

Incentives are the devices used to reward the appropriate managerial behaviour. Incentives are very ties to performance metrics, e.g. a bonus for exceeding performance targets.

Process

Process are the manners in which the decisions are made and work is performed within an organization. Examples are the processes for formulating strategy, for deciding how to allocate the resources within the firm, or for evaluating the performance of managers and giving feedback.

Origination culture

Origination culture are the norms and value systems that are shared among the employees of an organization. Just are societies having distinct patterns of culture and sub couture. The organizational culture can have a profound impact on how a firm performs.

Structure

People: means nor just the employees of the organization but also the strategy used to recruit, compensate and retain those individuals and the types of people that they are in terms of their skills values and orientation.

Original architecture-totality

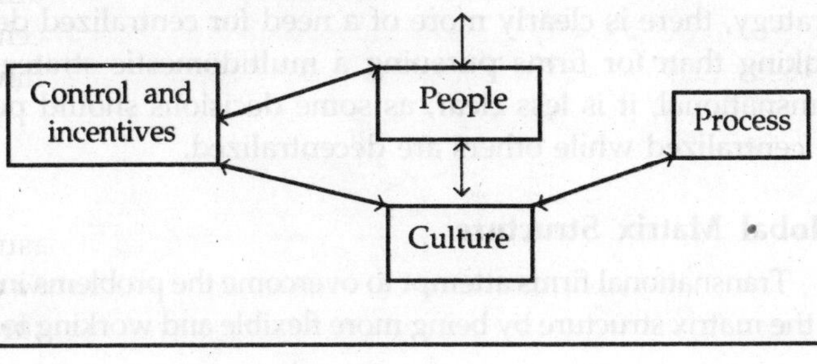

Just as there were trade-offs between different strategies, there are trade-offs between different organizational choices — advantages and disadvantages to different approaches.

Structure

Vertical differentiation is principally about the centralization and decentralization of decision-making responsibilities. It is concerned with identifying where in a hierarchy decision making power should be concentrated. There are four main arguments for centralization:

(1) Facilitating coordination,

(2) Ensuring consistency between decisions and organizational objectives,

(3) Providing top managers the means to push through major changes, and

(4) Avoiding duplication of activities.

There are five main arguments for decentralization:

(1) Overburdened and hence poor decision-making at the top of the organization,

(2) Increased motivation at lower levels,

(3) Greater flexibility,

(4) Better decisions on the spot by the people directly involved, and

(5) Increased accountability and control.

The choice between centralization and decentralization is not an absolute one. Frequently it makes sense to centralize some decisions and decentralize others depending upon the type of decision and the strategy of the firm. For firms pursuing a global strategy, there is clearly more of a need for centralized decision making than for firms pursuing a multidomestic strategy. For transnational, it is less clear, as some decisions should perhaps be centralized while others are decentralized.

Global Matrix Structure

Transnational firms attempt to overcome the problems inherent in the matrix structure by being more flexible and working to create networks of individuals and a shared culture. The Mixed Structure is most common in the Multinational Enterprises. It uses localization in product development, marketing, sales, and service. At the same time functions that benefit from scale advantages, like purchasing, are centralized

Subsidiary Roles and Imperatives

Corporations commonly have *subsidiaries* that operate in host environments. They play a key part in balancing integration and local responsiveness through playing an autonomous role, a receptive role, or an active role. The Autonomous Role has a subsidiary performing most activities of the value chain independently of HQ, selling output in a local market or in markets the autonomous subsidiary can arrange. This role is commonly used with Multi-Domestic Strategy. The Receptive Role has subsidiary functions that are integrated with HQ for other units. An example is where the subsidiary imports or exports components to other subsidiaries for redistribution or final assembly. Commonly used with Global Strategy. The Active Role has many activities performed locally, but coordinated with subsidiaries. Commonly used with Transnational Strategy, with mandate from HQ, and flexibility for adaptation.

Integrating Mechanisms

Both formal and informal mechanisms can be used to help achieve coordination. The need for coordination (and hence integrating mechanisms) varies systematically with the strategy of the firm. It is lowest in multidomestic firms, higher in international firms, higher still in global firms, and highest of all in transnational firms.

Integration is inhibited by a number of impediments to coordination, particularly different sub-unit orientations. To the extent that different sub-units have different objectives and ways of operating, integration becomes more difficult. Integration can be achieved through formal integrating mechanisms. Formal integrating mechanisms vary in complexity from direct contact and simple liaison roles, through teams, to a matrix structure. However, formal integrating mechanisms can become bureaucratic.

To overcome the bureaucracy associated with formal integrating mechanisms, firms often use informal mechanisms. These include management networks and organization culture. For a network to function effectively it must embrace as many managers within the organization as possible. Information systems and management development policies (including job rotation and management education programmes) can be used to establish firm wide networks.

For a network to function properly, managers in different sub-units must be committed to the same goals. One way of achieving this is to foster the development of a common organization culture. Leadership by example, management development programmes, and human relations policies are all-important considerations in building a common culture. Taken together, managerial networks and a common culture can serve as valuable coordination mechanisms in international firms that can help overcome the deficiencies of formal mechanisms.

Control Systems

One of the major tasks of a firm's headquarters is to control the various sub-units of the firm to ensure consistency with strategic goals. The headquarters can achieve this through its use of control systems. There are four main types of controls — personal controls, bureaucratic controls, output controls, and cultural controls. In most firms, all four are used, but the relative emphasis tends to vary with the strategy of the firm. Personal control involves control by personal contact with subordinates. This type of control system tends to be most widely used within small firms where it finds expression in the direct supervision of the actions of subordinates, but is also applicable in large international firms.

Bureaucratic control involves control through the establishment of a system of rules and procedures that are used to direct the actions of sub-units. With regard to headquarters control of sub-units within multinational firms, the most important form of bureaucratic controls are sub-unit budgets and capital spending rules. Output controls involve setting goals for sub-units to achieve, expressing those goals in terms of relatively objective criteria such as profitability, productivity, growth, market share, or quality, and then judging the performance of sub-unit management by their ability to achieve these goals.

Cultural controls exist when employees buy into the norms and value systems of the firm. When this occurs, employees tend to control their own behaviour, which reduces the need for direct management supervision. Cultural controls require substantial investments of time and money by the firm in building organization wide norms and value systems. The key to understanding the relationship between international strategy and control systems is the concept of performance ambiguity. Performance ambiguity arises when the causes of poor performance by a sub-unit are ambiguous — when there is a high degree of interdependence between sub-units within the organization. The degree of interdependence, and hence performance ambiguity and the costs of control, is a function of the international strategy of the firm. It is lowest in multidomestic firms, higher in international firms, higher still in global firms, and highest of all in transnational. The costs of control can be defined as the amount of time that top management has to devote to monitoring and evaluating the performance of sub-units. This will be greater the greater the amount of performance ambiguity.

Synthesis: Strategy and Structure

The implications of the four main strategies on organizational structure and control systems are identified. To underline the scheme is the notion that a *fit* between strategy and structure is necessary if the firm is going to achieve high performance. For a firm to succeed two conditions must be fulfilled. First, the strategy of the firm must be consistent with the environment in which the firm operates. Second, the organizational structure and control systems of the firm must be consistent with its strategy.

- What is a strategic alliance in International business?
- What are the factors to be considered in designing an organization structure of a MNC?
- What is global management?
- Discuss the different strategic choices available to compete in the international business.

Benefits of the Global Capital Market

In the case of international capital markets, there are simply more of players and a greater diversity in the players and the possible combinations. Firms can obtain funds via both debt and equity. To raise funds via debt, a firm owes investor money (They borrow). To raise funds via equity, a firm sells partial ownership (stock) to an investor. There are two main reasons why an international capital market offers an improvement over a purely domestic capital market:

(1) from a borrower's perspective, it increases the supply of funds available for borrowing and lowers the cost of capital; and

(2) from an investor's perspective, it provides a wider range of investment opportunities, thereby allowing investors to build a portfolio of international investments that diversifies risk.

If there is limited liquidity in a purely domestic capital market, the cost of capital is higher relative to what would be found in an international market. With an increase in the choices available to an investor, the investor is able to diversify holdings internationally, thereby reducing systematic risk below what could be achieved in a purely domestic market. While the systematic risks are reduced with international portfolio investments, exchange rate risks now come into play.

Growth of the Global Capital Market

De-regulation and improvements in technology have facilitated the growth of the international capital market. Due to advances in communications and data processing capabilities, the international capital markets are always active around the globe. International trading is an information intensive activity that would not have been possible only a few decades ago when computing and telecommunication capabilities were much less developed.

The deregulation of capital flows, a removal of limitations on the types services that can be provided by foreign financial services firms, and a reduction in the restrictions imposed on domestic financial services firms have all contributed to the growth of the international capital market.

While capital is generally free to move internationally, evidence to date suggests that most investors choose to make long term investments in their home country and only make short term opportunistic investments elsewhere. A lack of information about the fundamental quality of foreign investments may encourage speculative flows in the global capital market. The Country Focus on Mexico and the global capital markets shows that a country cannot count on capital inflows to finance its deficits, especially when the money that is being invested is not there for the long term.

The Eurocurrency Market

A Eurocurrency is any currency that is banked outside of its country of origin. Eurodollars, which account for about two-thirds of all Eurocurrencies, are dollars banked outside of the United States. The Eurocurrency got its origin as holders of dollars outside the USA, initially communist countries but later also middle eastern countries, wanted to deposit their dollars but were afraid that they may be confiscated if deposited in the USA.

The lack of government regulation makes the Eurocurrency market attractive to both depositors and borrowers. Due to the lack of regulation, the spread between the Eurocurrency deposit rate and the Eurocurrency lending rate is less than the spread between the domestic deposit rate and the domestic lending rate. This gives Eurobanks a competitive advantage.

The lack of regulation is also a drawback of Eurocurrency deposits, as the risk of forfeiture is greater than for domestic deposits. However, this is not a major problem. There is also a risk of currency fluctuations that would not arise if funds were held domestically in the domestic currency.

The Global Bond Market

The international bond market falls into two general classifications; the foreign bond market and the Eurobond market. Eurobonds account for the lion's share of international bond issues. Foreign bonds are sold outside of the borrower's country and are denominated in the currency of the country in which they are issued.

A Eurobond issue is normally underwritten by an international syndicate of banks and placed in countries other than the one in whose currency the bond is denominated. The Eurobond market is an attractive way for companies to raise funds due to the absence of regulatory interference, less stringent disclosure requirements than in most domestic bond markets, and the favorable tax status of Eurobonds. ECU and Euro denominated bonds became increasingly common in the 1990s. One advantage of these bonds is that the risks associated with exchange rates are lower, since the ECU and Euro are actually a basket of currencies.

The Global Equity Market

There is no international equity market in the same sense that there are international currency and bond markets. Instead there are a number of separate equity markets that are linked via specific equities and overall market fundamentals. Foreign investors are increasingly investing in different national equity markets, primarily as a way of diversifying risk by diversifying their portfolio of stock holdings across nations.

As firms are listed on multiple national exchanges and have their shares owned by an even greater number of shareholders from different nationalities, it is becoming increasingly meaningless to refer to firms as "American" or "Dutch." For example, the "nationality" of DaimlerChrysler does not matter.

Companies are beginning to list their stock in the equity markets of other nations, primarily as a prelude to issuing stock in the market to raise additional capital. Other reasons for foreign listings include facilitating future stock swaps, using the company's stock and stock options to compensate local management and employees, satisfying local ownership desires, providing access to funding for future acquisitions in a country, and increasing the company's visibility to local employees, customers, suppliers, and bankers

Foreign Exchange Risk and the Cost of Capital

When borrowing funds from the international capital market, companies must weigh the benefits of a lower interest rate against the risks of an increase in the real cost of capital due to adverse exchange rate movements. Using forward rates cannot typically remove the risk altogether, particularly in the case of long-term investments.

Implications for Business

By utilizing international capital markets, firms can often borrow funds at a lower cost than they could domestically — regardless of whether the funds are in the form of cash loans, equity, or bonds. The minimal regulation in international capital markets helps lower the cost of capital, but also increases risk in both currencies and security. For investors, the international capital market provides opportunities for portfolio diversification and the lowering of systematic risk. At the same time, it creates new currency risks.

Foreign Direct Investment

With FDI, a firm has a significant ownership in a foreign operation and the potential to affect managerial decisions of the operation. The goal of our coverage of FDI is to understand the pattern of FDI that occurs between countries, and why firms undertake FDI and become multinational in their operations. This chapter will describe some of the basic theories of FDI, and why firms undertake FDI rather than simply exporting products or licensing their know-how.

Foreign Direct Investment in the World Economy

When discussing foreign direct investment, it is important to distinguish between the flow of FDI and the stock of FDI. The flow of FDI refers to the amount of FDI undertaken over a given time period (normally one year). The stock of FDI refers to the total accumulated value of foreign owned assets at a given point in time. The significant growth in FDI during 1999-2001 has both to do with the political economy of trade as outlined and the political and economic changes that have been taking place in developing countries. The globalization of the world economy is causing firms to invest worldwide in order to assure their presence in every region of the world.

Another important trend is has been the rise of inflows into the US. The stock of foreign FDI in the US increased more rapidly than US FDI abroad. The rapid increase in FDI growth into the US may be due to the attractiveness of the US market, the falling value of the dollar, and a belief by some foreign corporations that they could manage US assets and workers more efficiently than their American managers could.

It is difficult to say whether the increase in the FDI into the US is good for the country or not. To the extent that foreigners are making more productive use of US assets and workers, it is probably good for the country. The management focus box details the techniques of Mexican cement manufacturer Cemex for its aggressive international expansion of cement manufacturing. Because cement is a product that is not easily exported due to its low ratio of value to weight, Cemex sought international expansion by acquisition.

Horizontal Foreign Direct Investment

Horizontal FDI is FDI in the same industry abroad as a firm operates in at home. A Japanese automobile manufacturer in Japan seeks to produce the same product in the USA. FDI would seem to be more expensive and risky than exporting or licensing, so there must be some other good reasons for firms to undertake FDI. Transportation costs can make export infeasible, especially for products that have a low value/weight ratio (i.e. cement, soft drinks), or would require refrigeration or similar controlled environments. For items like electronics, software, and medical equipment, transportation costs may not be an impediment to exporting.

The most accepted reason for horizontal FDI relates to market imperfections. By imposing quotas, tariffs, or impediments, governments can make FDI and licensing more attractive than exporting. Technological or managerial know-how can be difficult and dangerous to license, however, making it an infeasible alternative. A firm can lose control of critical competitive know-how, may not be able to optimize the flow and configuration of operations between countries, or simply may be unable to codify its knowledge in a way that would make licensing a practical option.

Firms may choose to undertake FDI simply to follow the lead of a competitor so as not be left behind or locked out of an opportunity. FDI may be most likely to occur in certain stages of a product's lifecycle — when other countries have a large enough market to justify local production or when there is a need to locate production in a low cost location.

A firm may choose to undertake FDI in a particular country or region due to location specific advantages. An obvious example occurs with respect to natural resources, but it also applies to the ability to tap into a particular expertise (e.g. silicon valley) or be located near customers or suppliers with unique characteristics. Porter's diamond, provides a partial explanation why firms in certain industries may find it attractive to invest in a particular country.

Vertical Foreign Direct Investment

Backward vertical FDI involves investment into an industry that provides inputs for a firm's domestic production processes. Forward vertical FDI involves investment in an industry that utilizes the outputs of a firm's domestic production processes.

The strategic behaviour explanation for vertical FDI suggests that firms try to either create new entry barriers or erode competitors' entry barriers. While there certainly are some examples where the strategic behaviour explanation seems to apply, the market imperfections explanation seems to present a more complete explanation.

Market imperfections can result from impediments to the sale of know-how and the need to invest in specialized assets. Because specialized know-how can be difficult to sell or license, a firm may have to integrate vertically to be successful.

The establishment of sales and services centers in high technology industries, or the investment in knowledge intensive extractive processes are two examples. When specialized assets must be invested in (i.e. the aluminum smelter), companies may need to secure a supply of the needed inputs to assure that those assets can be used efficiently.

Implications for Business

The market imperfections theory suggests that exporting should be preferred to licensing and horizontal FDI as long as transport costs are minor and tariff barriers are trivial. If that is not the case, then firms should consider licensing and FDI. FDI is more costly than licensing, but may be the most reasonable option. A decision tree suggesting when licensing, FDI, and exporting are most appropriate. Licensing tends not to be a good option in high technology industries where protecting firm specific know-how is critical, in industries where a firm must carefully coordinate and orchestrate its worldwide activities, or where there are intense cost pressures.

International Communication Management

Working with our clients on a basis of partnership, we develop unconventional and out-of-the-box strategies and methods to master today's international business challenges. We apply the full scope of our know-how and creativity to generating new concepts and fresh ideas. Our work is systematic, process and result-oriented.

Crisis and Communication Management

3C New York offers active support in crisis and communication management. Organizations and individual professionals profit from our expertise in representing their interests and advancing their projects. From PR, media liaison and investor relations to post-merger integration-3C is your partner in optimizing communications on all levels. Our targeted communications support is invaluable where legal issues are involved. At the same time, we make a point of leaving all legal advice to legal professionals. And since all aspects of business and communication are increasingly international, our approach is always sensitive to issues of intercultural communication.

Business Development

3C New York is a strong partner in building healthy business and promoting dynamic growth in a wide spectrum of companies acting in diverse sectors. Taking a comprehensive approach to the client company, its goals and its environment, we begin by designing a roadmap to success. This plan then points the way to clearly defined corporate objectives. Whether you are in charge of a major corporation or a small-to mid-size enterprise, whether you are aiming for a large-scale increase in your market share or require support for a single project, 3C New York has the know-how and the practice-proven tools to help you get results. Support for companies wishing to enter a foreign market is central to our business development services. Our consulting is built on the solid foundation of American business models, yet we are also equipped with a keen sensitivity to the needs, strengths and weaknesses of the European business world. We develop result-oriented strategies that address the host country's specific demands from all angles. And because we maintain offices in the US and in Germany, we are ideally positioned to facilitate transatlantic cooperation.

From strategic planning to hands-on implementation and beyond, we keep a finger on the pulse of the client company and its market at all times. That's why we remain able to make intelligent corrections throughout the implementation phase.

Investor Relations

3C New York is equipped with the international reach you need to access the investors most interested in your company-in North America or in Europe. With a focus on the most effective communications instruments and a keen sensitivity to intercultural differences, we help you and your staff prepare roadshows and presentations. We coach your top executives for public events and one-on-one meetings with potential investors. 3C New York supplies invaluable knowledge and experience to support you in achieving the highest standards of investor relations. We give you the tools to present your company successfully and meet the information needs of US or European sell-side analysts and buy-side investors.

Public Relations Management

3C New York uses proven PR tools that put you in charge of your media image. Whether you are active in business or in the political arena, we cover all the angles required to build awareness and fine-tune your image. We offer public relations management services designed for individuals, organizations and special interest groups, with a special focus on intercultural aspects. In order to be effective, PR must connect with the public on multiple levels.

That's why PR management has to adopt a proactive stance, anticipating new opinion trends before they affect public behaviour. By thorough analysis and evaluation of foreign and domestic media, 3C New York detects undercurrents before they surface. We then use this knowledge to create and update PR strategies and measures. Whether you are active abroad or in your own backyard, you can rely on 3C New York to help shape and communicate your visions.

CI Consulting-Corporate Identity and Image

A strong corporate identity is critical to the success of a company. This also applies to individual protagonists: the quality and clarity of the self-concept and the outwardly projected image determine a person's ability to perform effectively on a business or political platform.

3C New York takes all relevant factors into account in defining CI-from corporate visions and culture to the way an enterprise is perceived externally. Congruence of images from both vantage points is the key to a solid CI: in order to credibly communicate your message to the public, it is essential that it correspond with your internal identity. Creating unity between these components is our primary objective in CI consulting. The significance of an outward image cannot be overstated. Its impact depends directly on whether a company or an individual establishes and communicates a compelling CI. To consistently evoke positive associations with your visions, products or services, you and your organization must remain on message at all times and on all levels.

PR is an effective tool in shaping public opinion, yet it is possible only with in-depth contextual knowledge. 3C New York is equipped with the local insight you need to hone your corporate identity for presentation in an unfamiliar environment. Taking intercultural nuances into consideration, we will fine-tune your public appearance for new and traditional media in Europe and in the US. And help you leverage your potential at home and abroad.

Media Consulting

Whether in the political arena or in business, comprehensive media knowledge is essential to success. 3C New York provides in-depth media analysis and evaluation with regard to all topics relevant to you and your organization. As specialists in transatlantic relations, we pay particular attention to sensitive intercultural differences between the US, individual European countries, and the EU as a whole. Our targeted analysis form the basis for a focused strategy that lets you communicate your message on your own terms. We also coach individuals for public events, speaking engagements and interviews within a specific media context.

Political Consulting

Today more than ever, politics have great impact on economic climates. That's why no informed business decision can be reached without comprehensive knowledge of political developments. 3C New York offers in-depth political cross-cultural consulting, including research, analysis, evaluation and background information. We afford individual protagonists, organizations, businesses and special interest groups key insight into trends, policies and decision-making processes in the EU and US. The result: a deeper understanding of intercultural differences, underlying policies and political priorities, at home and abroad.

Cross Cultural Communication

Communication between people from different cultural backgrounds is always a collision of hidden thoughts, presumptions and intentions. A constructive exchange across international boundaries requires cross-cultural awareness on this invisible level. 3C New York offers specialized consulting designed to give you the insight you need to cultivate your transatlantic business and political relationships. We offer you practical guidance on all levels of intercultural communication-from developing individual presentations and consulting to the preparation of international events, roadshows or trade shows. We also assist in optimizing corporate structure as part of post-merger and multicultural integration. Tom Ernsing provides workshops, training and coaching on cross-cultural communication in Germany/Europe and the United States.

Material Development

Language is a powerful tool. Yet its impact can only be as strong as the communications instrument that carries your message. Whether print or electronic media, a special event, conference or PR initiative, 3C New York helps you determine the optimum media for your content. From drafting editorial articles and press releases, to speechwriting and generating copy for brochures and Websites, we turn complex and sensitive issues into concise and animated content. Where international communication is required, our intercultural expertise makes us your ideal partners in identifying the right platform and designing your presentation.

Relocation

There is more than meets the eye to relocation: setting up new businesses, subsidiaries and branch offices in a foreign country can also involve developing new corporate structures. Such a complex undertaking involves a variety of practical issues, each requiring individual attention and research. With its comprehensive skills and cross-cultural experience in American and European markets, 3C New York is your partner in facing these challenges. Whether you plan to establish a business presence in the United States, in Germany or elsewhere in the EU, we provide the hands-on support you need to succeed.

Research

A precise analysis of the marketplace is an indispensable prerequisite to effective marketing. Only after a detailed study of the market and the target group is it possible to fine-tune marketing instruments and to coordinate their application. 3C New York takes on responsibility for all preliminary steps-from surveys and interviews to full-scale market analyses. In addition, we will help you identify your target group, business partners or clients on both sides of the Atlantic.

Core Services

Most of the corporate communication management services we offer are intertwined and can rarely be isolated from each other. Our approach takes this into consideration:

1. intercultural project management and business development more
2. relocation assistance, location scouting, research and analysis-Germany, US more
3. CI-consulting & public relations, message development, issue & crisis management more
4. intercultural media training, political communications more
5. political consulting: analysis of political currents with respect to a specific initiative more
6. media consulting, media analysis and research-in Europe and the USA more
7. intercultural communications consulting and cross-culture training more
8. event planning & consulting: trade shows, conferences, roadshows-investor relations development.

Event Planning

When you launch a business or political event on foreign soil, you need to come prepared. With background information and support. Which platform is most appropriate? Does it make sense to exhibit at a particular trade fair? Would a roadshow or small-scale event be more effective? What impact can be realistically achieved and what will it cost? Which media representatives should be invited? To optimize the quality and cost-effectiveness of your event, you will need on-site organizational support. Only business professionals with in-depth local knowledge can ensure that your transaction and travel expenses are kept to a minimum. And to get the best results from contractors you need people who speak their language. From initial strategic planning to organization, execution and follow-up, we are at your side. We will help you choose the most suitable platform for your target group. In close cooperation with you, we will prepare your PR and promotional measures, direct mail and presentation material-with a keen focus on the unique culture in your target region.

3C Concept

3C New York uses innovative business development concepts, combining a systematic approach with a focus on dynamic growth and business success. The 3C method uses practice-proven tools to get sustainable results. Years of involvement in the European and American business environments have shown us the power of doing business "the American way." Our approach is based on three fundamental principals:

- transparency
- guidance
- results.

Consistently implementing strategies is the key to realizing visions. Yet traditional methods lack the agility to meet the challenges of today's constantly changing environment. To succeed in the real world of business, a strategy must do a great deal more than assume that a given set of measures will produce a predictable set of results. 3C New York is dedicated to creating result-oriented strategies that embrace this state of flux, minimizing its inherent risks and exploiting its opportunities.

Communications a Tool for Development

Prior to implementing a public communications campaign as part of a children's health programme in Ecuador, only 28 per cent of people surveyed had their children vaccinated. After the campaign had been in effect for 18 months, the number jumped to 52 per cent, according to a survey by the consulting firm HealthCom and the Academy for Educational Development (AED). Similarly dramatic results were reported by the consulting firm the Manoff Group during a reproductive health project in Cochabamba, Bolivia.

Before a communications campaign began, only 2 per cent of the women surveyed remembered that edema was a danger sign during pregnancy. After the campaign was underway, 64 per cent remembered that fact.

"The question is not 'Does it work?'" said AED Executive Vice President Dr. William Smith in his keynote presentation, "it's 'What kind of problem do I have?' and 'What kind of communications [mechanism] should I use to address it?'" Dr. Smith was the keynote speaker at a seminar hosted by the IDB on the role of strategic communications in development. The seminar, held on July 1st at the IDB's headquarters in Washington, DC, brought together a panel of experts from the IDB, the Academy for Education Development, the World Bank, and USAID to discuss best practices for integrating communications into development projects and achieving social change.

Elena Suarez, Chief of the IDB's Special Programs Section in the Office of External Relations, mentioned a couple of ways that the IDB incorporates strategic communications into its activities. "We provide technical assistance to develop communications strategies for IDB-financed operations, carry out public awareness campaigns such as the Don't Call Me Street Kid and Natural Disaster Awareness campaigns, and produce television programming on development topics such as domestic violence to sensitize public opinion in Latin America and the Caribbean."

Communications in Development Projects

Communications can be used many ways to advance development, according to Silvio Waisboard, Senior Program Officer at the Academy of Educational Development. For example, development professionals can use communications to promote behavioral changes, to educate, to mobilize communities, to advocate policy changes, to spark a community dialogue or public debate, or to increase participation in a project. Integrating top-down approaches (i.e. mass media) and bottom-up ones (i.e. town hall meetings) is one of the most effective means of strategic communications for development projects, panel members agreed. One way of doing that, according to Waisboard, is to have a tool-kit approach and combine media and interpersonal communications.

"You need to use techniques that fit your audience or target group, whether you use the mass media to mobilize large populations or do social marketing, or you use interpersonal communications to convince people to change their attitudes or behaviors." Waisboard continued, "Whatever you do, community empowerment should be the goal.

If you want your project to be sustainable, you need to build community ownership." The experts at the seminar also concurred that such communications efforts should be aimed at various levels-from individuals, families and communities to members of civil society organizations and governments from the municipal to the national level. Along those same lines, Cecilia Cabañero-Verzosa, head of knowledge and capacity building in the Development Communications Division of External Affairs at the World Bank, emphasized the importance of building partnerships in all sectors of society. Built partnerships at many levels, from internal networks at the World Bank, such as a 350 member development communications network, to sector-specific partnerships that focus on issues in the environment or the water sector, for example, to partnerships with civil society or the private sector.

A Few Caveats

The Center for Population, Health and Nutrition's senior advisor on health communications and behaviour change at USAID, Elizabeth Fox, warned that communications managers need to keep an eye on the structure of and participation in communications. "Who owns the media? How is it financed? How much competition is there [in each country in Latin America and the Caribbean]?" Fox asked. "The answers to those questions are going to influence who gets access to mass media communications and whether or not diverse opinions will get the chance to be heard." Experts also explained that investments in communications must be ongoing and long-term if they're going to bring sustained changes in behaviour.

If you drop your communications campaign, results are going to drop, too. A campaign encouraging seat belt use in North Carolina called Click it or ticket. Before the campaign began, 63 per cent of drivers used seat belts. Once the campaign was established, usage climbed to 80 per cent. The campaign was stopped for a time because local officials believed it had served its purpose. Afterward, usage dropped to 73 percent. They quickly realized what had happened and reinstated the campaign. At that point, usage again increased to 81 percent. The point is, using communications campaigns for short periods of time only brings short-term results.

Getting Results: Don't Call Me Street Kid Campaign

The specific impact that the Don't Call Me Street Kid campaign has already had in the region. The campaign has created new links between groups-at least 15 new government-NGO partnerships and alliances per country The IDB has taken the campaign to eleven countries. The campaign has also expanded public debate," Lobera said, "including 3 televised national debates in Bolivia that have catapulted the issue to the top of the political agenda. The campaign received an estimated $7 million in free on-air time, with our TV spot airing 30,000 times and the video documentary 416 times. Local policy changes that have resulted from the campaign include new local childhood policies in 50 municipalities in Colombia and the creation of action plans on the issue in Costa Rica, Honduras, El Salvador and Guatemala.

The Development of the World Trading System

Up until the Great Depression of the 1930s, most countries had some degree of protectionism. Great Britain, as a major trading nation, was one of the strongest supporters of free trade. Although the world was already in a depression, in 1930 the USA enacted the Smoot-Hawley tariff, which created significant import tariffs on foreign goods. As other nations took similar steps and the depression deepened, world trade fell further.

After WWII, the US and other nations realized the value of freer trade, and established the General Agreement on Tariffs and Trade (GATT).

The approach of GATT was to gradually eliminate barriers to trade. Over 100 countries became members of GATT, and worked together to further liberalize trade. The different rounds of GATT negotiations and the resulting reductions in tariffs.

During the 1980s and early 1990s, the world trading system as "managed" by GATT underwent strains. First, Japan's economic strength and huge trade surplus stressed what had been more equal trading patterns, and Japan's perceived protectionist (neo-mercantilist) policies created intense political pressures in other countries. Second, the persistent trade deficits by the US, the world's largest economy, caused significant economic problems for some industries and political problems for the government. Thirdly, many countries found that although limited by GATT from utilizing tariffs, there were many other more subtle forms of intervention that had the same effects and did not technically violate GATT (e.g. VERs). Against the background of rising protectionist pressures, in 1986 GATT members embarked on their eighth round of negotiations to reduce tariffs (called the Uruguay Round). This was the most ambitious round to date, as the goal was to expand beyond the regulation of manufactured goods and address trade issues related to intellectual property, agriculture, services, and enforcement mechanism.

The agreement, however, left several important matters unaddressed: financial services, broadcast entertainment, environmental matters, worker's rights, and foreign direct investment. Those items were left to further negotiations under the auspices of the World Trade Organization.

When the WTO was established, its creators hoped the WTO's enforcement mechanisms would make it a more effective policeman of the global trade rules than the GATT had been. The WTO has handed down a number of rulings that have led to changes in governmental policies that restricted trade; in other cases, governments had made changes in advance of WTO rulings.

Under the WTO, 68 countries that account for more than 90% of world telecommunications revenues pledged to open their markets to foreign competition and to abide by common rules for fair competition in telecommunications. The WTO has also made headway in liberalizing trade in financial services, although the current agreement still includes a number of exceptions. Substantial work still remains to be done on the international trade front. Environmental policies are one area of concern, as are regulations regarding foreign direct investment.

Implications for Business

Clearly, trade barriers negatively impact the ability of firms to locate activities in the economically optimal location or source materials from the best producers. Trade barriers can change the underlying costs and benefits of different locations, and force firms to undertake operations in specific locations rather than import or export. Even if specific quotas, tariffs, local content, etc. regulations do not specifically require that certain actions be taken, a firm may choose to locate facilities or buy from certain suppliers in order to reduce the threat of mandatory and more punitive governmental intervention.

Certain trade barriers may even make some operations no longer viable, and force a firm to give up particular markets or production sites. In general, international firms have an incentive to lobby for free trade, and keep protectionist pressures from causing them to have to change strategies. While there may be short-term benefits to having governmental protection in some situations, in the long-run, these can back fire and other governments can retaliate.

Communication in Business

Effective communication in business is not about creating the perfect PowerPoint presentation. It's not about writing the perfectly-pitched report. It's not even about assiduously alliterating <smile>. Sometimes effectively communicating in business can hinge on something really simple—the habits you bring to your interactions with others.

As we all know, we all have habitual behaviours that we carry around with us and use unconsciously. It could be the "um" you sandwich between every fourth word of your presentation. It could be the nervous 'fig-leaf' gestures of your hands. It could be your constant swaying and looking away from your audience, as if you should be somewhere else far more important right at that moment.

Whoever you are, whilst you may know your facts inside-out, whilst your work ethic is the standard by which others are measured, if you don't recognise and work on your personal presentation habits you might eventually destroy all that you have strived so hard to achieve.

Whatever your particular habit is, you can best find out what it is by two great methods:

- Ask your colleagues what you do in face-to-face encounters that annoys them
- Have someone video a presentation to a group that you give

We all have a communication habit that works against us in some small way. But the challenge we face is that, left unattended, they start adding up. The more you have, the more unprofessional you look. Here's eight interpersonal communication blunders that can wreck your career over time:

Owning a weak handshake: A weak handshake signals uncertainty, hesitation, a lack of integrity, a lack of confidence and a lack of courage. It quite possibly also triggers subconscious responses in the recipient that cause them to focus more and for longer on your handshake than on your message. To butcher Nike's slogan, "Just don't do it!" Displaying a nervous giggle: Just like a weak handshake, the nervous giggle, in the eyes and mind of your audience, turns you into a child. No one seriously does business with a child.

Over-using "I'm sorry": A 'killer' for undermining your authority, a phrase like, "I need your report on my desk by 5 o'clock, sorry" just knocks your professionalism, your communication and your career for six. You have no need to apologise if you are the boss or the client. There is a place for politeness in business, as there are for courtesy and humility. But in the shark-eat-shark world of nature and business, there is no room for the weak and mousy. Sorry to have to break that to you. . . .

Standing passively: Crossed arms, crossed legs . . . they signal just one thing—detachment, as if you really don't want to be there, listening to the other person, but you *have* to. Passively standing kicks down the building bricks of trust, over time reducing your career reputation to rubble. Avoiding eye contact: Whilst too much staring at someone can cause discomfort, so can too little. By not looking at your audience (of one of one thousand) in the eye, you come across as nervous and insincere. A reasonable period of eye contact is between 4 and 7 seconds at a time, per person, especially when you are talking to them.

Playing with your hands: Wringing your hands, or playing 'fig leaf' is a sure way of conveying insecurity about yourself or your message. And recently I was reminded by my Toastmasters club colleagues of a habit of mine that I need to break—twisting my wedding ring around my finger when I present. My colleagues found themselves focusing more on my ring-twiddling than my message.

Speaking too softly: A habit that is a sure sign in the eyes of others, that you are not confident about yourself, your message or your authority to deliver it. You come across as near-invisible, weak and insubstantial, as well as make yourself difficult to be heard by those who are hard of hearing. And as I get older, my hearing is definately getting worse—a legacy of spending years in front of PA stacks as a lighting manager for rock bands.

Using qualifying words: This is quite possibly one of the worst habits anyone could have. Absolutely nearly everyone qualifies their words, and most often the effect is to dilute the power and impact of your message. Seriously, using words such as "kind of", "sort of" and "maybe" make even the smartest of us appear unsure. If you are unsure if you have any or all of these habits when you communicate in a business setting, or if you are unsure about how to rid yourself of them, please do not hesitate to contact me. I can either point you in the direction of your nearest Toastmasters public speaking club (a fantastic organisation geared specifically to help you become a powerful public speaker), or else I can offer alternative resources, including analysing your business communication performance and subsequently coaching you to greater heights.

Communication Strategy

A critical element in the marketing mix is communication strategy. This is the process of communicating the attributes of a product to prospective customers. A number of different communications channels are available to a firm. These include direct selling, sales promotion, direct marketing, and advertising via many different media. A firm's communications strategy is partly defined by its choice of channel.

The effectiveness of international communication can be hindered by three potentially critical variables - cultural barriers, source effects, and noise levels. Cultural barriers arise from the difficulty of communicating messages across cultures. The best way for a firm to overcome cultural barriers is for it to develop cross-cultural literacy, although that is often difficult to achieve. Source effects occur when the receiver of the message (the potential consumer) evaluates the message based upon the status or image of the sender. Source effects can be either positive or negative. For example, think of some positive and negative source effects — such as German autos vs. French wine or Italian cuisine vs. British cuisine.

Noise tends to reduce the chance of effective communication. In this context, noise refers to the amount of other messages that are competing for a potential consumer's attention.

Push Strategy and a Pull Strategy

The main choice with regard to communication strategy is between a push strategy and a pull strategy. A push strategy emphasizes personnel selling which requires a competent sales force and is costly. Whereas a pull strategy emphasizes mass media advertising to communicate the marketing message to potential customers. The choice between push and pull strategies depends upon product type and consumer sophistication, channel length, and media availability.

Push strategies tend to be emphasized more in the following circumstances:

(1) for industrial products and/or complex new products,

(2) when distribution channels are short, and

(3) when few print or electronic media are available.

Pull strategies tend to be emphasized more in the following circumstances:

(1) for consumer goods products,
(2) when distribution channels are long, and when
(3) sufficient print and electronic media are available to carry the marketing message.

A globally standardized advertising campaign is one in which the same marketing message is used the world over. The major benefits of standard advertising are lower costs of ad creation, better utilization of creative talent, and the avoidance of confusion created by differences in message. While a standardized campaign has economic advantages, it usually fails to account for differences in culture and advertising regulations between countries.

Pricing Strategy

The concept of strategic pricing has tow aspects, which are refereed as predatory pricing and experience curve pricing. Price discrimination exists whenever consumers in different countries are charged different prices for the same product. Price discrimination can assist a firm in the procés of maximizing its profits.

For price discrimination to work, the firm must be able to keep national markets separate and different price elasticities of demand must exist in different countries. The elasticity of demand is determined by a number of factors, of which income level and competitive conditions are probably the most important. In general, price elasticities tend to be greater in countries with lower income levels and greater numbers of competitors. The concept of strategic pricing has two aspects, which are refereed as predatory pricing and experience curve pricing.

Predatory pricing involves using the profit gained in one market to support aggressive pricing in another market, the objective being to drive competitors out of the market. Here the price is used as competitive weapon to drive weaker competitors out of a national market by pricing very low. Once the competitors have left the market, the firm can raise prices and enjoy high profits. Many Japanese firms have been accused of pursuing this strategy. Experience curve pricing involves aggressive pricing to build up accumulated global volume as rapidly as possible, thereby moving the firm down the experience curve as rapidly as possible. A firm builds its accumulated production volume over time, unit costs fall due to "experience effects" due to learning curves and economies of scale.

The ability of a firm to engage in price discrimination or strategic pricing is limited by antidumping regulations and nation competition policy. Antidumping regulations limit firms' ability to price below cost or below the price in its domestic market. Competition regulations can limit firm's ability to charge monopoly prices.

Configuring the Marketing Mix

Standardization versus customization is not an all or nothing concept. In reality, most firms standardize some things and customize others. When looking at the overall marketing mix and message, one often finds some aspects of standardization and some aspects of customization in all products depending on local requirements and overall cost structures.

New Product Development

New product development is a high risk but high return activity. In order to build up a competency in new product development, the international business must do two things:

(1) disperse R&D activities to those countries where new products are being pioneered and

(2) integrate R&D with marketing.

Innovations can make established products obsolete overnight. At the same time, innovations can create a host of new product possibilities. To stay abreast of competitors' innovations, as well as develop their own, firms should have R&D activities in locations that are on the cutting edge of technology.

The need to adequately commercialize new technologies poses special problems in international businesses, since commercialization may require different versions of the product is produced for different countries. A firm's new product development efforts need to be closely coordinated with the marketing, production, and materials management functions. This integration is critical to making certain that customer needs are met and that the company performs all its value creation activities efficiently.

One way to achieve cross-functional integration is to have cross-functional product development teams. Effective cross-functional teams should be led by a heavyweight project manager with status in the organization, have members from all the critical functional areas, have members located together, have clear goals, and have an effective conflict resolution process. This all becomes more difficult when developing products for multiple worldwide markets. Many large firms have research centers in limited locations, with product development activities more dispersed.

Business Plan for an Established Business

This business plan consists of a narrative and several financial spreadsheets. The narrative template is the body of the business plan. It contains more than 150 questions divided into several sections. Work through the sections in any order you like, except for the *Executive Summary*, which should be done last. Skip any questions that do not apply to your business. When you are finished writing your first draft, you will have a collection of small essays on the various topics of the business plan. Then you will want to edit them into a flowing narrative. The real value of doing a business plan is not having the finished product in hand; rather, the value lies in the process of research and thinking about your business in a systematic way. The act of planning helps you to think things through thoroughly, to study and research when you are not sure of the facts, and to look at your ideas critically. It takes time, but avoids costly, perhaps disastrous, mistakes later.

The business plan narrative is a generic model suitable for all types of businesses. However, you should modify it to suit your particular circumstances. Before you begin, review the section titled *Refining the Plan*, found at the end of the business plan. It suggests emphasizing certain areas, depending upon your type of business (manufacturing, retail, service, etc.). It also has tips for fine-tuning your plan to make an effective presentation to investors or bankers. If this is why you are writing your plan, pay particular attention to your writing style. You will be judged by the quality and appearance of your work as well as your ideas. It typically takes several weeks to complete a good plan. Most of that time is spent in research and rethinking your ideas and assumptions. But then, that is the value of the process. So make time to do the job properly. Those who do never regret the effort. And finally, be sure to keep detailed notes on your sources of information and on the assumptions underlying your financial data.

Business Plan

Mission Statement: Many companies have a brief mission statement, usually 30 words or fewer, explaining their reason for being and their guiding principles. If you have a mission statement, this is a good place to put it in the plan, followed by company goals and objectives and business philosophy.

What business are you in? What do you do?

What is your target market? (Explain briefly here, because you will do a more thorough explanation in the *Marketing Plan* section.)

Describe your Industry. Is it a growth industry? What changes do you foresee in your industry, and how is your company poised to take advantage of them?

Now give a detailed description of the business:

Form of Ownership: Sole proprietor, partnership, corporation, or limited liability corporation (LLC)?

Company History: Years in business, previous owners, successes, failures, lessons learned, reputation in community, sales and profit history, number of employees, and events that affected success. Discuss significant past problems and how you solved and survived them.

Most important strengths and core competencies: What factors will make the company succeed? What are your major competitive strengths? What strengths do you personally bring to the business?

Significant challenges the company faces now and in the near future: If you are asking for funding, go on to explain how the new capital will help you meet these challenges.

Long Term: What are your plans for the future of the business? Growth? If so, at what rate and how will you achieve it?

Are you developing strategies for continued growth, increased production, diversification, or eventual sale of the business? What are your time frames for these?

Products and Services

Describe in depth your products and services. (Technical specifications, drawings, photos, sales brochures, and other bulky items belong in the *Appendices.*)

What factors give you competitive advantages or disadvantages? For example, the level of quality, or unique or proprietary features.

What is the pricing, fee, or leasing structure of your products and services?

Market Research: Why?

You spend so much time on marketing-related matters—customers, competitors, pricing, promotion, and advertising—that it is natural to assume that you have little to learn. However, every small business can benefit from doing market research to make sure it is on track. Use the business planning process as your opportunity to uncover data and to question your marketing efforts. It will be time well spent.

Market Research: How?

There are two kinds of market research: primary and secondary.

Primary market research means gathering your own data. For example, you could do your own traffic count at a proposed location, use the yellow pages to identify competitors, and do surveys or focus group interviews to learn about consumer preferences. Professional market research can be very costly, but there are many books that show small business owners how to do effective research.

Secondary research means using published information such as industry profiles, trade journals, newspapers, magazines, census data, and demographic profiles. This type of information is available from public libraries, industry associations, chambers of commerce, vendors who sell to your industry, and government agencies.

Start with your local library. Most librarians are pleased to guide you through their business data collection. You will be amazed at what is there. There are more online sources than you could possibly use. Your chamber of commerce has good information on the local area. Trade associations and trade publications often have excellent industry-specific data.

In your marketing plan, be as specific as possible; give statistics, numbers, and sources. The marketing plan will be the basis, later on, of the all-important sales projection.

4

Business Communication Methods

Telephony: VoIP

Voice over Internet Protocol (VoIP) technology allows users to communicate over the Internet. This calling option allows you to see your calling party and interact in real time. VoIP services also reduce the expenses that occur with standard local and long distance services since many VoIP services are free or low-cost.

Handheld Wireless Devices

Handheld wireless devices such as PDAs and smartphones combine the operations of a computer and phone into one device. These handheld devices provide phone, email, web browsing, calendar options and more. Some smartphones even allow you to sign into corporate databases and intranets. Business executives and employees have begun to use these devices to stay in touch with the office while they are away.

Video-conferencing

Videoconferencing has helped reduce business costs and expenses. Videoconferencing brings participants together from various locations with the help of cameras and screens. This communication method allows groups to see and interact with one another in real team.

This method allows businesses to reduce their overhead and expenses because they are no longer required to travel in order to meet with the business partners and clients.

Company Intranet

Intranet systems are widely used in business. Intranets house insider business information such as departmental information, product knowledge, events, meetings and contact information. The information is protected from external access and often provides interactive materials and access to business resources and software.

Blogs and Podcasts

Blogs and podcasts are becoming more popular in business. These communication methods allow customers and clients to express their experiences and concerns about the business with a journal entry (blog) or voice audio (podcast). Businesses use these communication methods to keep customers informed and to receive feedback. The received information can be highly informative and the information is obtained more quickly than when using surveys and feedback sheets.

Email, Internet Chat and Instant Messaging

Email has created a solid foundation in the business community, providing timely written conversations that can also be used as a record. Instant chat and instant messaging take the email method one step further, allowing for instant, real time responses. Many businesses have initiated chat and instant messaging options for customers seeking customer service and sales assistance on their company websites. These methods are advanced options that provide the customer with greater conveniences and less hassle. These options are also widely used within the business, allowing employees to immediate responses and assistance without losing productivity.

Business Communication: less is more

It may seem counter intuitive, but tearing yourself away from business communication tools like internet and email can actually make you more productive. We all know how much we rely on these business communication tools for running our work and personal life, but it's not until it's actually taken away from you for an extended period that you realise the full extent of your dependence.

For the first two weeks you were feeling pressured about your inability to respond to client enquiries, communicate with people and generally 'get things done'. But what you quickly discovered how much *actual work* you were doing because you didn't have the email or Internet to distract me! In fact, by the time three weeks had passed.

This experience truly opened my eyes to my own inefficiencies. Once you got over the feeling of being *out* of controlyou realised that actually you were very much *in* control. In today's world we're led to believe that we always need to be accessible - to our clients, our suppliers, family and friends. Not so. By choosing to control how frequently we communicate, and at what time, we put ourselves in the driver's seat.

Turn off automatic send/receive on your email programme

You used to have Outlook set up so it would check for new emails every 10 minutes. Really, I was just asking to be distracted. To turn this off (in Outlook) click on Tools, Mail Set Up, Send/ Receive. Then uncheck the box "schedule an automatic send/ receive every × minutes". Now you can decide when you want to read your emails.

Download emails no more than twice per day

Now you are in control, pick two times a day when you choose to hit the send/receive button and get all your emails delivered. Do this at the same time every day - make it a habit.

Schedule time to respond to emails, and stick to it

Our natural instinct when we get email is to reply immediately. That's extremely inefficient if you are constantly getting emails throughout the day. Set aside 30 to 45 minutes per day to respond to your emails, and you'll eliminate the problem of constant interruption.

Get better at managing junk email

Not having to read about Viagra, mortgages and surgical enhancement for 26 days was brilliant! Since being back online

I've used Outlook to filter out even more of my junk email. Two rules are highly recommend.

- create a rule putting all emails not addressed directly to you in a new folder called Junk Suspects.
- put all emails not from someone in your address book into the Junk Suspects folder.

To set these up in Outlook, select Tools, Rules and Alerts, New Rule. Then just use the suggested templates to create this and any other rule.

Set expectations with your customers about response times

The most difficult mental hurdle to overcome is about not feeling responsive to requests that come in from clients and customers. If your customers are used to getting a reply within one hour, then you need to communicate your new standards, or make them very clear up front. I suggest you 'induct' new clients and suppliers to your process by telling them when they can expect a reply from you. For example, "I read emails at 9am and 4pm every day, and will respond to you within 24 hours". This sets clear boundaries and removes the expectation of an immediate response.

Unsubscribe to everything that's unnecessary

If you're like me, you've signed up for all sorts of things over the years. It's amazing what you choose to spend time reading when you only have one hour per day. I used to waste so much time just scanning things through that I thought might be interesting. No more! This takes up huge amounts of time, so only read what is really of value. It may take you a week or so of feeling uncomfortable about these changes before you start to feel the benefits of more time. Stick with it. I'm totally converted.

Internet Communication Methods

How do we keep Internet communication simple? Let's start by taking a look at the different methods used to communicate on the web. It is important to understand the nuances and benefits of the different forms.

Email

This is the most popular communication method. Users typically use desktop software to receive, read and respond to messages. Some users use web-based mail and manage messages in a web browser like Internet Explorer. The downfall to email communication is that anyone can send email messages to anyone else if they have (or guess) the correct email address. This system's Achilles heel is its simplicity and universal popularity.

Email accounts are often burdened by spam or unsolicited email. Despite software developers having created complex spam filters and legislators having introduced new anti-spam legislation, the problem persists and spam continues to burden email as a messaging medium.

Instant Messaging

Instant messaging allows users to "chat" in real time. Users can send text messages to anyone online and receive instant replies if the user is also online. The "instant" fad gave way to parental fears as children made "friends" online. With no way to confirm if "friends" are who they represent themselves to be, and multiple security holes, instant messaging has taken a back seat in internet communication.

Blogs

Online journals and daily diaries have taken hold. Some blogs are interactive, allowing users to respond and comment on posts. Locating topic-specific blogs that provide relevant and interesting content on a daily basis can be a challenge. The nature of a blog is to contain fresh public content. As our lives become more complicated blogs are often abandoned, as they require constant updating.

RSS

RSS is the latest messaging medium and shows genuine promise as a means to communicate. RSS files are produced as XML files and are designed to provide content summaries of news or information. The biggest benefit to RSS is that it does not have the spam issues inherent to email; users opt-in to the RSS feeds that interest them.

Forums/Newsgroups

A forum is an online discussion group. Forums can be newsgroups, or they can be web-based discussion groups. Forums have proven themselves as valuable business resources - often creating communities of customers helping customers. Without moderation and oversight they can potentially create an unfriendly environment.

Listservs

Liststervs are mailing list programmes for communicating with other people who have subscribed to the same list. Using e-mail, you can participate in listservs pertaining to your topics of interest. When you submit a message to the server, your message is relayed to all on the listserv. You receive messages from other participants via e-mail.

What's Next?

Internet communication is intrinsically tied to the hardware options available. Wireless technology has accelerated the development of messaging software, opening the market to a dizzying array of devices for web access. Where we were once tied to a keyboard and mouse, we will soon be navigating the web with our voices from a moving automobile, or browsing via screens in our eyewear, with tiny cameras reading our eye movements to move the cursor and make selections. Our interactive conversations will include more and more participants at once. Evaluating the many options and choosing what works best for you is the first step to effectively communicating on the web.

Using Instant Messaging for Business

Instant messaging (IM) has become a popular way to communicate with clients and coworkers, and for good reason. Communicating over the Internet in real time can streamline communications and save you time and money. Plus, since most instant-messaging software is free, you don't need to invest more

But before you rush into using instant messaging, think about whether it will really improve your business communications or just serve as another distraction. First, consider reasons to use an instant messenger:

Save on long distance. Using instant messaging to communicate with employees and clients in other parts of the world can reduce your long-distance phone bills. And most instant message services now also support voice conversations as well as video. Conduct real-time interaction. When you work on a project with coworkers who have busy schedules or work in different offices, instant messaging facilitates quick and simple communication. Unlike e-mail, when you use an instant messenger you don't have to wait for messages to download from a mail server.

Reduce spam. Instant messengers get a lot fewer unwanted messages than e-mail. Host chats and conferences. Public chat rooms are often chaotic, and it's difficult to conduct a focused conversation — especially for business purposes. Although instant messengers are most commonly used for two-way conversations, most programmes offer a conference or chat setting where your workgroup can meet.

Now that you've considered the advantages of instant messaging, take a look at the disadvantages. Like most technologies, instant messaging does have some drawbacks: Proprietary software. While it is now possible to use software that lets you connect to multiple instant message services, most services only let you send messages to other users or add them to your contact list using the same instant messenger you do. Trying to mandate a particular messenger can be difficult, especially if employees are attached to specific programmes.

Word limits. Most messaging programmes have a character limit for messages. If you need to communicate a large amount of information, an e-mail or a phone call is a better choice. Security. Use caution with the information you share over chat or instant messengers. Take a look at your profile to see what information you've made public, and find out if the software creates public directories of its users.

Misuse. Employees may be tempted to communicate with their friends during work hours because instant messaging is easy and fun. You may want to adopt an instant-messaging policy (similar to your e-mail policy) that outlines how messaging should and should not be used for business.

Instant Messaging

Instant messaging (IM) is a form of real-time direct text-based communication between two or more people using shared clients. The text is conveyed via devices connected over a network such as the Internet.

Definition

Instant messaging falls under the umbrella of chat, as it is a real-time text-based networked communication system, but is distinct in that it is based on clients that facilitate connections between specified known users (often using "Buddy List", "Friend List" or "Contact List"), whereas Chat includes web-based applications that allow communication between (often anonymous) users in a multi-user environment. (an analogy would be comparing a telephone and a bar-room. With the telephone, you have to know the contact information to reach the other person, whereas you just show up at the bar and see who is there to chat with)

Overview

Instant messaging (IM) is a collection of technologies that create the possibility of real-time text-based communication between two or more participants over the internet or some form of internal network/intranet. It is important to understand that what separates chat and instant messaging from technologies such as e-mail is the perceived synchronicity of the communication by the user - Chat happens in real-time. Some systems allow the sending of messages to people not currently logged on (*offline messages*), thus removing some of the differences between Instant Messaging and e-mail (often this is done by sending the message to the associated e-mail account).

Instant messaging allows effective and efficient communication, allowing immediate receipt of acknowledgment or reply. In many cases Instant Messaging includes additional features, which make it even more popular. For example, users can see each other by using web-cams, or talk directly for free over the Internet using a microphone and headphones (or speakers). Many clients allow file transfer as well, although they are typically limited in the file-size allowed. It is typically possible to save a conversation for later reference. Instant messages are often logged in a local message history, making it similar to the persistent nature of e-mails.

History

Instant messaging predates the Internet, first appearing on multi-user operating systems like CTSS and Multics in the mid-1960s. Initially, some of these systems were used as notification systems for services like printing, but quickly were used to facilitate communication with other users logged in to the same machine. As networks developed, the protocols spread with the networks. Some of these used a peer-to-peer protocol (eg talk, ntalk and ytalk), while others required peers to connect to a server (see talker and IRC). During the Bulletin board system (BBS) phenomenon that peaked during the 1980s, some systems incorporated chat features which were similar to instant messaging; Freelancin' Roundtable was one prime example.

In the last half of the 1980s and into the early 1990s, the Quantum Link online service for Commodore 64 computers offered user-to-user messages between currently connected customers which they called "On-Line Messages" (or OLM for short). Quantum Link's better-known later incarnation, America Online, offers a similar product under the name "AOL Instant Messenger" (AIM). While the Quantum Link service ran on a Commodore 64, using only the Commodore's PETSCII text-graphics, the screen was visually divided up into sections and OLMs would appear as a yellow bar saying "Message From:" and the name of the sender along with the message across the top of whatever the user was already doing, and presented a list of options for responding. As such, it could be considered a sort of GUI, albeit much more primitive than the later Unix, Windows and Macintosh based GUI IM programmes. OLMs were what Q-Link called "Plus Services" meaning they charged an extra per-minute fee on top of the monthly Q-Link access costs.

Modern, Internet-wide, GUI-based messaging clients, as they are known today, began to take off in the mid 1990s with PowWow, ICQ, and AOL Instant Messenger (AOL Instant Messenger,). Similar functionality was offered by CU-SeeMe in 1992; though primarily an audio/video chat link, users could also type messages to each other. AOL later acquired Mirabilis, the creators of ICQ; a few years later ICQ (now owned by AOL) was awarded two patents for instant messaging by the U.S. patent office. Meanwhile, other companies developed their own applications (Excite, MSN, Ubique, and Yahoo), each with its own proprietary protocol and client; users therefore had to run multiple client applications if they wished to use more than one of these networks. In 1998 IBM released IBM Lotus Sametime, a product based on technology acquired when IBM bought Haifa-based Ubique and Lexington-based Databeam.

In 2000, an open source application and open standards-based protocol called XMPP was launched. XMPP servers could act as gateways to other IM protocols, reducing the need to run multiple clients. Multi-protocol clients can use any of the popular IM protocols by using additional local libraries for each protocol. IBM Lotus Sametime's November 2007 release added IBM Lotus Sametime Gateway support for XMPP.

Social networking providers (such as Facebook) often offer IM capabilities. Many instant messaging services offer video conferencing features, Voice Over IP (VoIP) and web conferencing services. Web conferencing services integrate both video conferencing and instant messaging capabilities. Some instant messaging companies are offering desktop sharing, IP radio, and IPTV to the voice and video features. The term "instant messenger" is a service mark of Time Warner and may not be used in software not affiliated with AOL in the United States. For this reason, the instant messaging client formerly known as Gaim or gaim announced in April 2007 that they would be renamed "Pidgin".

Clients

Each modern IM service generally provides its own client, either a separately installed piece of software, or a browser-based client. These typically only work with that companies service, although some (such as Google Talk) allow limited function with other services. There are also 3rd-party Client software applications that will connect with most of the major IM services. Pidgin (Windows/ Linux), Trillian (Windows/Browser-Based/iPhone/soon for OS X?), Meebo (Browser-based), Adium (Mac OS X) and Digsby (Windows), are a few of the common ones. Comparison_of_instant_ messaging_clients

Interoperability

Standard free instant messaging applications offer functions like file transfer, contact lists, the ability to have simultaneous conversations etc. These may be all the functions that a small business needs but larger organisations will require more sophisticated applications that can work together. The solution to finding applications capable of this is to use enterprise versions of instant messaging applications. These include titles like XMPP, Lotus Sametime, Microsoft Office Communicator, etc., which are often integrated with other enterprise applications such as workflow systems. These enterprise applications, or Enterprise Application Integration (EAI), are built to certain constraints, namely storing data in a common format. There have been several attempts to create a unified standard for instant messaging: IETF's SIP (Session Initiation Protocol) and SIMPLE (SIP for Instant Messaging and Presence Leveraging Extensions), APEX (Application Exchange), Prim (Presence and Instant Messaging Protocol), the open XML-based XMPP (Extensible Messaging and Presence Protocol), and OMA's (Open Mobile Alliance) IMPS (Instant Messaging and Presence Service) created specifically for mobile devices.

Most attempts at creating a unified standard for the major IM providers (AOL, Yahoo! and Microsoft) have failed, and each continues to use its own proprietary protocol. However, while discussions at IETF were stalled, Reuters head of collaboration services, David Gurle (the founder of Microsoft's Real Time Communication and Collaboration business), signed the first inter-service provider connectivity agreement on September 2003. This agreement enabled AIM, ICQ and MSN Messenger users to talk with Reuters Messaging counterparts and vice-versa. Following this, Microsoft, Yahoo! and AOL came to a deal where Microsoft's Live Communication Server 2005 users would also have the possibility to talk to public instant messaging users. This deal established SIP/SIMPLE as a standard for protocol interoperability and established a connectivity fee for accessing public instant messaging clouds. Separately, on October 13, 2005 Microsoft and Yahoo! announced that by the 3rd quarter of 2006 they would interoperate using SIP/SIMPLE which was followed on December 2005 by the AOL and Google strategic partnership deal where Google Talk users would be able to talk with AIM and ICQ users provided they have an AIM account.

There are two ways to combine the many disparate protocols:

1. One way is to combine the many disparate protocols inside the IM client application.
2. The other way is to combine the many disparate protocols inside the IM *server* application. This approach moves the task of communicating to the other services to the server. Clients need not know or care about other IM protocols. For example, LCS 2005 Public IM Connectivity. This approach is popular in XMPP servers however the so-called transport projects suffer the same reverse engineering difficulties as any other project involved with closed protocols or formats.

Some approaches allow organizations to create their own private instant messaging network by enabling them to limit access to the server (often with the IM network entirely behind their firewall) and administer user permissions. Other corporate messaging systems allow registered users to also connect from outside the corporation LAN, by using a secure firewall-friendly HTTPS based protocol. Typically, a dedicated corporate IM server has several advantages such as pre-populated contact lists, integrated authentication, and better security and privacy. Some networks have made changes to prevent them from being utilized by such multi-network IM clients. For example, Trillian had to release several revisions and patches to allow its users to access the MSN, AOL, and Yahoo! networks, after changes were made to these networks. The major IM providers typically cite the need for formal agreements as well as security concerns as reasons for making these changes.

Mobile Instant Messaging

Mobile Instant Messaging (MIM) is the technology that allows Instant Messaging services to be accessed from a mobile/cellular device, ranging from a standard cell phone to an iPhone, to a Blackberry, to an Android-based device. It is done two ways:

- Embedded Clients - tailored IM client for every specific device.
- Clientless Platform – a browser based application that does not require downloading any software to the handset, which enables all users, all devices, from any network to connect to their Internet IM service (theoretically. There are sometimes issues with browser capabilities that can limit this).

Friend-to-friend Networks

Instant Messaging may be done in a Friend-to-friend network, in which each node connects to the friends on the friends list. This allows for communication with friends of friends and for the building of chatrooms for instant messages with all friends on that network.

IM language

Users sometimes make use of internet slang or text speak to abbreviate common words or expressions in order to quicken conversations or to reduce keystrokes.

The language has become universal, with well-known expressions such as 'lol' translated over to face to face language. Emotions are often expressed in shorthand, such as the abbreviation LOL, BRB, TTYL.

Some, however, attempt to be more accurate with emotional expression over IM. Real time reactions such as (chortle) (snort) (guffaw) or (eye-roll) are becoming more popular.

Also there are certain standards that are being introduced into mainstream conversations including, '#' indicates the use of sarcasm in a statement (alternatively (!) after the statement) and '*' which indicates a spelling mistake and/or grammatical error in the previous message, followed by a correction.

Business Application

Instant messaging has proven to be similar to personal computers, e-mail, and the World Wide Web, in that its adoption for use as a business communications medium was driven primarily by individual employees using consumer software at work, rather than by formal mandate or provisioning by corporate information technology departments. Tens of millions of the consumer IM accounts in use are being used for business purposes by employees of companies and other organizations.

In response to the demand for business-grade IM and the need to ensure security and legal compliance, a new type of instant messaging, called "Enterprise Instant Messaging" ("EIM") was created when Lotus Software launched IBM Lotus Sametime in 1998. Microsoft followed suit shortly thereafter with Microsoft Exchange Instant Messaging, later created a new platform called Microsoft Office Live Communications Server, and released Office Communications Server 2007 in October 2007. Oracle Corporation has also jumped into the market recently with its Oracle Beehive unified collaboration software. Both IBM Lotus and Microsoft have introduced federation between their EIM systems and some of the public IM networks so that employees may use a single interface to both their internal EIM system and their contacts on AOL, MSN, and Yahoo!. Current leading EIM platforms include IBM Lotus Sametime, Microsoft Office Communications Server, and Jabber XCP. In addition, industry-focused EIM platforms as Reuters Messaging and Bloomberg Messaging provide enhanced IM capabilities to financial services companies.

The adoption of IM across corporate networks outside of the control of IT organizations creates risks and liabilities for companies who do not effectively manage and support IM use. Companies implement specialized IM archiving and security products and services to mitigate these risks and provide safe, secure, productive instant messaging capabilities to their employees.

Practical use in Enterprise

The popular embrace of IM technology for sharing information has quickly led to organizations adopting IM solutions for the perceived advantages that can be brought by it. As organizations are becoming more information based the need for effective knowledge sharing, team working and collaborative environments amongst employees has become vital, especially within more geographically dispersed teams.

Typically, IM conversations tend to have a certain "character"; they are often short and only cover one topic. Media-switching and multitasking are common throughout, however IM might also be used between established coworkers and friends for longer, more intermittent conversation. In their report of IM use at the workplace it is identifies the four primary functions of IM which are often cited in other reports. These primary functions are:

- Quick questions and clarifications
- Coordinating and scheduling tasks
- Coordinating impromptu social meetings
- Keeping in touch with friends and family

Instant messaging is perhaps best suited to "Quick questions and clarifications" as this is the most often mentioned attribute in other reports. A user can "respond rapidly without the overhead of telephone or FTF interaction. For example, IDC reports, "Users see IM as a medium for quick, semi-permanent 'flashes' that beg a near-immediate response". Nardi's second and third observations are enabled in part due to the "Presence Awareness" feature of IM clients in which the user knows who is "available". This is the most relevant for colleagues who share the same physical space as each other and even paves the way for other mediums to take up the task of communication e.g. F2F or Phone. The implication is that viable communication of any sort can in someway be encouraged through IM's "Presence Awareness" feature. IM in business might not be the main tool for of communication, it could just be the meeting point for another type of media e.g. conference calls.

Nardi's third and fourth observations focus on the social use of IM, which have also been widely publicized in other report.

That IM is used for keeping in touch with friends and arranging social events has led some employers to believe that it is used primarily for this purpose. According to a market study found that:

> "'Fear of losing employee productivity' was the greatest concern of businesses in regards to instant messaging. The study by goes on to suggest this fear is unfounded as it was found that on average 'only 13% of conversations contained personal topics', and 'only 6.4% were exclusively personal'."

A study published in 2008 in the *Journal of Computer Mediated Communication* found that workers who used instant messaging on the job reported less interruption than colleagues who did not. Research showed that instant messaging was often used as a substitute for other, more disruptive forms of communication such as the telephone, e-mail, and face-to-face conversations. They found that the conversations were briefer between co-workers when using instant messaging than with the other forms of communications. Because of its unique setup, instant messaging allows users to control how and when they communicate with their coworkers. This technology gives people the ability to flag their availability or postpone responses to a more convenient time, according to one of the researchers. The study also notes that the ability to manage interruptions is most clear with the modality of text-based IM, and that such benefits are less likely with VOIP - or video-conference-based IM.

Review of Products

IM products can typically be categorised into two types: Enterprise Instant Messaging (EIM) and Consumer Instant Messaging (CIM). Enterprise solutions use an internal IM server, however this isn't always feasible, particularly for smaller businesses with limited budgets. The second option, using a CIM provides the advantage of being inexpensive to implement and has little need for investing in new hardware or server software. For corporate use encryption and conversation archiving are usually regarded as important features due to security concerns. Sometimes the use of different operating systems in organizations calls for the use of software that supports more than one platform. For example many software companies use Windows XP in administration departments but have software developers who use Linux.

Risks and Liabilities

Although instant messaging delivers many benefits, it also carries with it certain risks and liabilities, particularly when used in workplaces. Among these risks and liabilities are:

- Security risks (e.g. IM used to infect computers with spyware, viruses, trojans, worms)
- Compliance risks
- Inappropriate use
- Intellectual property leakage.

Security Risks

Crackers (malicious "hacker" or black hat hacker) have consistently used IM networks as vectors for delivering phishing attempts, "poison URLs", and virus-laden file attachments from 2004 to the present, with over 1100 discrete attacks listed by the IM Security Center in 2004-2007. Hackers use two methods of delivering malicious code through IM: delivery of virus, trojan, or spyware within an infected file, and the use of "socially engineered" text with a web address that entices the recipient to click on a URL that connects him or her to a website that then downloads malicious code. Viruses, worms, and trojans typically propagate by sending themselves rapidly through the infected user's buddy list. An effective attack using a poison URL may reach tens of thousands of people in minutes when each person's buddy list receives messages appearing to be from a trusted friend. The recipients click on the web address, and the entire cycle starts again. Infections may range from nuisance to criminal, and are becoming more sophisticated each year. IM connections usually take place in plain text, making them susceptible to eavesdropping. In addition, IM client software often requires the user to expose open UDP ports to the world, increasing the threat posed by potential security vulnerabilities.

Compliance Risks

In addition to the malicious code threat, the use of instant messaging at work also creates a risk of non-compliance to laws and regulations governing the use of electronic communications in businesses. In the United States alone there are over 10,000 laws and regulations related to electronic messaging and records retention. The better-known of these include the Sarbanes-Oxley Act, HIPAA, and SEC 17a-3. Clarification from the Financial Industry Regulatory Authority ("FINRA") was issued to member firms in the financial services industry in December, 2007, noting that "electronic communications", "email", and "electronic correspondence" may be used interchangeably and can include such forms of electronic messaging as *instant messaging* and text messaging. Changes to Federal Rules of Civil Procedure, effective December 1, 2006, created a new category for electronic records which may be requested during discovery in legal proceedings. Most countries around the world also regulate the use of electronic messaging and electronic records retention in similar fashion to the United States. The most common regulations related to IM at work involve the need to produce archived business communications to satisfy government or judicial requests under law. Many instant messaging communications fall into the category of business communications that must be archived and retrievable.

Inappropriate Use

Organizations of all types must protect themselves from the liability of their employees' inappropriate use of IM. The informal, immediate, and ostensibly anonymous nature of instant messaging makes it a candidate for abuse in the workplace. The topic of inappropriate IM use became front page news in October 2006 when Congressman Mark Foley resigned his seat after admitting sending offensive instant messages of a sexual nature to underage former House pages from his Congressional office PC.

The Mark Foley Scandal led to media coverage and mainstream newspaper articles warning of the risks of inappropriate IM use in workplaces. In most countries, corporations have a legal responsibility to ensure harassment-free work environment for employees. The use of corporate-owned computers, networks, and software to harass an individual or spread inappropriate jokes or language creates a liability for not only the offender but also the employer. A survey by IM archiving and security provider Akonix Systems, Inc. in March 2007 showed that 31% of respondents had been harassed over IM at work. Companies now include instant messaging as an integral component of their policies on appropriate use of the World Wide Web, e-mail, and other corporate assets.

Intellectual Property Leakage

Within the company there is also the risk of employees using instant messaging to release confidential information and project details to an outside source. This issue is best controlled by a combination of written policy and technology. An organization's policies on use of IM in the workplace could be an integral part of the overall computing and network use policies, and should be published and communicated at least annually. In addition to written policy, organizations should implement "gateways" or IM security products to monitor content of inbound and outbound messages. Products from IM security providers typically allow administrators to set alerts and enforce policy (i.e. allow or block messages) based on keywords and regular expressions within instant messages.

Security and Archiving

In the early 2000s, a new class of IT security provider emerged to provide remedies for the risks and liabilities faced by corporations who chose to use IM for business communications. The IM security providers created new products to be installed in corporate networks for the purpose of archiving, content-scanning, and security-scanning IM traffic moving in and out of the corporation. Similar to the e-mail filtering vendors, the IM security providers focus on the risks and liabilities described above.

With rapid adoption of IM in the workplace, demand for IM security products began to grow in the mid-2000s. By 2007, the preferred platform for the purchase of security software had become the "computer appliance", according to IDC, who estimate that by 2008, 80% of network security products will be delivered via an appliance.

User Base

Note that many of the numbers listed in this section are not directly comparable, and some are speculative. Some instant messaging systems are distributed among many different instances and thus difficult to measure in total (e.g. XMPP). While some numbers are given by the owners of a complete instant messaging system, others are provided by commercial vendors of a part of a distributed system. Some companies may be motivated to inflate their numbers in order to increase advertisement earnings or to attract partners, clients, or customers. Importantly, some numbers are reported as the number of "active" users (without a shared standard of that activity), others indicate total user accounts, while others indicate only the users logged in during an instance of peak usage.

5

Business Performance Management

Business performance management (BPM) is a set of processes that help organizations optimize their business performance. It is a framework for organizing, automating and analyzing business methodologies, metrics, processes and systems that drive business performance. BPM is seen as the next generation of business intelligence (BI). BPM helps businesses make efficient use of their financial, human, material and other resources.

History

An early reference to non-business performance management occurs in Sun Tzu's The Art of War. Sun Tzu claims that to succeed in war, one should have full knowledge of one's own strengths and weaknesses and full knowledge of one's enemy's strengths and weaknesses. Lack of either one might result in defeat. A certain school of thought draws parallels between the challenges in business and those of war, specifically:

- collecting data-both internal and external
- discerning patterns and meaning in the data (analyzing)
- responding to the resultant information

Prior to the start of the Information Age in the late 20th century, businesses sometimes took the trouble to laboriously collect data from non-automated sources. As they lacked computing resources to properly analyze the data they often made commercial decisions primarily on the basis of intuition. As businesses started automating more and more systems, more and more data became available. However, collection remained a challenge due to a lack of infrastructure for data exchange or due to incompatibilities between systems. Reports on the data gathered sometimes took months to generate. Such reports allowed informed long-term strategic decision-making. However, short-term tactical decision-making continued to rely on intuition.

In modern businesses, increasing standards, automation, and technologies have led to vast amounts of data becoming available. Data warehouse technologies have set up repositories to store this data. Improved ETL and even recently Enterprise Application Integration tools have increased the speedy collecting of data. OLAP reporting technologies have allowed faster generation of new reports which analyze the data. Business intelligence has now become the art of sieving through large amounts of data, extracting useful information and turning that information into actionable knowledge. In 1989 Howard Dresner, a research analyst at Gartner, popularized "Business Intelligence" as an umbrella term to describe a set of concepts and methods to improve business decision-making by using fact-based support systems. Performance Management is built on a foundation of BI, but marries it to the planning and control cycle of the enterprise-with enterprise planning, consolidation and modeling capabilities.

The term "BPM" is now becoming confused with "Business Process Management", and many are converting to the term "Corporate Performance Management" or "Enterprise Performance Management".

What is BPM?

BPM involves consolidation of data from various sources, querying, and analysis of the data, and putting the results into practice. BPM enhances processes by creating better feedback loops. Continuous and real-time reviews help to identify and eliminate problems before they grow. BPM's forecasting abilities help the company take corrective action in time to meet earnings projections. Forecasting is characterized by a high degree of predictability which is put into good use to answer what-if scenarios. BPM is useful in risk analysis and predicting outcomes of merger and acquisition scenarios and coming up with a plan to overcome potential problems. BPM provides key performance indicators (KPIs) that help companies monitor efficiency of projects and employees against operational targets.

Metrics/Key Performance Indicators

For business data analysis to become a useful tool, however, it is essential that an enterprise understand its goals and objectives-essentially, that they know the direction in which they want the enterprise to progress. To help with this analysis key performance indicators (KPIs) are laid down to assess the present state of the business and to prescribe a course of action. More and more organizations have started to speed up the availability of data. In the past, data only became available after a month or two, which did not help managers react swiftly enough. Recently, banks have tried to make data available at shorter intervals and have reduced delays. For example, for businesses which have higher operational/ credit risk loading (for example, credit cards and "wealth management"), A large multi-national bank makes KPI-related data available weekly, and sometimes offers a daily analysis of numbers and realtime dashboards are also provided. This means data usually becomes available within 24 hours, necessitating automation and the use of IT systems.

Most of the time, BPM simply means use of several financial/ nonfinancial metrics/key performance indicators to assess the present state of the business and to prescribe a course of action. Some of the areas from which top management analysis could gain knowledge by using BPM:

Customer-related numbers:

1. New customers acquired
2. Status of existing customers
3. Attrition of customers (including breakup by reason for attrition)
2. Turnover generated by segments of the Customers-these could be demographic filters.
3. Outstanding balances held by segments of customers and terms of payment-these could be demographic filters.

4. Collection of bad debts within customer relationships.
5. Demographic analysis of individuals (potential customers) applying to become customers, and the levels of approval, rejections and pending numbers.
6. Delinquency analysis of customers behind on payments.
7. Profitability of customers by demographic segments and segmentation of customers by profitability.
8. Campaign management
9. Realtime Dashboard on Key operational metrics such
10. Clickstream analysis on a website
11. Key product portfolio trackers
12. Marketing Channel analysis
13. Sales Data analysis by product segments
14. Callcenter metrics

This is more an inclusive list than an exclusive one. The above more or less describes what a bank would do, but could also refer to a telephone company or similar service sector company.

What is important is:

1. KPI related data which is consistent, correct and provide an insight into operational aspects of a company.
2. Timely availability of KPI-related data.
3. KPIs designed to directly reflect the efficiency and effectiveness of a business
4. Information presented in a format which aids decision making for top management and decision makers
5. Ability to discern patterns or trends from organised information

BPM integrates the company's processes with CRM or ERP. Companies become able to gauge customer satisfaction, control customer trends and influence shareholder value.

Application Software Types

People working in business intelligence have developed tools that ease the work, especially when the intelligence task involves gathering and analyzing large amounts of unstructured data.

Tool categories commonly used for business performance management include:

- OLAP-Online Analytical Processing, sometimes simply called "Analytics" (based on dimensional analysis and the so-called "hypercube" or "cube")
- Scorecarding, dashboarding and data visualization
- Data warehouses
- Document warehouses
- Text mining
- DM-Data mining
- BPM-Business performance management
- EIS-Executive information systems
- DSS-Decision support systems
- MIS-Management information systems
- SEMS-Strategic Enterprise Management Software
- Business Dashboards.

Designing and implementing a business performance management programme

When implementing a BPM programme one might like to pose a number of questions and take a number of resultant decisions, such as:

- *Goal Alignment queries*: The first step is determining what the short and medium term purpose of the programme will be. What strategic goal(s) of the organization will be addressed by the programme? What organizational mission/vision does it relate to? A hypothesis needs to be crafted that details how this initiative will eventually improve results/performance (i.e. a strategy map).
- *Baseline queries*: Current information gathering competency needs to be assessed. Do we have the capability to monitor important sources of information? What data are being collected and how is it being stored? What are the statistical parameters of this data, e.g., how much random variation does it contain? Is this being measured?

- *Cost and risk queries*: The financial consequences of a new BI initiative should be estimated. It is necessary to assess the cost of the present operations and the increase in costs associated with the BPM initiative? What is the risk that the initiative will fail? This risk assessment should be converted into a financial metric and included in the planning.
- *Customer and stakeholder queries*: Determine who will benefit from the initiative and who will pay. Who has a stake in the current procedure? What kinds of customers/ stakeholders will benefit directly from this initiative? Who will benefit indirectly? What are the quantitative/qualitative benefits? Is the specified initiative the best way to increase satisfaction for all kinds of customers, or is there a better way? How will customer benefits be monitored? What about employees, shareholders, and distribution channel members?
- *Metrics-related queries*: These information requirements must be operationalized into clearly defined metrics. One must decide what metrics to use for each piece of information being gathered. Are these the best metrics? How do we know that? How many metrics need to be tracked? If this is a large number (it usually is), what kind of system can be used to track them? Are the metrics standardized, so they can be benchmarked against performance in other organizations? What are the industry standard metrics available?
- *Measurement Methodology-related queries*: One should establish a methodology or a procedure to determine the best (or acceptable) way of measuring the required metrics. What methods will be used, and how frequently will data be collected? Are there any industry standards for this? Is this the best way to do the measurements? How do we know that?
- *Results-related queries*: The BPM programme should be monitored to ensure that objectives are being met. Adjustments in the programme may be necessary. The programme should be tested for accuracy, reliability, and

validity. How can it be demonstrated that the BI initiative, and not something else, contributed to a change in results? How much of the change was probably random?

Business Rule

Business rules or business rulesets describe the operations, definitions and constraints that apply to an organization in achieving its goals. For example a business rule might state that no credit check is to be performed on return customers. Others could define a tenant in terms of solvency or list preferred suppliers and supply schedules. These rules are then used to help the organization to better achieve goals, communicate among principals and agents, communicate between the organization and interested third parties, demonstrate fulfillment of legal obligations, operate more efficiently, automate operations, perform analysis on current practices, etc. Strategic management is distinct from business rules. Business rules are a means by which strategies are implemented. The rules tell an organization what it can do in detailed tactics, while the strategy tells it how to focus the business at a macro level to optimize results. Put differently, a strategy provides high-level direction about what an organization should do. Business rules can provide the tactical detail about exactly how a strategy will translate to actions.

Example business rule domains include:

- marketing strategies
- pricing policies
- customer relationship management practices
- human resources activities
- regulatory forces, either to ensure compliance with regulations, or to make decisions under regulations (e.g. determining someone's tax bill or whether they are eligible for a government benefit)
- product and service offerings or operation workflows.

How Business Rules are Gathered

Business rules exist for an organization whether or not they are ever written down, talked about or even part of the organization's consciousness. However it is a fairly common practice for organizations to gather business rules in at least a very informal manner. Organizations may choose to proactively describe their business practices in a database of rules. For example, they might hire a consultant to come through the organization to document and consolidate the various standards and methods currently in practice. More commonly, business rules are discovered as part of a formal requirement gathering process during the initial stages of a project. In this case the collecting of the business rules are coincidental. Projects, such as the launching of a new product, might lead to a new body of business rules for an organization, i.e. this new product would require the employees to conceptualize about what the purpose of the organization is in a new way. This practice of coincidental business rule gathering is vulnerable to the creation of inconsistent or even conflicting business rules within different organizational units, or within the same organizational unit over time. Business Rules Methodology is the process of capturing business rules in English, in real-time while empowering users to manage rules with a few simple steps.

Real World Applications and Obstacles

Despite many software vendors, consultants and research institutions offering business rules solutions, business rules are usually only gathered when dictated by law, as the first step in the automation process or as an ephemeral aid to engineers. This is mostly due to the overhead and effort required to maintain this database of rules. This becomes most severe the more dynamic and fluid the business rules for an organization are, for example in start-up companies. Another factor mitigating usage is the lack of incentive for employees to part with their most valuable asset to the organization; their knowledge of the business rules. A third factor is access to viable technology for maintaining business rules. A classic solution is the business rules engine. Rules engine products have been gaining traction in the market place.

Software packages automate business rules using business logic. The term business rule is sometimes used interchangeably with business logic; however the latter connotes an engineering practice and the former an intrinsic business practice. There is value in outlining an organization's business rules regardless of whether this information is used to automate its operations.

Best Practices

1. *Declarative*: A business rule is a statement of truth about an organization. It is an attempt to describe the operations of an organization, not an attempt to prescribe how an organization should operate. This is why business rules are said to be discovered or observed and not created.
2. *Atomic*: A rule is either completely true or completely false; there are no shades of gray. For example a rule for an airline that states passengers may upgrade to first class round-trip tickets if seats are available and they pay the fare increase does not imply that this deal is available for just one leg of the journey.
3. *Distinct, independent constructs*: Separate the things that define your business (the rules) from the processes (i.e. strategies and tactics). Don't build complex and cyclical dependencies-simplify and flatten the constructs.
4. *Expressed in natural language*: In order to appeal to the broadest audience, it is almost always best to express business rules in a natural language without the use of a lot of technical jargon.
5. *Business, not technology, oriented*: For example, a company's business rules should not be foreign to a knowledgeable customer.
6. *Business, not technology, owned*: Business rules come from business decisions. These are independent from implementation decisions.

Formal Specification

Business rules can be expressed in a very formal language. An example of when this rigour is required is in highly technical enterprises such as the building of a bridge. Another example is a project trying to automate the business rules gathering process. Example languages include Unified Modelling Language, Z notation, Business Process Execution Language, Web Services

Policy Framework, Business Process Modelling Notation, or Semantics of Business Vocabulary and Business Rules (SBVR).

Business Model

The term business model describes a broad range of informal and formal models that are used by enterprises to represent various aspects of business, such as operational processes, organizational structures, and financial forecasts. Although the term can be traced to the 1950s, it achieved mainstream usage only in the 1990s. Many informal definitions of the term can be found in popular business literature, such as the following:

> "A business model is a conceptual tool that contains a big set of elements and their relationships and allows expressing the business logic of a specific firm. It is a description of the value a company offers to one or several segments of customers and of the architecture of the firm and its network of partners for creating, marketing, and delivering this value and relationship capital, to generate profitable and sustainable revenue streams".

More recently, researchers build definitions based on economic and organizational theories and show that the definitions are econometrically sound. For example, at MIT propose an operational definition of business model, based on theories such as those from transaction cost economics. Simply put: What problem does this business solve and how does it do so profitably?

Components of a Business Model

They all have various degrees of resemblance or difference. The model synthesises the different conceptualizations into a single reference model based on the similarities of a large range of models. The author's conceptualization describes a business model as consisting of nine related business model building blocks. Thus, a business model describes a company's business:

Infrastructure

- core capabilities: The capabilities and competencies necessary to execute a company's business model.

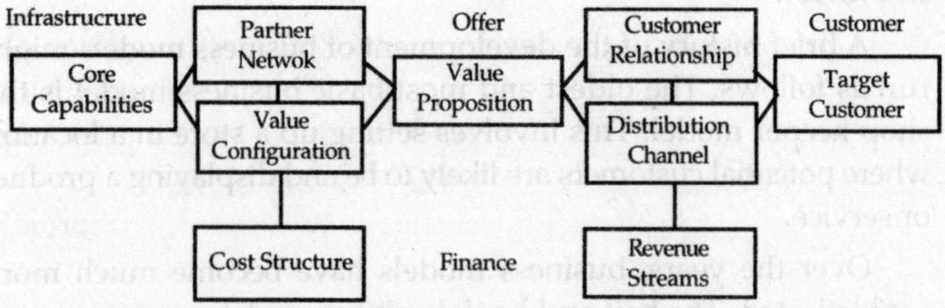

- *partner network*: The business alliances which complement other aspects of the business model.
- *value configuration*: The rationale which makes a business mutually beneficial for a business and its customers.

Offering

- *value proposition*: The products and services a business offers.

Customers

- *target customer*: The target audience for a business' products and services.
- *distribution channel*: The means by which a company delivers products and services to customers. This includes the company's marketing and distribution strategy.
- *customer relationship*: The links a company establishes between itself and its different customer segments. The process of managing customer relationships is referred to as customer relationship management.

Finances

- *cost structure*: The monetary consequences of the means employed in the business model. A company's DOC.
- *revenue*: The way a company makes money through a variety of revenue flows. A company's income.

These nine business model building blocks constitute a business model design template which allows companies to describe their business model.

Evolution

A brief history of the development of business models might run as follows. The oldest and most basic business model is the shop keeper model. This involves setting up a store in a location where potential customers are likely to be and displaying a product or service.

Over the years, business models have become much more sophisticated. The bait and hook business model was introduced in the early 20th century. This involves offering a basic product at a very low cost, often at a loss (the "bait"), then charging compensatory recurring amounts for refills or associated products or services (the "hook"). Examples include: razor (bait) and blades (hook); cell phones (bait) and air time (hook); computer printers (bait) and ink cartridge refills (hook); and cameras (bait) and prints (hook). An interesting variant of this model is a software developer that gives away its word processor reader for free but charges several hundred dollars for its word processor writer.

In the 1950s, new business models came from McDonald's Restaurants and Toyota. In the 1960s, the innovators were Wal-Mart and Hypermarkets. The 1970s saw new business models from FedEx and Toys R Us; the 1980s from Blockbuster, Home Depot, Intel, and Dell Computer; the 1990s from Southwest Airlines, Netflix, eBay, Amazon.com, and Starbucks. Poorly thought out business models were a problem with many dot-coms.

Today, the type of business models might depend on how technology is used. For example, entrepreneurs on the internet have also created entirely new models that depend entirely on existing or emergent technology. Using technology, businesses can reach a large number of customers with minimal costs.

Example Business Models over the Years

- The open business model
- The subscription business model
- The razor and blades business model (bait and hook)
- The pyramid scheme business model
- The multi-level marketing business model

- The network effects business model
- The monopolistic business model
- The cutting out the middleman model
- The auction business model
- The online auction business model
- The bricks and clicks business model
- The loyalty business models
- The Collective business models
- The industrialization of services business model
- The servitization of products business model
- The low-cost carrier business model
- The online content business model
- The freemium business model
- The premium business model
- The direct sales model
- The professional open-source model
- Various distribution business models.

Do Business Models Matter?

Some business models, indeed performed better than others in a dataset consisting of the largest U.S. firms, in the period 1998 through 2002. Business models to performance, in the context of 190 young, growth-oriented firms in the US and Europe that had gone public between 1996 and 2000. Business Model Innovation has become increasingly important as the recent IBM CEO survey 2006 shows.

Related Concepts

The process of business model design is part of business strategy. The implementation of a company's business model into organizational structures (e.g. organigrams, workflows, human resources) and systems (e.g. information technology architecture, production lines) is part of a company's business operations. It is important to understand that business modeling commonly refers to business process design at the operational level, whereas business models and business model design refer to defining the business logic of a company at the strategic level.

Business Model Design

Business model design refers to the activity of designing a company's business model. It is part of the business development and business strategy process and involves design methods. Business model design includes the modeling and description of a company's:

- value propositions
- target customer segments
- distribution channels
- customer relationships
- value configurations
- core capabilities
- partner network
- cost structure
- revenue model.

Business model design is distinct from business modeling. The former refers to defining the business logic of a company at the strategic level, whereas the latter refers to business process design at the operational level. A business model design template can facilitate the process of designing and describing a company's business model.

Business Plan

This is a summary article that covers many topics related to business plans-their content, how they are used, legal issues, and spoofs of business plans, among others. A business plan is a formal statement of a set of business goals, the reasons why they are believed attainable, and the plan for reaching those goals. It may also contain background information about the organization or team attempting to reach those goals.

The business goals being attempted may be for-profit or non-profit. For-profit business plans typically focus on financial goals. Non-profit and government agency business plans tend to focus on service goals. Business plans may also target changes in perception and branding by the customer, client, tax-payer, or larger community. A business plan that has changes in perception and branding as its primary goals is called a marketing plan.

Business plans may be internally or externally focused. Externally focused plans target goals that are important to external stakeholders, particularly financial stakeholders. They typically have detailed information about the organization or team attempting to reach the goals. With for-profit entities, external stakeholders include investors and customers. External stakeholders of non-profits include donors and the clients of the non-profit's services. For government agencies, external stakeholders include tax-payers, higher-level government agencies, and international lending bodies such as the IMF, the World Bank, various economic agencies of the UN, and development banks.

Internally focused business plans target intermediate goals required to reach the external goals. They may cover the development of a new product, a new service, a new IT system, a restructuring of finance, the refurbishing of a factory or a restructuring of the organization. An internal business is often developed in conjunction with a balanced scorecard or a list of critical success factors. This allows success of the plan to be measured using non-financial measures. Business plans that identify and target internal goals, but provide only general guidance on how they will be met are called strategic plans. Operational plans describe the goals of an internal organization, working group or department. Project plans, sometimes known as project frameworks, describe the goals of a particular project. They may also address the project's place within the organization's larger strategic goals.

Business Plan Content

Business plans are decision making tools. There is no fixed content for a business plan. Rather the content and format of the business plan is determined by the goals and audience. A business plan should contain whatever information is needed to decide whether or not to pursue a goal. For example, a business plan for a non-profit might discuss the fit between the business plan and the organization's mission. Banks are quite concerned about defaults, so a business plan for a bank loan will build a convincing case for the organization's ability to repay the loan. Venture capitalists are primarily concerned about initial investment, feasibility, and exit valuation. A business plan for a project requiring equity financing will need to explain why current resources, upcoming growth opportunities, and sustainable competitive advantage will lead to a high exit valuation.

Preparing a business plan draws on a wide range of knowledge from many different business disciplines: finance, human resource management, intellectual property management, supply chain management, operations management, and marketing, among others.. It can be helpful to view the business plan as a collection of sub-plans, one for each of the main business disciplines.

Business Plan Preparation

Support Services

- books, portals, and other sources of written information
- consultancies
- electronic planning templates (software)
- face to face help: mentoring programmes, training courses
  - USA: SCORE, SBA centers
  - Morocco: CRI (Centre Régional d'Investisment)
  - England: Business Link
  - Pakistan: SMEDA (Small and medium enterprise development authority)
  - Other countries: needs research.

Resources for Researching Facts and Figures

Internal Corporate Records

Free Information

- published statistics on the web
- free articles and abstracts from consulting firms
- alumni resources-many undergraduate and graduate programmes provide access to library and/or campus

business center services as part of their package of alumni services.

Fee-based services

- marketing reports from subscription services
- archive and journal services
- books

Strategic Analysis

- Industry Assessment
  - — The macroenvironment
  - — Customer Strategy & Market Analysis
- Competitor Analysis
  - — Porter 5 forces analysis.

Forecasts: Modelling Techniques

Presentation Formats

The format of a business plan depends on its presentation context. It is not uncommon for businesses, especially start-ups to have three or four formats for the same business plan:

- *an "elevator pitch"* - a three minute summary of the business plan's executive summary. This is often used as a teaser to awaken the interest of potential funders, customers, or strategic partners.
- *an oral presentation* - a hopefully entertaining slide show and oral narrative that is meant to trigger discussion and interest potential investors in reading the written presentation. The content of the presentation is usually limited to the executive summary and a few key graphs showing financial trends and key decision making benchmarks. If a new product is being proposed and time permits, a demonstration of the product may also be included.
- *a written presentation for external stakeholders* - a detailed, well written, and pleasingly formatted plan targeted at external stakeholders.

- *an internal operational plan* - a detailed plan describing planning details that are needed by management but may not be of interest to external stakeholders. Such plans have a somewhat higher degree of candor and informality than the version targeted at external stakeholders.

Revisiting the Business Plan

Cost overruns and revenue shortfalls

Cost and revenue estimates are central to any business plan for deciding the viability of the planned venture. But costs are often underestimated and revenues overestimated resulting in later cost overruns, revenue shortfalls, and possibly non-viability. During the dot-com bubble 1997-2001 this was a problem for many technology start-ups. However, the problem is not limited to technology or the private sector; public works projects also routinely suffer from cost overruns and/or revenue shortfalls. The main causes of cost overruns and revenue shortfalls are optimism bias and strategic misrepresentation.

Legal and Liability Issues

Disclosure requirements

An externally targeted business plan should list all legal concerns and financial liabilities that might negatively affect investors. Depending on the amount of funds being raised and the audience to whom the plan is presented, failure to do this may have severe legal consequences.

Limitations on content and audience

Non disclosure agreements (NDAs) with third parties, non-compete agreements, conflicts of interest, privacy concerns, and the protection of one's trade secrets may severely limit the audience to which one might show the business plan. Alternatively, they may require each party receiving the business plan to sign a contract accepting special clauses and conditions. This situation is complicated by the fact that many venture capitalists will refuse to sign an NDA before looking at a business plan, lest it put them in the untenable position of looking at two independently developed look-alike business plans, both claiming originality. In such situations one may need to develop two versions of the business plan: a stripped down plan that can be used to develop a relationship and a detail plan that is only shown when investors have sufficient interest and trust to sign an NDA.

How Business Plans are Used

Venture Capital

- business plan contests-provides a way for venture capitals to find promising projects
- venture capital assessment of business plans-focus on qualitative factors such as team.

Education

K-12

Business plans are used in some primary and secondary programmes to teach economic principles. Wikiversity has a v:Lunar Boom Town project where students of all ages can collaborate with designing and revising business models and practice evaluating them to learn practical business planning techniques and methodology.

Higher Education

- BA, MBA programmes
  - — integrative team projects
  - — projects for specific course work
  - — Business plan contests.

Satires of Business Plans

The business plan is the subject of many satires. Satires are used both to express cynicism about business plans and as an educational tool to improve the quality of business plans. For example,

- Five Criteria for a successful business plan in biotech uses Dilbert comic strips to remind people of what not to do when researching and writing a business plan for a biotech start-up. Scott Adams, the author of Dilbert, is an MBA graduate (U.C. Berkeley) who sees humour as a critical tool that can improve the behaviour of businesses and their managers. He has written numerous critiques of business practices, including business planning. The website Dilbert.com-Games has a mission statement generator that satires the wording often found in mission statements. His book *The Dilbert Principle - A Cubicle's Eye View of Bosses, Meetings, Management Fads & Other Workplace Afflictions* discusses the foibles of management and their plans as depicted in the Dilbert comic strips by Scott Adams.

- In the article "South Park's" Investing Lesson, the The Motley Fool columnist "Fool on the Hill" uses the Underpants Gnomes to illustrate the fallacy of focusing on goals without a clear implementation strategy. The Underpants Gnomes episode satires the business plans of the Dot.com era. It features a three-part business plan for a new coffee shop:
    1. Collect underpants
    2. Profit!

Business Marketing

Marketing is a societal process that is needed to discern consumers' wants; focusing on a product/service to those wants, and to mould the consumers towards the products/services. Marketing is fundamental to any businesses growth. The marketing teams (Marketers) have the task to create the consumer awareness of the products/services through marketing techniques; if a business does not pay attention to their products/services and their consumers' demographics, the business would not be able to endure longevity. Marketing tends to be seen as a creative industry, which includes advertising, distribution and selling. It is also concerned with anticipating the customers' future needs and wants, often through market research.

Its specialist areas include:

- Advertising and Branding
- Direct Marketing

- International Marketing
- Public Relations
- Communications
- Strategic Management
- Market Research
- Events Organisation
- Database Marketing
- Search Engine Marketing.

A market-focused, or customer-focused, organization first determines what its potential customers desire, and then builds the product or service. Marketing theory and practice is justified in the belief that customers use a product or service because they have a need, or because it provides a perceived benefit.

Two major factors of marketing are the recruitment of new customers (acquisition) and the retention and expansion of relationships with existing customers (base management). Once a marketer has converted the prospective buyer, base management marketing takes over. The process for base management shifts the marketer to building a relationship, nurturing the links, enhancing the benefits that sold the buyer in the first place, and improving the product/service continuously to protect the business from competitive encroachments. For a marketing plan to be successful, the mix of the four "Ps" must reflect the wants and desires of the consumers in the target market. Trying to convince a market segment to buy something they don't want is extremely expensive and seldom successful. Marketers depend on marketing research, both formal and informal, to determine what consumers want and what they are willing to pay for it. Marketers hope that this process will give them a sustainable competitive advantage. Marketing management is the practical application of this process. The offer is also an important addition to the 4P's theory.

Within most organizations, the activities encompassed by the marketing function are led by a Vice President or Director of Marketing. A growing number of organizations, especially large US companies, have a Chief Marketing Officer position, reporting to the Chief Executive Officer. The American Marketing Association (AMA) states,

> "Marketing is the process of planning and executing the conception, pricing, promotion, and distribution of ideas, goods, and services to create exchanges that satisfy individual and organizational objectives".

Marketing methods are informed by many of the social sciences, particularly psychology, sociology, and economics. Anthropology is also a small, but growing, influence. Market research underpins these activities. Through advertising, it is also related to many of the creative arts. Marketing is a wide and heavily interconnected subject with extensive publications. It is also an area of activity infamous for re-inventing itself and its vocabulary according to the times and the culture. Marketing is a very essential part of any business.

Two Levels of Marketing

Strategic Marketing attempts to determine how an organization competes against its competitors in a market place. In particular, it aims at generating a competitive advantage relative to its competitors. Operational Marketing executes marketing functions to attract and keep customers and to maximize the value derived for them, as well as to satisfy the customer with prompt services and meeting the customer expectations. Operational Marketing includes the determination of the marketing mix.

Four Ps

In popular usage, "marketing" is the promotion of products, especially advertising and branding. However, in professional usage the term has a wider meaning which recognizes that marketing is customer centered. Products are often developed to meet the desires of groups of customers or even, in some cases, for specific customers. E. Jerome McCarthy divided marketing into four general sets of activities. His typology has become so universally recognized that his four activity sets, the Four Ps, have passed into the language.

The four Ps are:

- *Product*: The product aspects of marketing deal with the specifications of the actual goods or services, and how it relates to the end-user's needs and wants. The scope of a product generally includes supporting elements such as warranties, guarantees, and support.
- *Pricing*: This refers to the process of setting a price for a product, including discounts. The price need not be monetary-it can simply be what is exchanged for the product or services, e.g. time, energy, psychology or attention.
- *Promotion*: This includes advertising, sales promotion, publicity, and personal selling, and refers to the various methods of promoting the product, brand, or company.
- *Placement or distribution* refers to how the product gets to the customer; for example, point of sale placement or retailing. This fourth P has also sometimes been called Place, referring to the channel by which a product or services is sold (e.g. online vs. retail), which geographic region or industry, to which segment (young adults, families, business people), etc.

These four elements are often referred to as the marketing mix, which a marketer can use to craft a marketing plan. The four Ps model is most useful when marketing low value consumer products. Industrial products, services, high value consumer products require adjustments to this model. Services marketing must account for the unique nature of services. Industrial or B2B marketing must account for the long term contractual agreements that are typical in supply chain transactions. Relationship marketing attempts to do this by looking at marketing from a long term relationship perspective rather than individual transactions.

As a counter to this, one of the greatest limitations of the 4 Ps approach "is that it unconsciously emphasizes the inside-out view (looking from the company outwards), whereas the essence of marketing should be the outside-in approach". Nevertheless, the 4 Ps offer a memorable and workable guide to the major categories of marketing activity, as well as a framework within which these can be used.

Seven Ps

As well as the standard four Ps (Product, Pricing, Promotion and Place), services marketing calls upon an extra three, totalling seven and known together as the extended marketing mix. These are:

- *People*: Any person coming into contact with customers can have an impact on overall satisfaction. Whether as part of a supporting service to a product or involved in a total service, people are particularly important because, in the customer's eyes, they are generally inseparable from the total service. As a result of this, they must be appropriately trained, well motivated and the right type of person. Fellow customers are also sometimes referred to under 'people', as they too can affect the customer's service experience, (e.g., at a sporting event).
- *Process*: This is the process(es) involved in providing a service and the behaviour of people, which can be crucial to customer satisfaction.
- *Physical evidence*: Unlike a product, a service cannot be experienced before it is delivered, which makes it intangible. This, therefore, means that potential customers could perceive greater risk when deciding whether to use a service. To reduce the feeling of risk, thus improving the chance for success, it is often vital to offer potential customers the chance to see what a service would be like. This is done by providing physical evidence, such as case studies, testimonials or demonstrations.

Web 2.0 and Marketing New 4Ps

The original 4Ps concept idea was developed to help marketers manage the four most important aspect of marketing. With the Internet and the Web 2.0, marketers have needed to adapt a broader perspective on these elements. Idris Mootee devised a "New 4Ps" model in 2001 to supplement the traditional marketing 4Ps. They are Personalization, Participation, Peer-to-Peer and Predictive Modeling.

- *Personalization*: The author here refers to customization of products and services through the use of the Internet. Early examples include Dell on-line and Amazon.com, but this concept is further extended with emerging social media and advanced algorithms. Emerging technologies will continue to push this idea forward.
- *Participation*: This is to allow customer to participate in what the brand should stand for; what should be the product directions and even which ads to run. This concept is laying the foundation for disruptive change through democratization of information.
- *Peer-to-Peer*: This refers to customer networks and communities where advocacy happens. The historical problem with marketing is that it is "interruptive" in nature, trying to impose a brand on the customer. This is most apparent in TV advertising. These "passive customer bases" will ultimately be replaced by the "active customer communities". Brand engagement happens within those conversations. P2P is now being referred as Social Computing and will likely to be the most disruptive force in the future of marketing.
- *Predictive modelling*: This refers to predictive algorithms, such as neural network, that are being successfully applied in marketing problems (both a regression as well as a classification problem).

Product

Scope

- *Breadth*--number of product lines in a range.
- *Depth*--number of product items in a product line.

Steps in product design

- Design and development of product ideas.
- Selection of and sifting through product ideas.
- Design and testing of product concept.
- Analysis of profitability of product concept.

- Design and testing of physical product.

Packaging and trademarks

Requirements of good packaging

- Appropriately designed for target market
- Eye-catching
- Suitable to product
- Compliant with retailers' requirements
- Promotes image of enterprise
- Distinguishable from competitors' products
- Strong, convenient, well-designed
- Point of difference in service and supply of product.

Forms of packaging

- Specialty packaging-emphasizes the elegant character of the product
- Packaging for double-use
- Combination packaging two or more products packaged in the same container
- Kaleidoscopic packaging-packaging changes continually to reflect a series or particular theme
- Packaging for immediate consumption-to be thrown away after use
- Packaging for resale-packed, into appropriate quantities, for the retailer or wholesaler

Significance of a trademark

- Distinguishes one company's goods from those of another
- Serves as advertisement for quality
- Protects both consumers and manufacturers
- Used in displays and advertising campaigns
- Used to market new products

Requirements of a good trademark

- Reflects products' advantages

- Good, simple language
- Easily pronounced and remembered
- Distinct from names of other products
- Easily added to an existing range
- Easily registered for legal protection

Pricing

Pricing refers to the amount of money exchanged for a product. This value is determined by utility to the consumer in terms of money and/or sacrifice that he is prepared to give for it.

Objectives

- Definite sales volume
- Achieve profit
- Larger market share
- Maintain market share
- Eliminate competition
- Advantages of mass production
- Satisfactory return on capital

Factors influencing price-determination

- Production and distribution costs
- Substitute goods available
- Normal trade practices
- Fixed prices
- Reaction of distributors
- Reaction of consumers
- Nature of demand:
  - — Elastic
  - — Inelastic
- Form of market:

— Perfect competition

— Monopolistic competition

— Monopoly

— Oligopoly

Steps to determine price

- Determine market share to be captured
- Set up price strategy
- Estimate demand
- Evaluate competitors' reactions

Distribution

Channels

- Manufacturer to consumer (most direct)
- Manufacturer to wholesaler to retailer to consumer (traditional)
- Manufacturer to agent to retailer to consumer (current)
- Manufacturer to agent to wholesaler to retailer to consumer
- Manufacturer to agent to customer (ex: AMWAY)

Manufacturers

Reasons for direct selling methods

- Manufacturer wants to demonstrate goods.
- Wholesalers, retailers and agents not actively selling.
- Manufacturer unable to convince wholesalers or retailers to stock product.
- High profit margin added to goods by wholesalers and retailers.
- Middlemen unable to transport.

Reasons for indirect selling methods

- Manufacturer does not have the financial resources to distribute goods.
- Distribution channels already established.
- Manufacturer has no knowledge of efficient distribution.
- Manufacturer wishes to use capital for further production.
- Too many consumers in a large area; difficult to reach.
- Manufacturer does not have a wide assortment of goods to enable efficient marketing.

Wholesalers

Reasons for using wholesalers

- Bear risk of selling goods to retailer or consumer
- Storage space
- Decrease transport costs
- Grant credit to retailers
- Able to sell for the manufacturers
- Give advice to manufacturers
- Break down products into smaller quantities

Reasons for bypassing wholesalers

- Limited storage facilities
- Retailers' preferences
- Wholesaler cannot promote products successfully
- Development of wholesalers' own brands
- Desire for closer market contact
- Position of power
- Cost of wholesalers' services
- Price stabilisation
- Need for rapid distribution
- Make more money

Ways of bypassing wholesalers

- Sales offices or branches
- Mail orders
- Direct sales to retailers
- Travelling agents
- Direct Orders

Agents

- Commission agents work for anyone who needs their services. They do not acquire ownership of goods but receive del credere commission.
- Selling agents act on an extended contractual basis, selling all of the products of the manufacturer. They have full

authority regarding price and terms of sale.

- Buying agents buy goods on behalf of producers and retailers. They have an expert knowledge of the purchasing function.
- Brokers specialize in the sale of one specific product. They receive a brokerage.
- Factory representatives represent more than one manufacturer. They operate within a specific area and sell related lines of goods but have limited authority regarding price and sales terms.

Marketing Communications

Marketing communications breaks down the strategies involved with marketing messages into categories based on the goals of each message. There are distinct stages in converting strangers to customers that govern the communication medium that should be used.

Advertising

- Paid form of public presentation and expressive promotion of ideas
- Aimed at masses
- Manufacturer may determine what goes into advertisement
- Pervasive and impersonal medium

Functions and advantages of successful advertising

- Task of the salesman made easier
- Forces manufacturer to live up to conveyed image
- Protects and warns customers against false claims and inferior products
- Enables manufacturer to mass-produce product
- Continuous reminder
- Uninterrupted production a possibility
- Increases goodwill
- Raises standards of living (or perceptions thereof)
- Prices decrease with increased popularity

- Educates manufacturer and wholesaler about competitors' offerings as well as shortcomings in their own.

Objectives

- Maintain demand for well-known goods
- Introduce new and unknown goods
- Increase demand for well-known goods

Requirements of a good advertisement

- Attract attention
- Stimulate interest
- Create a desire
- Bring about action
- Create Awareness

Eight steps in an advertising campaign

- Market research
- Setting out aims
- Budgeting
- Choice of media (TV,newspaper,radio)
- Choice of actors (New Trend)
- Design and wording
- Coordination
- Test results.

Personal Sales

Oral presentation given by a salesman who approaches individuals or a group of potential customers:

- Live, interactive relationship
- Personal interest
- Attention and response.

Sales Promotion

Short-term incentives to encourage buying of products:

- Instant appeal
- Anxiety to sell.

Publicity

- Stimulation of demand through press release giving a favourable report to a product
- Higher degree of credibility
- Effectively news
- Boosts enterprise's image.

Customer Focus

Many companies today have a customer focus (or customer orientation). This implies that the company focuses its activities and products on consumer demands. Generally there are three ways of doing this: the customer-driven approach, the sense of identifying market changes and the product innovation approach.

In the consumer-driven approach, consumer wants are the drivers of all strategic marketing decisions. No strategy is pursued until it passes the test of consumer research. Every aspect of a market offering, including the nature of the product itself, is driven by the needs of potential consumers. The starting point is always the consumer. The rationale for this approach is that there is no point spending R&D funds developing products that people will not buy. History attests to many products that were commercial failures in spite of being technological breakthroughs. A formal approach to this customer-focused marketing is known as SIVA (Solution, Information, Value, Access). This system is basically the four Ps renamed and reworded to provide a customer focus.

The SIVA Model provides a demand/customer centric version alternative to the well-known 4Ps supply side model (product, price, place, promotion) of marketing management.

Product-> Solution

Promotion-> Information

Price-> Value

Place->Access

The four elements of the SIVA model are:

1. *Solution*: How appropriate is the solution to the customers problem/need?

2. *Information*: Does the customer know about the solution, and if so how, who from, do they know enough to let them make a buying decision?
3. *Value*: Does the customer know the value of the transaction, what it will cost, what are the benefits, what might they have to sacrifice, what will be their reward?
4. *Access*: Where can the customer find the solution? How easily/locally/remotely can they buy it and take delivery?

This model was proposed by Chekitan Dev and Don Schultz in the Marketing Management Journal of the American Marketing Association, and presented by them in Market Leader-the journal of the Marketing Society in the UK. The model focuses heavily on the customer and how they view the transaction.

Product Focus

In a product innovation approach, the company pursues product innovation, then tries to develop a market for the product. Product innovation drives the process and marketing research is conducted primarily to ensure that a profitable market segment(s) exists for the innovation. The rationale is that customers may not know what options will be available to them in the future so we should not expect them to tell us what they will buy in the future. However, marketers can aggressively over-pursue product innovation and try to overcapitalize on a niche. When pursuing a product innovation approach, marketers must ensure that they have a varied and multi-tiered approach to product innovation. It is claimed that if Thomas Edison depended on marketing research he would have produced larger candles rather than inventing light bulbs. Many firms, such as research and development focused companies, successfully focus on product innovation (Such as Nintendo who constantly change the way Video games are played). Many purists doubt whether this is really a form of marketing orientation at all, because of the ex post status of consumer research. Some even question whether it is marketing.

- An emerging area of study and practice concerns internal marketing, or how employees are trained and managed to deliver the brand in a way that positively impacts the acquisition and retention of customers (employer branding).

- Diffusion of innovations research explores how and why people adopt new products, services and ideas.
- A relatively new form of marketing uses the Internet and is called internet marketing or more generally e-marketing, affiliate marketing, desktop advertising or online marketing. It typically tries to perfect the segmentation strategy used in traditional marketing. It targets its audience more precisely, and is sometimes called personalized marketing or one-to-one marketing.
- With consumers' eroding attention span and willingness to give time to advertising messages, marketers are turning to forms of Permission marketing such as Branded content, Custom media and Reality marketing.
- The use of herd behaviour in marketing.

In an article entitled "Swarming the shelves: How shops can exploit people's herd mentality to increase sales", The Economist recently reported a recent conference in Rome on the subject of the simulation of adaptive human behaviour. Mechanisms to increase impulse buying and get people "to buy more by playing on the herd instinct" were shared. The basic idea is that people will buy more of products that are seen to be popular, and several feedback mechanisms to get product popularity information to consumers are mentioned, including smart-cart technology and the use of Radio Frequency Identification Tag technology. A "swarm-moves" model was introduced by a Princeton researcher, which is appealing to supermarkets because it can "increase sales without the need to give people discounts." Large retailers Wal-Mart in the United States and Tesco in Britain plan to test the technology in spring 2007.

Other recent studies on the "power of social influence" include an "artificial music market in which some 14,000 people downloaded previously unknown songs" (Columbia University, New York); a Japanese chain of convenience stores which orders its products based on "sales data from department stores and research companies;" a Massachusetts company exploiting knowledge of social networking to improve sales; and online retailers who are increasingly informing consumers about "which products are popular with like-minded consumers" (e.g., Amazon, eBay).

Criticism of Marketing

Some aspects of marketing, especially promotion, are the subject of criticism. It is especially problematic in classical economic theory, which is based on the assumption that supply and demand are independent. However, product promotion is an attempt coming from the supply side to influence demand. In this way producer market power is attained as measured by profits that would not be realized under a free market. Then the argument follows that non-free markets are imperfect and lead to production and consumption of suboptimal amounts of the product.

Critics acknowledge that marketing has legitimate uses in connecting goods and services to the consumers who want them. Critics also point out that marketing techniques have been used to achieve morally dubious ends by businesses, governments and criminals. Critics see a systemic social evil inherent in marketing. Marketing is accused of creating ruthless exploitation of both consumers and workers by treating people as commodities whose purpose is to consume.

Most marketers believe that marketing techniques themselves are amoral. While it is ethically neutral, it can be used for negative purposes, such as selling unhealthy food to obese people or selling SUVs in a time of global warming, but it can also have a positive influence on consumer welfare.

The Observer's survey among 1,206 UK adult consumers in 2001 highlighted some of the stark changes our society has gone through in the last two decades. This raises a question on the effectiveness of the CIM's definition of marketing (anticipating, identifying and satisfying customer needs profitably), mainly in consumer marketing. There are similar concerns in industrial markets, also known as business-to-business or B2B. Industrial market segmentation attempts to provide some answers. Core marketing elements such as segmentation, targeting and positioning are still relevant in the modern (or post-modern) world. However, they are complex topics that need a high level of effort, intelligent thinking as well as resources to be implemented successfully. A definitive statement cannot be made whether the conventional marketing concept is applicable in today's environment. Its relevance is very much situational and depends on many factors such as the product, the segment, time, location, political and economic conditions and the inner workings of a company.

However, some scholars such as Stephen Brown challenge the marketing concept in an extreme language. Their statements, sometimes unfair, are relevant, which is why Post-Modern Marketing 2 was chosen as a key reference point for this chapter. On the one hand Brown makes positive statements about marketing, e.g. "marketing is endowed with considerable personal charm and has enjoyed more than its fair share of conquests" (Brown, 1998:16); and "indeed, the increasing academic attention that is being devoted to marketing and consumption-related phenomena by non-business disciplines such as sociology, anthropology and history; far from being the second-hand rose of the scholarship, marketing is now something of a fashion leader".

On the other hand, he condemns marketing by saying "marketing has to decide whether to expose its intellectual nakedness or press itself against the searing heat of postmodernism"; and using quotes such as "mid-life crisis"; "in decline; failing; anachronistic; being abandoned; no longer appropriate; in an unprecedented state of crisis; delivered nothing of value; failure; confusion; misunderstanding; occasional inexplicable hitting of the jackpot".

This apparent love-hate relationship is proof in itself that even a skeptics find it difficult to deny the contribution that marketing has made and can make to customer satisfaction and economic value. It has contributed to both customers' and suppliers' quality of life by selecting profitable customer satisfaction as its sole objective. The marketing concept, together with other business disciplines, helped the UK to make the transition from a 19th-century manufacturing economy to a modern model of success in the service industry, creating an economic growth period never seen before in the United Kingdom.

Marketing has helped create value through customized products, no-questions-asked refund policies, comfortable cars, environmental attention, shopkeepers' smile, and guaranteed delivery dates. Even some government departments address the public not as 'the Queen's subjects' or 'the applicants' any more but as 'customers.' Of course all of the above is done for economic or political gain, for better or worse. Despite all this achievement, to dismiss marketing as a failure is unfair.

Marketing also helps companies avoid unnecessary R&D, operational and sales costs by helping to develop products because customers want them, not for the sake of innovation. Another success is the now commonly implemented value-pricing principle, whereby a product or service is sold for the price the customer is willing to pay, not on a cost-plus basis. This way, both suppliers and customers get a fair deal. In the context of segmentation, Brown suggests that "the traditional, linear, step-by-step marketing model of analysis, planning, implementation and control no longer seems applicable, appropriate or even pertinent to what is actually happening on the ground". If Mr. Brown had studied "the ground" before making his statement, he would have realised that companies are successful the world over precisely because they implement this model.

They segment their markets, relate their products and services to them, define their value proposition and serve their customers accordingly. Examples are General Electric, HSBC, PriceWaterhouseCoopers, Smiths Aerospace, BAE Systems, BOC Edwards, Weir Group and the BT Group to name but a few. A brief visit to their websites can make this point clear.

Stephen Brown also has a constructive suggestion: "I reckon we need more passion in marketing, not less; it is time we banished banishing passion from works of marketing scholarship". This refers mainly to promotion, which is only one element within the marketing concept. The truth is that marketing today leads the way in segmentation, innovation, pricing, product management, distribution, and last but not least, promotion. After all the contribution as well as further potential, to deny its successes and try to reduce it to only promotion is a great injustice to the marketing profession as well as to academic insight. Contrary to Brown's suggestion in his final paragraph, we need objectivity, rigour, quantification, models, relationships, paradigm shifts and (some application of) science.

Construction Marketing

Due to increased competition, privatisation and globalisation, marketing and business development have become increasingly important functions in all construction organisations. Marketing research, corporate branding and public relations are increasingly being seen as vital in a marketplace typified by sophisticated and demanding clients and customers, and a socially and environmentally aware general public and media.

6

Business Presentations

Is your ability to speak confidently and persuasively to a group an important part of your function as a manager or an executive? Countless surveys of employers and executives over the past two decades have consistently placed oral communication skills among the top five most desired characteristics for a manager. It is no longer possible to advance in a company or graduate programme without solid communication ability. Because today's work and academic environments emphasize teams, meetings, and extensive information sharing, oral and written skills are essential. In this part, you'll learn the key process steps and tasks involved in preparing and delivering business presentations:

* Defining your purpose
* Analyzing your audience
* Gathering supporting materials
* Organizing your ideas
* Planning your visual support
* Practicing your delivery
* Preparing for the question-and-answer session
* Evaluating your presentation.

In addition, we also discuss how to handle speech anxiety. While this may not be part of the preparation and delivery process for every speaker or every situation, it is a very common concern, and we address it in detail. We described a writing and editing process that can help you write more efficiently and effectively. We advocated using such a process to improve your writing and save you and your company time and money. We advocate that you use a similar, multistep process when preparing your business presentations. Recognizing the parallels between the writing and editing and presentation processes can be very helpful when you need to create a document and then present it. Mentally linking the two processes should help you recognize and break ineffective habits and establish new ways of preparing more integrated presentations and documents.

Effective presentations will help you:

* Convey information more efficiently and effectively
* Motivate work teams and groups to make faster and better decisions
* Demonstrate proficiency in subject matter to supervisors and clients
* Increase your professional profile and value to the company
* Provide confidence in all areas of communication.

By strengthening your skills and improving your understanding of the presentation process, you will be a more efficient and effective speaker in interpersonal, group, and business settings.

Defining Your Purpose

Imagine the following scenario: When you arrive at work, your manager mentions that you need to be in Chicago on the 15th for an important meeting. You note the meeting on your calendar and go on to other business. On the morning of the 15th, you get in your car and drive to the airport, hoping to find a flight to Chicago. You're lucky! You find one. When you arrive in Chicago, you go to the rental car counter, hoping a car will be available. You're lucky! You find one. When you get in the car, you drive aimlessly around the city, looking for your meeting. You're lucky! You see your manager walking into a hotel and you find the meeting.

Sound pretty implausible? It is, but many executives use a similar approach when they "plan" a presentation or a report. They make a note of it, and when the times comes, they plunge right in without planning ahead, without a good idea of where they are going, what they need to accomplish, or how they are going to accomplish it. From a process perspective, they are ignoring a key preparation step of the presentation process. The first step is to define your purpose. In order to get to where you want to go, it helps to plan your itinerary, make appropriate reservations, and get directions. Moreover, if you're going to a meeting in Chicago, wouldn't it be nice to know the purpose of the meeting, why you were invited, and your role? Similarly, when you need to write a document or make a presentation, it's best to consider where you want to go rather than just plunging right in. Because you can't rely on luck, in this chapter we discuss the following three key ideas related to planning business communication:

* Defining your general purpose
* Defining your specific purpose
* Defining your desired results.

Defining Your General Purpose

People in business communicate to fulfill a basic need—typically to inform or persuade. It is important to know what you're trying to accomplish:

* Does your audience want to be informed, persuaded, or both? Do they want objective information? Do they want to know all the pros and the cons?
* Do they prefer a subjective evaluation of a problem? When you know your audience's expectations and requirements, you can better define your purpose and organize your ideas.

When you're presenting or writing to inform (for example, conveying the results of a market research study), you goal should be to provide information in the most objective way possible. The presenter (or writer) should present facts and use verifiable data.

In a persuasive presentation, on the other hand, your goal is to support a particular viewpoint for your audience. Your goal is to present those facts and ideas that build support for your appeal. For example, in a persuasive proposal designed to increase your sales force, you might include sales figures, as well as workload and sales call information that support your recommendation. Your general purpose will be your initial guide as you plan your presentation. Knowing whether you'll be informing or persuading your audience will help you decide if your purpose is primarily to teach (to impart knowledge and facts) or to guide (to interpret the facts and present alternatives). Next, we will show how your general purpose may also guide your selection of patterns of organization for your writing and speaking.

Determining Your Specific Purpose

After you've determined whether your writing or presentation is to be informative or persuasive, you need to better define your purpose by writing a specific, straightforward statement of purpose. This statement of purpose, or basic thesis sentence, will focus your efforts as you zero in on what you are trying to do in your presentation or document. In a document, this sentence should help your readers understand what you are trying to accomplish. In a presentation, it should perform the same function, and it should also stand out: If we asked your audience to hit a buzzer when they heard the thesis, all the buzzers should ring at the same time.

Some people use very blunt statements: "The purpose of this memo is . . ." or "The purpose of my speech is . . ." Less obvious examples might be phrased as follows:

* "I intend to demonstrate why our no-load mutual fund is the best place for your investment dollars."
* "Our market research shows that the population of our target country is getting younger, and in this presentation we will explore ways to attract this younger audience to our product."
* "This afternoon we will describe three key ways in which the new software can streamline our billing processes."

Defining Your Desired Results

You will find it helpful to define the results you expect to see. This will make you further clarify and focus your message.

Typically, you do not state your operational definition to your audience. You use it to help plan your message and evaluate the response, or lack of response, that you receive. Here are some examples of how you might phrase the desired results of your presentation:

* "After this presentation, 50 percent of the audience will invest in our mutual fund."
* "After this presentation, a majority of managers will vote in favour of the proposal to add staff to the marketing division."
* "This report will clarify the goals of the assessment team, and as a result, every member will be able to participate fully in the next planning session."

Presenting as a Team

Team presentations may derive from written documents or they may be initiated solely as stand-alone projects, without previously written documents as guidelines. Obviously, preparing a presentation from an existing document will give you a head start.

A Team Presentation from a Team-Written Document

If your assignment is to present a written document as a team, you've already tackled the biggest part of the job: defining your purpose, analyzing your audience, organizing your ideas, and gathering supporting materials. And you have probably worked on the layout and design of visuals where appropriate. So the first four steps of the presentation have already been completed. However, as a team, you need to review these steps to make sure everyone is working from the same game plan. Once you have done this, you need to do some very specific work to transform that document into an oral presentation. Some of the issues you need to work through with your team are as follows:

* *What material will we select for presentation*? A team presenting a report or proposal can rarely cover the entire document in an oral presentation. If you were to assume the audience members would also be reading the document, what are the most significant things that you would select to highlight for the presentation?

* *What format will we use to present the material*? Sometimes, past experience and/or corporate culture will tell you how to present the material. At some companies, presenters rarely stand in front of a group, but rather sit around a conference table, often with a built-in projection system. In other situations, a presenter would be expected to stand in front of a group that sits in formal rows of chairs. If your team has the option to choose a delivery style, discuss how you might be most effective. Many excellent presenters feel more comfortable on their feet, since they can move around and put more physical energy into their presentations. Others might find more receptive listeners with a less formal style. Your goal for your team presentation should help to guide you in this decision.
* *Who will present this presentation*? The temptation for many teams is to select the team member who is the best speaker and nominate that person to do the entire presentation. This is, of course, one option, but it is rarely one that works best. If this is truly a team effort, the whole team should be involved in the preparation of the material, and, unless it's a very large team, all team members should speak during the presentation and/or the question-and-answer session. Even though presentation skill levels may vary considerably within your team, the expertise that each individual brings to the project can generally compensate for less-than-perfect delivery skills. Furthermore, demonstrating the commitment of all team members to the presentation can enhance team and message credibility.

International Team Members

Some of our international students and clients have been reluctant to participate in team presentations because they feel their language skills are not good enough for an American audience. We have always encouraged these people to participate fully in their team presentations, usually with excellent results. We have found two interesting things happen:

* First, most managers and executives today are becoming familiar with Asian, European, and South American

dialects because corporate culture in general is becoming so international. Once an audience becomes used to the differences in pronunciation of a speaker, it generally is not a distraction.

* Second, a business audience is there to hear the content of your message. With the exception of speech instructors or consultants, listeners are rarely there to critique a speaker's delivery skills—they want to focus on your message. Unless an individual's skills are so poor as to make him or her unintelligible, international speakers rarely present a problem for business teams.

A Team Presentation without a Written Document

Obviously, if you are beginning a presentation from scratch, you will need to do a considerable amount of work in planning the presentation before you get to the aspects of team delivery described in the preceding section. We recommend that you go back and work through the seven steps in the presentation process, from defining your purpose to handling questions and answers. While some of the work may be divided among members of the team, you need to keep all team members informed and involved through each step of this process. This ensures that your presentation can be supported by everyone and that everyone can participate fully.

General Guidelines for Presenting As a Team

Following are the guidelines for presenting as a team:

* *Practice the presentation together as a team.* While you may be familiar with the material, especially if you are presenting from a team-written document, the team presentation should appear as a unified whole—not as a series of minipresentations. Additionally, practicing team presentations helps you to revisit the content of the presentation for accuracy, as well as to identify any areas of overlap or redundancy. It gives you a chance to make sure your visual aids work well from a mechanical standpoint (e.g., "Can this computer projection system read my PowerPoint disk?") as well as a visual standpoint

("Oops, the fluorescent colors really don't look too professional, do they?"). You can also use rehearsal time to help one another on delivery skills (as in, "Joe, be sure not to block the screen with your body when you show that slide.") and improve overall comfort level within the team.

* *Introduce yourself and the members of the team.* Where appropriate, provide some background on your involvement with the project. Unless you can be 100 percent sure that everyone in the room knows each presenter, this step is essential. It will establish some familiarity with the team and enhance your credibility as speakers.
* Use the introduction to preview the content of the presentation and how the team will present it. This preview will give your audience a framework demonstrating how you will proceed, making it easier to follow. The preview could be something as simple as this: "First, I'll be describing some background information on the project and how we approached our study. Then Joe will described the data we collected and our forecast for the next year. Next, Mary will discuss some of the liabilities of going along with this project. And I'll be back at the end to talk about some of our recommendations."
* *Plan clear transitions between speaker segments.* Transitions serve as signposts for your listeners so they can follow the presentation more easily. A common team transition is the internal summary, where the speaker might say something like, "Now that I have shown you how the data supports this project, I'll turn this over to Mary, who will discuss some concerns about liabilities."
* *Visual aids used in the presentation should all follow the same format.* Many speakers today use Microsoft PowerPoint, and if you do, the presentation slides should be done in a consistent template, as a package. We have seen teams where each speaker did his or her own visuals, and the results generally appear unprofessional and uncoordinated. If this is indeed a team presentation, then there needs to

be consistency among medium, format, and appearance to help tie the parts of the presentation together.

* All team members should be available for the question-and-answer session at the end of the presentation. In addition to following the guidelines for handling the Q&A, the team members should discuss ahead of time who will handle questions in specific areas. It is helpful to have all team members participate in the Q&A, but they should be neither competing to answer questions nor reluctant to respond to a concern.
* As with individual presentations, the team presentation should not drift lamely to a close at the end of the Q&A. One team member should signal when time is up and offer an appropriate closing comment on behalf of the group.

Guidelines for Special-Occasion Presentations

While most managers and executives spend most of their presentation time informing or persuading audiences and workgroups, there are times when you will be called upon to deliver a special-occasion presentation. These kinds of presentations include:

* Speeches of introduction
* Speeches to pay tribute or present an award
* Speeches of gratitude or to acknowledge an award
* Eulogies at funerals and memorial services
* Toasts at recognition banquets and weddings.

While each of these occasions is different and special in its own right, the general guidelines for all of these presentations are the same.

1. For special-occasion presentations, you should still go through the presentation preparation process. The early steps are the most important—determining your purpose and analyzing your audience. You need to know these things in order to determine what kinds of remarks are appropriate for the occasion and what your audience would like and needs to hear.

2. Your role as the speaker is to focus on two specific tasks: reflecting the tone of the occasion and making a connection with the audience. Your remarks should appropriately reflect the feelings evoked by this occasion (for example, jubilance at a colleague receiving an award for outstanding sales performance, solemnity at the untimely death of a junior executive in a car crash). It is also your job to connect the occasion to the audience, to draw them into the spirit and feeling of the event (for example, an amusing anecdote that reflects how this salesperson achieved her success, a few lines from a poem that the executive kept on the wall of his office for inspiration).
3. Keep your remarks short. Most special-occasion presentations should take no more than 2 to 3 minutes. Most often, you are not the main focus of the occasion, so let your audience appreciate your remarks as a supplement to their overall listening experience.
4. Here are some basic guidelines specific to each type of special-occasion presentation.

Avoid the trite, "Here's a person who needs no introduction..." in favour of a well-prepared and thoughtful speech. Be sure to get some background information on the person you will be introducing, and use that information in the most glowing terms. While light humor may be appropriate if your speaker is somewhat humorous or fun-loving, it is inappropriate to make fun at the speaker's expense (unless this is a "roast"). You don't need to give a person's complete history, but outline the points most relevant to the talk, state why the individual is an appropriate speaker for this group, and introduce the speaker's topic or the title of the talk.

Paying Tribute or Presenting an Award: These speeches are very focused. You are there to acknowledge the accomplishments of a colleague and present some recognition of those accomplishments. You should definitely gather information about the person's background as it relates to the recognition he or she is receiving. It is also appropriate to personalize the attributes of the award recipient for your audience, perhaps by relating a personal experience you had with the recipient or an anecdote related to you by a colleague.

Giving Speeches of Gratitude or Accepting an Award: When you are the recipient of an award, you should thank the group or organization sponsoring the award. You should also thank coworkers, team members, or even family and friends in some cases—those who supported you and made it possible for you to win this recognition. You can also go beyond the standard thank-you remarks and share a lesson, an idea, or a brief inspirational story that will connect you with the audience.

Eulogies at Funerals and Memorial Services: These can be among the most difficult presentations to plan. There is generally so much emotion involved in the death of a close family member or coworker that many find it difficult to speak publicly at these times. If you have accepted the invitation to deliver a eulogy, you should spend much of your preparation time reflecting on the deceased and on the words that would bring most comfort to your audience. The eulogy is one place where the sincere speaker is always appreciated, even if the delivery is not the most articulate or polished.

Toasts at Recognition Banquets and Weddings: Most of us have been to enough banquets and weddings to see examples of how not to deliver a toast. Some of the most common don'ts are as follows:

- Don't deliver a toast with no preparation: "Here's to Harry and his lovely bride what's-her-name. . . ."
- Don't deliver a toast after you have been partaking of the open bar with great enthusiasm.
- Don't deliver a toast with private jokes and references that only a few people in the audience can understand. A corollary: Don't deliver a toast in a language only a few attendees can understand.

You should consider it an honor to be asked to deliver a toast, and you should put as much thought and preparation into this speech as you would other presentations.

Once again, you should think of the person or couple who is receiving the toast and the reason for the occasion. Consider the special attributes of the people involved and consider the audience and what they want to hear.

Special-occasion presentations are often not a routine part of an executive's speaking calendar, and yet they can be significant in your personal and professional development. With the proper preparation and practice, they can become a natural part of your professional portfolio.

Evaluating Your Presentation

As you're packing up your notes and visuals following your presentation, you probably feel a great sense of relief—and hopefully, a sense of accomplishment for a job well done. However, you shouldn't let these fleeting emotions be your final contact with this presentation. The best presenters add a final step to the process: a post presentation evaluation. In this step, you evaluate each aspect of the presentation process and plan for future improvement. You need to do this specifically in three key areas: purpose, audience analysis, and delivery.

Did You Achieve Your Purpose?

Early in the presentation process, you specified your general purpose, your specific purpose, and what you would like to have happen as a result of this presentation. Now you need to examine the outcome of your presentation: Did you achieve your purpose? Did you accomplish your goals for the presentation? If you did, why were you successful? If not, why not? What factors contributed to the audience's acceptance or failure of your proposal?

Audience Analysis

If you followed a systematic presentation process, you probably spent a good bit of time doing audience analysis. You looked at what your audience knew, what you wanted them to know, and what they needed to know. How successful were you in reaching this particular audience? If you didn't reach them, why not? Go through the questions we asked you to explore in to identify the source of the communication breakdown. Did the audience know more than you realized they knew? Were they bored by your presentation? Did they know less than you realized? Were they lost during your presentation? What might you have done differently to better connect with this group of people?

Delivery

This is probably the area most frequently used for a postpresentation evaluation. In this step, you evaluate the verbal and nonverbal communication that contributed to the success or failure of your presentation. Did you use your voice, posture, gestures, and facial expressions to maximum effectiveness? Did your visual aids work smoothly and enhance your presentation? Did you control your anxiety? Did you seem knowledgeable and confident in the question-and-answer session?

You may not be able to complete the postpresentation evaluation totally on your own. If you have a videotape of the presentation, this may help in your self-assessment. However, you may need to enlist the help of close colleagues to give you guidance on how well you met your objectives in the presentation. Certainly, if you are involved in a team project, team members should be open to constructive comments for improvement from others on the team.

One of our most memorable examples of thorough self-evaluation comes from a former MBA student at St. John Fisher College. Alan was an excellent presenter with a high-visibility job in county government, and he was always looking for ways to improve his performance. During his final presentation, he used a large poster board on an easel as a visual aid. When he was through referencing the chart, he took it down, as is appropriate.

However, he hadn't decided what he was going to do with the chart. He held it awkwardly for a few moments and then laid it down on the floor. For a few moments, the audience could hear Alan's voice, but we saw only his back as he leaned down to lay his visual on the floor. It wasn't a major issue in what was otherwise an excellent presentation. However, when Alan saw the videotape, he was appalled by what he had done. Not only had he not planned how to remove his visual, he kept speaking while he lost visual contact with the audience. His written self-evaluation included two pages on the correct use of visual aids.

We aren't recommending that you get overly scrupulous about every aspect of your presentation delivery. However, you can be sure that Alan will never make that same mistake again. He evaluated his performance, didn't like what he saw, and developed a strategy for dealing with it in the future.

Summary

Unless you evaluate your preparation and performance after the presentation, you won't be able to adjust your strategy for the next presentation. You may be condemned to repeat fatal errors or annoying distractions that can test the patience of your audience. Even if your presentation was successful in achieving your purpose, it is good to know just what you did correctly so you can capitalize on those strengths next time. Doing a presentation without systematic evaluation afterward is like not calling the doctor to find out if your child's throat culture is positive for strep: It leaves too much to chance and allows mistakes to multiply. The evaluation doesn't take long, and the insights will be well worth the effort.

Communication and its Presentation

Presentation is the process of presenting the content of a topic to an audience. Presentation software, such as OpenOffice.org Impress, Apple Keynote or Microsoft PowerPoint, is often used to generate the presentation content.

Useful Illustrations

- *BCG Diagram*: This diagram is extremely useful in marketing, although most people only learn the basics of the diagram at undergraduate level.
- *SWOT Analysis*: This is clear and precise, and states the problem effectively.

Telecommuting

Telecommuting, e-commuting, e-work, telework, or working from home (WFH) is a work arrangement in which employees enjoy limited flexibility in working location and hours. In other words, the daily commute to a central place of work is replaced by telecommunication links. Telework is a broader term, referring to substituting telecommunications for any form of work-related travel, thereby eliminating the distance restrictions of telecommuting. All telecommuters are teleworkers but not all teleworkers are telecommuters. A frequently repeated motto is that "work is something you do, not something you travel to". A successful telecommuting programme requires a management style which is based on results and not on close scrutiny of individual employees. This is referred to as 'managing by objective' as opposed to 'managing by observation'. The terms 'telecommuting' and 'telework' were coined by American Jack Nilles in 1973. Long distance telework is facilitated by such tools as virtual private networks, videoconferencing, and Voice over IP. It can be efficient and useful for companies as it allows staff and workers to communicate over a large distance, saving significant amounts of travel time and cost. As broadband Internet connections become more commonplace, more and more workers have enough bandwidth at home to use these tools to link their home office to their corporate intranet and internal phone networks.

Technology

The roots of telecommuting lay early 1970s technology, linking satellite offices to downtown mainframes by dumb terminals using telephone lines as a network bridge. The massive ongoing decrease in cost and increase in performance and usability of personal computers forged the way to decentralize even further, moving the office to the home. By the early 1980s, these branch offices and home workers were able to connect to the company mainframe using personal computers and terminal emulation. The adoption of local area networks promoted sharing of resources, and client server computing allowed for even greater decentralization. Today, telecommuters can carry laptop PCs around which they can use both at the office and at home (and almost anywhere else). Telecommuters are linked to their home office by use groupware, virtual private networks, and similar technologies to collaborate and interact with team members. As the price of VPN-capable routers, high-speed Internet connections to the home, and VOIP technology has plummeted in recent years, the cost to connect a telecommuter to their employer's intranet and telecommunications system has become negligible when compared with the operating costs of conventional offices.

Benefits

Telecommuting, options increase the employability of marginalized groups, such as mothers and fathers with small children, the handicapped and people living in remote areas. It can also reduce an individual's carbon footprint, through minimizing daily commuting. The set up also offers possibilities for increased service and internationalisation, since telecommuters in different time zones can ensure that a company is virtually open for business around the clock. Telework has also enabled offshore outsourcing. Telecommuting provides employee flexibility, eases the working parent's burden, increases employee productivity, and reduces absenteeism. Virtual offices allow employers to keep valuable employees, allow employers to hire employees otherwise not available, and have facilitated productive re-engineering of order-management and customer service processes.

Environmental Advantages

Telecommuting gained more ground in the United States in 1996 after "the Clean Air Act amendments were adopted with the expectation of reducing carbon dioxide and ground-level ozone levels by 25 percent". The act required companies with over 100 employees to encourage car pools, public transportation, shortened workweeks, and telecommuting. In 2004, an appropriations bill was enacted by Congress to encourage telecommuting for certain Federal agencies. The bill threatened to withhold money from agencies that failed to provide telecommuting options to all eligible employees.

Telecommuting is seen as a solution to traffic congestion caused by single-car commuting, and the resulting urban air pollution and petroleum use. Initial investments in the network infrastructure and hardware are balanced by an increased productivity and overall greater well-being of telecommuting staff (more quality family time, less travel-related stress), which makes the arrangement attractive to companies, especially those who face large operating costs related to the need for a central office. Even so, telecommuting has not been as widely adopted as expected. "The number of U.S. telecommuters falls somewhere between 9 million and 24 million-far short of the 55 million telecommuters that some forecasters predicted would be in place in the early 2000s. Although the majority of Fortune 1,000 firms offer telecommuting, more than half say that only between 1 percent and 5 percent of employees participate in such programmes".

Current Trends

Distributed Work

Telecommuters need not necessarily work from the home. A more recent extension of telecommuting is distributed work. Distributed work entails the conduct of organizational tasks in places that extends beyond the confines of traditional offices. It can refer to organizational arrangements that permit or require workers to perform work more effectively at any appropriate locations, such as their homes and customers' sites-through the application of information and communication technology. An example is financial planners who meet clients during lunchtime with access to various financial planning tools and offerings on their mobile computers, or publishing executives who recommend and place orders for the latest book offerings to libraries and university professors, among others. These work arrangements are likely to become more popular with current trends towards greater customization of services and virtual organizing. Distributed work offers great potential for firms to reduce costs, enhance competitive advantage and agility, access a greater variety of scarce talents, and improve employee flexibility, effectiveness and productivity e.g., it has gained in popularity in the West, particularly in Europe. While increasing in importance, distributed work has not yet gained widespread acceptance in Asia.

Virtual Offices

Virtual offices please management because they reduce overheads, reduce office space needs, increase productivity, and reduce staff turnover. However, managers (whose roles are varied and not well defined) in telecommuting roles typically receive fewer promotions due to the lack of direct contact they need. From that aspect, telecommuting seems to work best for professionals such as engineers.

Microjobs

Telecommuters who begin working from home part time for one company tend to acquire self employed status through agreement or necessity, and from that position it is less of a step to seek a little more work from other sources. Ultimately, The size of the job unit reduces such that many more people are working in small chunks for multiple clients. These chunks have been named microjobs.

Potential Drawbacks

- Telecommuting has come to be viewed as more a "complement rather than a substitute for work in the workplace". Thus, some workers may find their work load increased to the point where they are under more stress than before. Distractions at home can have a similar effect, especially among workers that leave the office to be better able to care for small children and the infirm.
- The home telecommuter becomes socially isolated and further job advancement is more difficult to achieve. Fellow employees in the home office sometimes resent home telecommuters. Corporate culture, loyalty, communication, access to people, and managerial control can be difficult to adapt to the new workplace.
- Even when a company successfully implements telecommuting practices, increasing productivity and decreasing stress, they face an increased risk of confidential data loss and risks to data integrity resulting from the increased geographical diversity of their network and the loss of direct corporate control over the telecommuter's physical work environment. For instance, a major breach of privacy by the United States Department of Veterans Affairs resulted from a laptop being stolen from a worker who took his work home. The result was described as

"potentially the largest loss of Social Security numbers to date."

- Initially, managers may view the teleworker as experiencing a drop in productivity during the first few months. This drop occurs as "the employee, his peers, and the manager adjust to the new work regimen". The drop could also be accountable to inadequate office setup. Managers need to be patient and let the teleworker adapt. It can be claimed that as much as "70 minutes of each day in a regular office are wasted by interruptions, yakking around the photocopier, and other distractions". Eventually, productivity of the teleworker will climb.
- Management needs to recognise the communication barriers that telecommuters experience. The feeling of alienation can be very difficult for the teleworker. The job should be clearly defined as well as its objectives. Performance measures should be thorough and apparent.
- Managers need to be aware that although overhead decreases, the cost of technology becomes greater. Information Technology (IT) managers experience greater demands because of user requirements for remote access through laptops, personal digital assistants, and home computers. Use of non-standard software can create problems. Setting up security and virtual private networks increase the demands for IT.
- Traditional line managers are accustomed to managing by observation and not necessarily by results. This causes a serious obstacle in organizations attempting to adopt telecommuting. Liability and workers' compensation can become serious issues as well. Companies considering telecommuting should be sure to check on local legal issues, union issues, and zoning laws. Telecommuting should incorporate training and development that includes evaluation, simulation programmes, team meetings, written materials, and forums. Information sharing should be considered synchronous in a virtual office and building processes to handle conflicts should be developed. Operational and administrative support should be

redesigned to support the virtual office environment. Facilities need to be coordinated properly in order to support the virtual office and technical support should be coordinated properly. The conclusion for managers working within telecommuting organizations is that new approaches to "evaluating, educating, organizing, and informing workers" should be adopted.

Telecommuting Jobs

The proliferation of many smaller Internet companies has resulted in an increase of data entry related telecommuting jobs. The tight budgets of many of these companies make it economically impossible to carry full time staff. Contracting with home based free-lancers is a cost effective way of meeting the demands of daily data entry tasks. These tasks may include the preparation of correspondence, reports, spreadsheets, lists, records and databases. Below are profiles of some of the most popular telecommuting data entry jobs:

- *Litigation Coding*: A growing category, litigation coding involves the capture of information from scanned documents to assist legal professionals in not only storing their documents electronically but locating the documents using keyword search criteria.
- *Medical and Legal Transcription*: Medical and/or legal transcription requires the entry of information as heard on an audio file. The contractor will listen to a recording and type everything that they hear. There is specialized equipment available such as headphones and even foot pedals that can slow down or speed up what you're listening to, as well as training courses that can teach and certify you in these types of data entry jobs.
- *Medical Coding*: Ensures the proper entry and management of sensitive medical data. There are correspondence courses that can teach you how to do this from home.

Graphical user Interface

A graphical user interface (GUI) allows for interaction with a computer or other media formats which employs graphical images, special graphical element devices called "widgets", along with text to represent the information and actions available to a user. The actions are usually performed through direct manipulation of the graphical elements.

History

Precursors to GUIs

The precursor to GUIs was invented by researchers at the Stanford Research Institute, led by Doug Engelbart. They developed the use of text-based hyperlinks manipulated with a mouse for the On-Line System. The concept of hyperlinks was further refined and extended to graphics by researchers at Xerox PARC, who went beyond text-based hyperlinks and used GUIs as the primary interface for the Xerox Alto computer. Most modern general-purpose GUIs are derived from this system. As a result, some people call this class of interface a PARC User Interface (PUI) (note that PUI is also an acronym for perceptual user interface).

PARC User Interface (PUI)

The PUI consists of graphical widgets (often provided by widget toolkit libraries) such as windows, menus, radio buttons. PUIs employ a pointing device in addition to a keyboard. These aspects of PUIs can be emphasized by using the alternative acronym WIMP, which stands for Windows, Icons, Menus and Pointing device.

Evolution of Graphic user Interfaces

The GUIs familiar to most people today are the Microsoft Windows, Mac OS X, or the X Window System interfaces. Their applications originated at the Xerox PARC (Palo Alto Research Center) in the late 1970s and was copied by Apple who used it in their first Macintosh computers. Later IBM and Microsoft borrowed many of Apple's ideas to develop the Common User Access specifications, that formed the basis of the user interface found in Microsoft Windows, IBM OS/2 Presentation Manager, and the Unix Motif toolkit and window manager. These ideas evolved to create the interface found in current versions of the

Windows operating system, as well as in Mac OS X and various desktop environments for Unix-like systems. Thus most current graphical user interfaces have largely common idioms.

GUI Design

GUI design is an important adjunct to application programming. Its goal is to enhance the usability of the underlying logical design of a stored programme. The visible graphical interface features of an application are sometimes referred to as "chrome". They include graphical elements (widgets) that may be used to interact with the programme. Common widgets are: windows, buttons, menus, and scroll bars. Larger widgets, such as windows, usually provide a frame or container for the main presentation content such as a web page, email message or drawing. Smaller ones usually act as a user-input tool. The widgets of a well-designed system are functionally independent from and indirectly linked to programme functionality, so the GUI can be easily customized, allowing the user to select or design a different skin at will.

PUIs

Rare kinds of GUI including PUIs are most notably found in computer games, and advanced GUIs based on virtual reality are now frequently found in research.

Zooming user Interface

Many research groups in North America and Europe are currently working on the Zooming User Interface (ZUI) which is a logical advancement on the GUI, blending some 3D movement with 2D or "2.5D" vectorial objects.

Some GUIs are designed for the rigorous requirements of vertical markets. These are known as "application specific GUIs." One example of such an application specific GUI is the now familiar touchscreen point of sale software found in restaurants worldwide and being introduced into self-service retail checkouts. First pioneered by Gene Mosher on the Atari ST computer in 1986, the application specific touchscreen GUI has spearheaded a worldwide revolution in the use of computers throughout the food and beverage industry and in general retail. Other examples of application specific touchscreen GUIs include the most recent automatic teller machines, airline self-ticketing, information kiosks and the monitor/control screens in embedded industrial applications which employ a real time operating system (RTOS). The latest cell phones and handheld game systems also employ application specific touchscreen GUIs.

GUI vs. CLI

GUIs were introduced in reaction to the steep learning curve of command line interfaces (CLI), text-based user interfaces that require commands to be typed on the keyboard. Since the command words in CLIs are often numerous, very complicated operations can be completed using a relatively short sequence of words and symbols. This allows for great efficiency, once the many commands are learned, but reaching this level takes some time because the command words are not easily discoverable. WIMPs ("window, icon, menu, pointing device"), on the other hand, present the user with numerous widgets that represent and can trigger some of the system's available commands.

WIMPs extensively use modes as the meaning of all keys and clicks on specific positions on the screen are redefined all the time. CLIs use modes only in the form of a current directory.

Most modern operating systems provide both a GUI and some level of a CLI, although the GUIs usually receive more attention. The GUI is usually WIMP-based, although occasionally other metaphors surface, such as those used in Microsoft Bob, 3dwm or File System Visualizer or FSV.

Applications may also provide both interfaces, and when they do the GUI is usually a WIMP wrapper around the CLI version. This is especially common with applications designed for Unix-like operating systems. The latter used to be implemented first because it allowed the developers to focus exclusively on their product's functionality without bothering about interface details such as designing icons and placing buttons. Designing programmes this way also allows users to run the programme non-interactively, such as in a shell script.

GUI vs. TUI

3D user Interfaces

For commonly-available computer displays, 3D is a misnomer. Their displays are two-dimensional. Three-dimensional images are projected on them in two dimensions. Since this technique has been in use for many years, the recent use of the term 3D must be considered a declaration by equipment marketers that the speed of 3D to 2D projection is adequate to use in standard GUIs.

3D GUIs are very common in science fiction literature and movies, such as in Jurassic Park, which features Silicon Graphics' 3D Filemanager, "File system navigator", an actual file manager that never got any widespread use as the user interface of a Unix computer.

In science fiction, 3D user interfaces are often immersible environments like William Gibson's Cyberspace or Neal Stephenson's Metaverse. 3D graphics is currently mostly used in computer games, art and computer aided design. There have been several attempts at making 3D desktop environments like Sun's Project Looking Glass or SphereXP from Sphere Inc. A 3D computing environment could possibly be used for collaborative work, for example scientists may study 3D models of molecules in a virtual reality environment or engineers may work on assembling a 3D model of an airplane. This is a goal of the Croquet project and Project Looking Glass by Java.

The use of 3D has become increasingly common in mainstream operating systems, but its use has mainly been confined to creating eye candy. For example, user switching is in the form of a rotating cube and window management in the form of Exposé on Mac OS X, or via a Rolodex-style flipping mechanism in Windows Vista. In both cases, the operating system resizes and relocates windows on-the-fly, whilst continuing to update the content of those windows.

Linux operating systems, such as Ubuntu, have also begun implementing basic 3D user interfaces through the XGL architecture, which uses OpenGL to perform tasks such as user switching in a similar fashion to Mac OS X.

Another branch in the 3D desktop environment is the 3D GUIs that take the desktop metaphor a step further, like the BumpTop, where a user can manipulate documents and windows as if they were "real world" documents, with realistic movement and physics. With the current pace on 3D and related hardware evolution, we can expect that projects such these reach an operational level soon.

Simulation

A simulation is an imitation of some real thing, state of affairs, or process. The act of simulating something generally entails representing certain key characteristics or behaviors of a selected physical or abstract system. Historically, the word had negative connotations: . . . for Distinction Sake, a Deceiving by Words, is commonly called a Lye, and a Deceiving by Actions, Gestures, or Behaviour, is called Simulation. However, the connection between simulation and dissembling later faded out and is now only of linguistic interest.

Simulation is used in many contexts, including the modeling of natural systems or human systems in order to gain insight into their functioning. Other contexts include simulation of technology for performance optimization, safety engineering, testing, training and education. Simulation can be used to show the eventual real effects of alternative conditions and courses of action. Key issues in simulation include acquisition of valid source information about the referent, selection of key characteristics and behaviours, the use of simplifying approximations and assumptions within the simulation, and fidelity and validity of the simulation outcomes.

Types of Simulation

Historically, simulations used in different fields developed largely independently, but 20th century studies of Systems theory and Cybernetics combined with spreading use of computers across all those fields have led to some unification and a more systematic view of the concept.

Physical and Interactive Simulation

Physical simulation refers to simulation in which physical objects are substituted for the real thing. These physical objects are often chosen because they are smaller or cheaper than the actual object or system. Interactive simulation is a special kind of physical simulation, often referred to as a human in the loop simulation, in which physical simulations include human operators, such as in a flight simulator.

Computer Simulation

A computer simulation is an attempt to model a real-life situation on a computer so that it can be studied to see how the system works. By changing variables, predictions may be made about the behaviour of the system. An interesting application of computer simulation is to simulate computers using computers.

The related software is called computer architecture simulators, which can be further divided into instruction set simulators or full system simulators. Computer simulation has become a useful part of modeling many natural systems in physics, chemistry and biology, and human systems in economics and social science (the computational sociology) as well as in engineering to gain insight into the operation of those systems. A good example of the usefulness of using computers to simulate can be found in the field of network traffic simulation. In such simulations the model behaviour will change each simulation according to the set of initial parameters assumed for the environment. Computer simulations are often considered to be human out of the loop simulations.

Traditionally, the formal modeling of systems has been via a mathematical model, which attempts to find analytical solutions enabling the prediction of the behaviour of the system from a set of parameters and initial conditions. Computer simulation is often used as an adjunct to, or substitution for, modeling systems for which simple closed form analytic solutions are not possible.

There are many different types of computer simulation, the common feature they all share is the attempt to generate a sample of representative scenarios for a model in which a complete enumeration of all possible states would be prohibitive or impossible. In finance, for example, the risk-adjusted net present value is computed from well-defined but not always known (or fixed) inputs. By imitating the performance of the project under evaluation, simulation can provide a distribution of NPV over a range of discount rates and other inputs. Several software packages exist for running computer-based simulation modeling (e.g. Monte Carlo simulation and stochastic modeling) that makes the modeling almost effortless. It is increasingly common to hear simulations of many kinds referred to as "synthetic environments". This label has been adopted to broaden the definition of "simulation" to encompass virtually any computer-based representation.

Simulation in Computer Science

In computer science, simulation has an even more specialized meaning: Scholars use the term "simulation" to refer to what happens when a digital computer runs a state transition table (runs a programme) that describes the state transitions, inputs and outputs of a subject discrete-state machine. The computer simulates the subject machine. In computer architecture, a simulator is often used to execute a programme that has to run on some inconvenient type of computer, or in a tightly controlled testing environment. For example, simulators are usually used to debug a microprogram or sometimes commercial application programmes. Since the operation of the computer is simulated, all of the information about the computer's operation is directly available to the programmer, and the speed and execution of the simulation can be varied at will. Simulators may also be used to interpret fault trees, or test VLSI logic designs before they are constructed. Symbolic simulation is a form of simulation that is also an abstract interpretation of the concrete system under analysis. In theoretical computer science the term simulation represents a relation between state transition systems. This is useful in the study of operational semantics.

Simulation in Training

Simulation is often used in the training of civilian and military personnel. This usually occurs when it is prohibitively expensive or simply too dangerous to allow trainees to use the real equipment in the real world. In such situations they will spend time learning valuable lessons in a "safe" virtual environment. Often the convenience is to permit mistakes during training for a safety-critical system.

Training simulations typically come in one of three categories:

- "live" simulation (where real people use simulated (or "dummy") equipment in the real world);
- "virtual" simulation (where real people use simulated equipment in a simulated world (or "virtual environment")), or
- "constructive" simulation (where simulated people use simulated equipment in a simulated environment). Constructive simulation is often referred to as "wargaming" since it bears some resemblance to table-top war games in which players command armies of soldiers and equipment that move around a board. Cognitive Simulations constitute a sub-type, in which the goal of the simulation is to engage and train the same brain areas that are deployed in the real performance, in order to ensure maximum transfer to the real environment.

Simulation in Education

Simulations in education are somewhat like training simulations. They focus on specific tasks. In the past, video has been used for teachers and education students to observe, problem solve and role play; however, a more recent use of simulations in education include animated narrative vignettes (ANV). ANVs are cartoon-like video narratives of hypothetical and reality-based stories involving classroom teaching and learning. ANVs have been used to assess knowledge, problem solving skills and dispositions of children, and pre-service and in-service teachers. Another form of simulation has been finding favour in business education in recent years. Business simulations that incorporate a dynamic model enables experimentation with business strategies in a risk free environment and provide a useful extension to case study discussions.

Medical Simulators

Medical simulators are increasingly being developed and deployed to teach therapeutic and diagnostic procedures as well as medical concepts and decision making to personnel in the health professions. Simulators have been developed for training procedures ranging from the basics such as blood draw, to laparoscopic surgery and trauma care. They are also important to help on prototyping new devices for biomedical engineering problems. Currently, simulators are applied to research and development of tools for new therapies, treatments and early diagnosis in medicine. Many medical simulators involve a computer connected to a plastic simulation of the relevant anatomy. Sophisticated simulators of this type employ a life size mannequin that responds to injected drugs and can be programmed to create simulations of life-threatening emergencies. In others simulations, visual components of the procedure are reproduced by computer graphics techniques, while touch-based components are reproduced by haptic feedback devices combined with physical simulation routines computed in response to the user's actions. Medical simulations of this sort will often use 3D CT or MRI scans of patient data to enhance realism. Some medical simulations are developed to be widely distributed (such as via the web) and can be interacted with using standard computer interfaces, such as the keyboard and mouse.

Another important medical application of a simulator - although, perhaps, denoting a slightly different meaning of simulator - is the use of a placebo drug, a formulation that simulates the active drug in trials of drug efficacy.

History of Medical Simulation

The first medical simulators were simple models of human patients. Since antiquity, these representations in clay and stone were used to demonstrate clinical features of disease states and their effects on humans. Models have been found from many cultures and continents. These models have been used in some cultures (e.g., Chinese culture) as a "diagnostic" instrument, allowing women to consult male physicians while maintaining social laws of modesty. Models are used today to help students learn the anatomy of the musculoskeletal system and organ systems.

Active Models

Active models that attempt to reproduce living anatomy or physiology are recent developments. The famous "Harvey" mannikin was developed at the University of Miami and is able to recreate many of the physical findings of the cardiology examination, including palpation, auscultation, and electrocardiography.

Interactive Models

More recently, interactive models have been developed that respond to actions taken by a student or physician. Until recently, these simulations were two dimensional computer programmes that acted more like a textbook than a patient. Computer simulations have the advantage of allowing a student to make judgements, and also to make errors. The process of iterative learning through assessment, evaluation, decision making, and error correction creates a much stronger learning environment than passive instruction.

Computer Simulators

Simulators have been proposed as an ideal tool for assessment of students for clinical skills. Programmed patients and simulated clinical situations, including mock disaster drills, have been used extensively for education and evaluation. These "lifelike" simulations are expensive, and lack reproducibility. A fully functional "3Pi" simulator would be the most specific tool available for teaching and measurement of clinical skills.

Such a simulator meets the goals of an objective and standardized examination for clinical competence. This system is superior to examinations that use "standard patients" because it permits the quantitative measurement of competence, as well as reproducing the same objective findings.

The "Classroom of the Future"

The "classroom of the future" will probably contain several kinds of simulators, in addition to textual and visual learning tools. This will allow students to enter the clinical years better prepared, and with a higher skill level.

The advanced student or postgraduate will have a more concise and comprehensive method of retraining - or of incorporating new clinical procedures into their skill set-and regulatory bodies and medical institutions will find it easier to assess the proficiency and competency of individuals.

The classroom of the future will also form the basis of a clinical skills unit for continuing education of medical personnel; and in the same way that the use of periodic flight training assists airline pilots, this technology will assist practitioners throughout their career.

The simulator will be more than a "living" textbook, it will become an integral a part of the practice of medicine. The simulator environment will also provide a standard platform for curriculum development in institutions of medical education.

City Simulators/Urban Simulation

A City Simulator can be a game but can also be a tool used by urban planners to understand how cities are likely to evolve in response to various policy decisions. UrbanSim (developed at the University of Washington), ILUTE (developed at the University of Toronto) and Distrimobs (developed at the University of Bologna) are examples of modern, large-scale urban simulators designed for use by urban planners. City simulators are generally agent-based simulations with explicit representations for land use and transportation.

Flight Simulators

A flight simulator is used to train pilots on the ground. It permits a pilot to crash his simulated "aircraft" without being hurt. Flight simulators are often used to train pilots to operate aircraft in extremely hazardous situations, such as landings with no engines, or complete electrical or hydraulic failures. The most advanced simulators have high-fidelity visual systems and hydraulic motion systems. The simulator is normally cheaper to operate than a real trainer aircraft.

Home-built Flight Simulators

Some people who use simulator software, especially flight simulator software, build their own simulator at home. Some people in order to further the realism of their homemade simulator, buy used cards and racks that still run the exact same software they did before they were disassembled from the actual machine itself. Though this brings along the problem of matching hardware and software, and the fact that hundreds of cards plug into many different racks, still, many find that is it well worth it. Some are very serious in building their simulator by buying real aircraft parts like complete nose sectionals of written off aircraft at aircraft boneyards. This permits people who are unable to perform their hobby in real life to simulate it.

Marine Simulators

Bearing resemblance to flight simulators, marine simulators train a ships' personnel. Simulators like these are mostly used to simulate large or complex vessels, such as cruise-ships and dredging ships. They often consist of a replication of a ships' bridge, with operating desk(s), and a number of screens on which the virtual surroundings are projected.

Process Simulation

Simulation is an important feature in engineering systems or any system that involves many processes. For example in electrical engineering, delay lines may be used to simulate propagation delay and phase shift caused by an actual transmission line. Similarly, dummy loads may be used to simulate impedance without simulating propagation, and is used in situations where propagation is unwanted. A simulator may imitate only a few of the operations and functions of the unit it simulates. Most engineering simulations entail mathematical modeling and computer assisted investigation. There are many cases, however, where mathematical modeling is not reliable. Simulation of fluid dynamics problems often require both mathematical and physical simulations. In these cases the physical models require dynamic similitude. Physical and chemical simulations have also direct realistic uses, rather than research uses; in chemical engineering, for example, process simulations are used to give the process parameters immediately used for operating chemical plants, such as oil refineries.

For example, discrete event simulation is often used in industrial engineering, operations management and operational research to model many systems (commerce, health, defence, manufacturing, logistics, etc.) for example, the value-adding transformation processes in businesses, and optimize business performance. Imagine a business, where each person could do 30 tasks, where thousands of products or services involved dozens of tasks in a sequence, where customer demand varied seasonally and forecasting was inaccurate-this is the domain where such simulation helps with business decisions across all functions. Related topics include Theory of Constraints, bottlenecks, and management consulting.

Games

Strategy games-both traditional and modern-may be viewed as simulations of abstracted decision-making for the purpose of training military and political leaders. In a narrower sense, many video games are also simulators, implemented inexpensively. These are sometimes called "sim games". Such games can simulate various aspects of reality, from economics to piloting vehicles, such as flight simulators. Another type of simulation is a government simulation, which can be used to help the player understand certain aspects of political science-specifically cause and effect.

7

Business Policy of Strategic Management

Deming Prize Winners in Auto-component Companies

Sona Koyo Steering Systems Ltd., India

Sona Group had technical collaboration agreement with Koyo Seiko Co. Ltd., Japan in 1985, for manufacture of manual steering, gear assemblies and steering column assemblies. From October 1987 this company started its production. In 1992 equity participation of 8% by Koyo and it was increased to equity participation to 20.5%. In 1998, Sona Steering systems changed to Sona Koyo Steering Systems Ltd. Since 1994 Koyo certified Sona as an approved vendor for export of steering parts to Japan.

Policy management is the process of formulating, deploying and implementing the company policy of the year related to high priority to lower levels in the organization. Policy Deployment starts from the Top Management and goes down to Plant Manager, Departmental Manager and to the Section Manager level. The process has been improved over the years based on the learning during implementation using the Plan, Do, Check, Act (PDCA) Cycle as propagated by Guru's like Shewart and Deming.

Implementation of Objectives & Action Plans At Sona Koyo Steering Systems Ltd. the implementation of objectives and action plans is briefly highlighted as:

* Weekly review of action plan in Managing Committee meetings

* Monthly review of Divisional Objectives
* Quarterly review of Chief Level Objectives
* Half yearly review of Company Objectives
* Daily, weekly and monthly gap analysis of Checking Points, and
* Monthly review of Managing Points.

This has given better results in terms of reducing the manufacturing expenses as % of net sales from 2000 year onwards. Fuel consumption per unit of power has gone down since year 2000. Inventory Turnover ratio has improved; In-house rejection have declined customer returns Per Part Million (PPM) has decreased since year 2000. After implementing the concept of policy management in the company. Some highlights of the company from the primary source are given which gives us an idea how this company has achieved competitive advantage in the field of auto component business.

New competitions will be coming through supplier power and price level sensitivity in the market. New opportunity for the company will be in Western Europe and North America as well as new challenges in Indian market. Some of the aspect of the competitive advantage in this company is:

* Shared costs between several products
* Quality & knowledge of work force
* Experience and knowledge of business & organizational learning culture
* Production technology upgradation
* Strategic outsourcing
* Standardization of product and pricing policy
* Good relationship with suppliers computerized management of information flows and material flows
* Quick response to unscheduled production demand
* Just-in-Time (JIT) concept of manufacturing
* Customer service contract
* After sales service and availability of spare parts
* Regular assessment of customer satisfaction

* Product purchased from the company vs. competition, services required from time-to-time by the customers
* Trends or future possible change in customer requirement for product and services monitoring
* Good financial management systems
* Good policy management systems in the company.

New strategic goals of the company are:

* Development of new knowledge and technologies
* Increase of the sales turnover
* To be present in the global market
* Research and development reinforcement & development of unique capabilities within the company for innovation.

The company won the prestigious Deming Application Prize for Business Excellence awarded by Japanese Union of Scientists and Engineers (JUSE) in 2003.

This company has become globally competitive by applying the principles of Total Quality and Excellence.

(B) Sundaram-Clayton Limited Brakes Division (Chennai), India This company was established in 1962 as a joint venture with Clayton Devandre, UK (Now WABCO Automotive UK).

WABCO Automotive is part of American Standard Inc.--a fortune 500 company. Sundaram Clayton-Brakes Division is located at Chennai and is part of the TVS group, which was established in India in 1911.

SCL Products:

* Air brake systems for medium and heavy commercial vehicles
* Vacuum brake products for light commercial vehicles.
* Anti-lock braking systems (ABS) and Anti-spin Regulation Systems.

In 1983-87 there was a recession in the Automobile Industry and Emergence of Competition in Sundaram Clayton Business. There was a drop in market share and profitability. Thus in 1987-88 there was a wakeup call for the company to gear up and faced competition. Sundaram Clayton embraced the TQM philosophy and the Deming model for improving performance and manufacturing excellence.

1987-90 Phase the Introduction Phase

The first issues was to be tackled in this phase was bringing about a cultural change in the organization by having common uniform for all employees, open offices, total employee involvement, where quality circles and suggestion schemes were encouraged among the employees. Restructuring Manufacturing process was done to have product layout, self-contained units, and operator's ownership of Quality.

1990-1994: The Promotion Phase

The Policy Management philosophy was employed to have goal congruence among all the levels of management. Measures and targets were fixed and monitored/reviewed and achieved. The audit reviews were carried out throughout the organization. The concept of cellular manufacturing--emphasizing Productivity Improvements, Lead--Time Reduction, settings up of operation standards for all key processes were done. Massive efforts towards Education and Training where problem solving skills were imparted to company wide employers at all levels.

1994-1998: Deployment Phase

Standardization was adopted for all processes and operating procedures were written for every activity specially all manufacturing activity & related activities. Poka-Yoke (Mistake Proofing) was implemented for various machines in the manufacturing process. New Product Development was taken up very seriously applying a multidisciplinary task force full time and New Product Development (NPD) process was well defined and all the tools and techniques were applied for New Product Development.

Supplier Development was emphasized for the whole manufacturing function. Manufacturing cells were created at the suppliers' sites and training of suppliers or vendors of the company was done by the specialists. In 1998 Sundaram Clayton--Brakes Division was awarded "Deming Application Price" for distinctive performance improvement through the application of Company-wide Quality Control. This company became the forth company outside Japan and the very first in India to receive this prestigious award.

Continuos Improvement Phase (1998--Present)

Responding to the External changes and the Internal changes, the Deming examiner's feedback with TVS corporate values in mind, efforts began to own new products, sustain product quality and productivity with social responsibility for improved customer satisfaction and business results. Concepts like Total Productivity Maintenance (TPM), Lean Manufacturing, Application of IT as enabling processes Productivity Improvement, Establishing Environmental Management Standards (EMS) as per ISO 14001 standard were taken up. Development work for electronic control system for air brakes was taken up during this period. Development of new customers has also being given importance. For sustaining profit, product mix optimization and cost management have been made very effective throughout the company. With the above two case study, from the auto component industry in India, we have seen how policy management as part of the Deming way of implementing Total Quality Management (TQM) for achieving business excellence has been implemented in the two case studies.

Tata Business Excellence Model (TBEM) at Tata Steel

Now we look at the genesis of the Tata Business Excellence Model (TBEM) applied by one of the largest diversified and admired private group in India the Tata Group. Based on the American Model, The Malcolm Baldrige Award for business Excellence, The TBEM is applied in one of the oldest companies of the group, Tata Steel, the first Steel Company in Asia, which started in 1907 in India. By applying this integrated model for excellence, has become one of the best steel companies of the world now. Tata Business Excellence Model at Tata Steel: One of the largest business groups in India consists of 85 companies and 7 business sectors worth about Rs. 50, 000 crores i.e. about US $11. 213 billion in revenues.

Tata Group of companies have taken upon themselves one of the largest strategic change initiatives in their companies through the Tata Business Excellence Model (TBEM) launched in 1998 to grapple with the challenges and transformation, the competitive environment was throwing upon the different companies in the Group. Post 1991--when the liberalization era had just begun in India, there was a change in the competitive scenario in India and companies had to adopt their strategies and philosophies which would make them more competitive in the market place.

Between December 1998 and early 2000, about 30 companies in the Tata Group signed up to implement the Tata Business Excellence Model (TBEM) and from July 2000, these companies are being annually evaluated on the 7 criteria that constitute the TBEM:

1. Leadership
2. Strategic Planning
3. Customer and Market Focus
4. Information and Analysis
5. Human Resource Management
6. Process Management and
7. Business Results.

Origin of TBEM

The genesis of the Tata Business Excellence Model (TBEM) lies in the JRD Quality Value (JRDQV) Award launched after the death of the group chairman Mr. J.R.D. Tata in 1994 in his memory for the Tata group companies. This model is based on Malcolm Baldrige National Quality Award that jump-started the Quality movement in USA in 1988. The TBEM, which was adopted in Tata Group, companies including Tata Steel, was adopted in 1998. It has all the same criteria as the Malcolm Baldrige Award criteria plus it also incorporates the Tata Brand equity promotion and Tata Code of conduct.

JRDQV Award Quest at Tata Steel

Tata Steel, the oldest Integrated Steel Company India, which was, founded in 1907 at Jamshedpur in the Bihar State (Now called Jharkhand State) produces about 3 Million Tons/year of saleable steel. Tata Steel is Asia's first and country's largest private sector integrated steel plant. The company has played a pioneering role in integrating professional business practices with exemplary corporate citizenship programmes in India.

In mid of year 2000, the company has started operating a 1 Million-Ton Cold Rolling Plant with the collaboration with Nippon Steel, Japan. In 1999-2000, the company had a sales turnover of Rs. 6,943.33 Crores i.e. about $1.47 Billion and Profit after Taxes as Rs. 422.59 Crores i.e. about $8.93 Million. In the year 2000-2001, the sales turnover was Rs.7814.58 Crores i.e. about $1.65 Billion with a net profit of Rs.553.44 Crores i.e. $11.71 Million. Year 2001-2002 was a very difficult year for the steel industry.

All the companies in the world made losses but Tata Steel made a profit of Rs 205 crores and in 2002-2003, The company has done exceedingly well by making a net profit of Rs. 1012 crores i.e. about $18.72 Million. Tata Steel in its new vision statement in 1998 had taken up the challenge to become the lowest cost producer of steel in the world. Till the year 2000, it was second to the leading Korean Steel Company, Posco Steel.

In year 2001-2002 as per the World Steel Dynamics, Tata Steel of India has become the lowest cost producer of steel in the whole world.

This is the only company among the Tata Group, which has crossed 600 points out of 1000 points to qualify for the JRDQV award in July 2000. Tata Steel is way ahead of the other companies because it's quest for Total Quality and Excellence, which started in the late 1989, when it started its Total Quality Management (TQM) movement. In early 1992, it adopted the Malcolm Baldrige Award Criteria for implementing TQM in various divisions of the company and called it the JN Tata Quality Award, where various divisions within the company were competing with each other on Total Quality Implementation. In 1994, Tata Steel adopted the JRDQV guidelines again based on Malcolm Baldrige guidelines for moving towards Total Quality or Business Excellence, and started competing with other Tata group companies. From 1998 onwards it has been leading in the JRDQV award total scores in the Tara group. The need for TBEM and what it does are given in the next sections.

The Need for the TBEM

The following issues were considered before the Tata Group felt the need for adopting the Tata Business Excellence Model (TBEM). They are:

* Processes and practices were not customer-centric in the companies
* Tata Group Companies pursued size instead of agility
* Performance standards varied between organizations
* Knowledge and best practices were not being shared
* There was no unified management strategy for the Tata Group.

What the TBEM Does?

* Provides a framework for the group to become competitive
* Uses quality as the route to acquiring competitiveness
* Works as a competition to ensure participation
* Becomes a transformational tool for every company.

The TBEM Model

Beyond the broad guidelines, the model has no prescriptions, and is extensively adaptable. The choices of the tools of implementation lie entirely with the company, as does the method of deployment. Here is how the TBEM drives excellence across functions:

* The leadership criteria checks how senior leaders create a leadership system based on Group Values
* The customer and Market Focus checks how the company determines customer groups, key customer needs, and complaint-management issues
* The Strategic Planning criteria examines how the company develops strategic-objectives, action plans and resource allocation
* The information and Analysis criteria check whether the organization has key metrics in place to measure and analyze performance
* The human resources management checks the appraisal-

system, the work environment, and the training and development of employees

* The process management examines the product-design, production and delivery process and supply-chain management
* The business results criteria measures the organization's performance in business areas like customer satisfaction, human resource results and company's financial results.

The foundation on which the Tata Business Excellence Model (TBEM) is built upon is the 1) JRDQV Award guidelines (based on Malcolm Baldrige Quality Award), which emphasizes on quality practices, customer focus and process improvement and 2) the Tata Brand Equity Business Promotion (BEBP) which lays down the criteria for using the Tata Brand and 3) the code of conduct for the Tata group and ethical practices for the Tata Group. Beyond the broad guidelines, the model has no prescriptions and is extremely adaptable. The choices of tools of implementation lie entirely with the company, as does the method of deployment. TBEM drives excellence across functions. Every group company with different business is applying this model for business excellence in their own way.

Massive education and training effort is in place in the company to take care of the minimum training needs for each employee and the developmental need for every employee. This is achieved through in-house Management Development Center and Technical Training Institute for the company. Every Department in the company has Training and Educational Executive and coordinates the Education and Training function with the central company facilities.

The Human Resource Division has now an organizational learning wing, which caters to the employee's learning needs. When Tata Steel won the JRDQV awards in July 2000, its highest scores were in the category of "Customer and Market-Knowledge" and Public Responsibility and Citizenship" Now, Knowledge Management structures has been created for the benefit of integration of knowledge within the company. The measures based on Customer, In-process, Financial and Innovation and Learning are monitored at the top management level. It also percolates to each department and division and individual employee.

Tata Steel started positioning itself as a more competitive and customer-oriented steel manufacturer. For this, a process was needed which could be used by the managers throughout the organization to improve their performance and hence the competitiveness of the organization. In order to achieve such a goal, the company incorporated Benchmarking into its corporate strategy and started Reengineering its core Business processes.

Journey for Business Excellence at Tata Steel

Prior to globalization of Indian economy in 1991, the competition in steel industry was limited. By adopting measures leading to marginal improvements, Tara Steel was ahead of its Indian competitors. However, the company was primarily inward looking and was not affected much with the happenings beyond Indian economy with globalization, the environment changed dramatically and the company had to think 'out of the box'.

It became necessary to redefine the business elements (technology, products, market-segment, human resource, input materials, plant location, etc.), business priorities, vision, strategies, management tool and techniques etc. In effect, the company redefined and reoriented itself in a turbulent environment. First adopting the Total Quality Management (TQM) philosophy as a part of Competitive Strategy was formally launched in the company in late 1989. It started with massive effort on education and training on TQM. It started with ISO 9001 and ISO 9002 certification of various manufacturing and later service units. Process Improvements through Quality Improvement Projects (QIP's), Value Engineering Projects and Statistical Process Control projects and Operations Research Projects by managerial teams was making great contributions in various departments and divisions of the company.

Quality Circles and 5S as strategic tool for employee involvement and improvement were adopted in all departments of the company. It adopted the J N Tata Quality Award Model based on Malcolm Baldrige Model for its various divisions in the company in 1992. Later it adopted the JRDQV Model for Business Excellence in 1994 for competing with other group companies.

Benchmarking and Business Process Reengineering (BPR) emerged as powerful Management Tools in this direction complimenting the TQM efforts at Tata Steel in terms of continuous improvement in process and practices. Concept of Balanced Score Card was integrated with the TQM strategy of the company in 1998. It was integrated with the Annual quality Improvement Plans (AQUIP's) of various departments.

New Thrust Areas at Tata Steel

In the quest for further increasing their benchmark and improving their processes, Tata Steel has signed an Automotive Steel Technology Cooperation with Nippon Steel of Japan and Arcelor of Europe. This will help Tata Steel get the technology of making high quality sheets for the Indian automotive market. The top management of Tata Steel has created the new vision 2007 after Tata Steel became the world's lowest cost producer of hot-rolled coils at $160 per tonne in the year 2001.

The New Vision 2007

"To seize the opportunities of tomorrow and create a future that will make us an EVA +ve company. To continue to improve the quality of life of our employees and communities we serve." This vision will uphold the spirit and values of the Tata's towards nation building. It will realize the core business for a sustainable future and venture into new business that will own a share of the company's future. Applying and adopting the strategic issues as discussed in this paper, Tata Steel, has been able to achieve the JRDQV Award in July 2000. This is the only company among the Tata Group of companies to have got this award for excellence based on the Malcolm Baldrige Award criteria for Organizational Excellence.

The judges for the award found that Tata Steel exhibited the following strengths:

* System based approaches in addressing many areas of the TBEM

* Demonstrable strength in processes addressing key customer and stakeholder needs
* Fact-based evaluation and improvement processes

Tata Steel also won the CII-EXIM Award for Business Excellence in November 2000. This award is based on the European Model for Business Excellence (EFQM). Tata Steel become the third company in India to win this award after Hewlett Packard India and Maruti Udyog Ltd., (the biggest car manufacturer in India) who have a Japanese collaboration with Suzuki Motors. In 2003 Tata Steel has won the TBEM sustainable award by getting 675 marks out of 1000 points based on Malcolm Baldrige criteria for Excellence assessed by experienced Baldrige Assessors along with the Tata Group Assessors. Despite difficult times in Steel industry worldwide as well as in India, Tata Steel has been always making net profit every year since its inception. World Steel Dynamics has identified 12 companies as World Class Steel Makers. Tata Steel of India has been rated on the top above Posco of South Korea, Nucor of USA and Nippon of Japan and other such companies.

Conclusion

By applying the Japanese Business Excellence Model, the Deming Prize as shown by two small auto component companies in India namely Sona Steering Limited and Sundaram Clayton which have won the Deming Prize in India have become globally competitive companies. It has been seen that by applying the principles of the American Model for Business Excellence and fine-tuning to the needs of an old and culturally strong Steel Company, Tata Steel, has inculcated the philosophy of Total Quality Management and Business Excellence as part of the company's Corporate Business Strategy. Any company can gain competitive advantage and move towards Business Excellence as described in this paper. Tata Steel, Sona Koyo Steerings Limited and Sundaram Clayton Limited in India have done this because of its foresight and the vision it had among the Top Management Leadership and support from all its employees in the company. These companies have as prepared themselves to compete and be successful in a competitive globalized world.

8

Making Presentations

Overview

Imagine, for a moment, that you are an area sales manager with a company that produces fast-moving consumer goods. Last quarter– January to March – the results for your region were very bad. In fact, sales were 10 per cent below target. Understandably, the sales director wants to know why there was such a serious shortfall, and how you propose to reverse the situation next quarter. He has asked you to make a presentation to him and the finance director between 10.00 and 10.30 next Monday morning.

There were a number of reasons for your area's poor performance and none of them was your fault. You have all the facts and figures to show what went wrong and why. The overriding problem, however, was that you simply don't have enough sales representatives to cover the region. You pointed this out last October when you submitted your budget, but HQ rejected your proposal to recruit extra staff.

As you sit down to prepare your presentation, which of the approaches below do you instinctively feel it would be better to take?

A. Spend most of the presentation looking back over the last quarter making sure that your bosses understand exactly what went wrong and why.

B. Say very little about the last three months; concentrate, instead, on explaining how, with one or two extra sales representatives, you'll be able to meet, and most probably exceed, next quarter's target.

And how do you propose to give your bosses all the facts and figures you've prepared?

A. Show a series of slides as you are making your presentation.

B. Give them a written handout to study at their leisure afterwards.

And what about timing? How do you plan to use the 30 minutes you've got?

A. Spend most of the time presenting with five minutes or so at the end for questions.

B. Make a brief speech and leave at least 20 minutes for questions and discussion.

Clearly your decisions would depend, to a large extent, on how well you know the bosses, what kind of people they are, and what they're interested in. What's gone before and how much is *at stake* (to be gained or lost) would be key factors too. But if you found yourself in a similar position to this area manager, which of these approaches would come more naturally to you? And if you were one of the bosses, what would you expect from this presentation? Which of the approaches would you be more inclined to listen to?

It's quite possible that you are wondering why we're asking these questions. *It's perfectly obvious which of the approaches is right*, you may be thinking. *Why are these people insulting my intelligence?*

Well, actually, we aren't trying to insult your intelligence. The fact is, what people expect from a presentation varies from culture to culture. For example, some people think the best presentations are thorough and detailed with plenty of supporting facts and documentation; others will only listen to you if you're brief and selective. Some audiences are impressed by a logical structure; others by a creative one. Some presenters instinctively aim to inform; others to persuade or entertain. So while it may have been immediately obvious to you that approach A or B was the right one, you can't assume that your international colleagues will share your view.

But surely, you may say, there must be some rights and wrongs that are universal; some presentation styles and techniques that are guaranteed to succeed with any audience? Well, we wouldn't go so far as to say there are universal rights and wrongs. But there is one golden rule that successful presenters the world over follow: no matter what message they're trying to get across, they put the audience first. That may sound simple and obvious. But, as our international clients often tell us, it isn't always easy to do.

When you're having a conversation with someone, you can see or hear their reactions. And, provided you're willing to try to put yourself in their position, you can adapt what you say and the way you say it as the conversation progresses. But when you sit down to prepare a presentation, the members of your audience aren't around. You have to put the whole thing together, from start to finish, without any input or feedback from them. And you may well be tempted to concentrate on the message you want to deliver and what *you* want to achieve. As we keep repeating, however, focusing on yourself and your own agenda is the major block to successful communication, whatever context you're operating in. If you want your audience to really sit up and listen, you have to make sure that everything you say and every visual you show is interesting and relevant to them. And you can only do that if you put yourself in their *shoes* (position) at every stage.

Planning and delivering an effective presentation is hard work – even if you know your audience well and they're from the same national and corporate culture as you. When they're from a different country and you don't know them personally, it can be harder still. In our experience, the greatest challenges for an international presenter are: choosing a style that will suit the audience's expectations; putting the message you want to deliver into a concrete context that your audience can relate to; and speaking in a way that will be clear and accessible.

Choosing the Right Style

The management techniques that businesses adopt originate in the USA. So, too, do many of the techniques that are taught on international presentation skills courses. The Americans, perhaps more than any other culture, seem instinctively to try to build a personal rapport with their audience and to put their message across persuasively and positively. In this respect, we believe, they have a lot to teach the rest of the world. But, as our international clients often tell us, they also have a lot to learn: When a Swiss company decided to award 'loyalty' points to their customers, they asked their in-house IT department to develop the software they needed to operate the scheme. The project was scheduled to take two years. After 18 months, however, it ran into serious difficulties. Two and a half years later, they were still trying to solve them. The company moved Connie, one of their brightest and most competent Swiss managers, on to the team. They gave her six months to get the system up and running. By June – the new deadline – she had indeed established the basic framework and solved the major difficulties. The relatively minor problems that remained could, she decided, be sorted out gradually over the next two years – at a cost of 5 million Swiss francs per year. The Swiss manager who was responsible for the loyalty scheme accepted Connie's proposal. A couple of months later, however, he left the company and was replaced by an American called Robert. One of the first things Robert did was to ask Connie for a progress report on the project. She prepared a well-structured, informative and clear presentation.

She had, in fact, performed a miracle during her six months on the team. But, being Swiss, it didn't occur to her to 'sell' herself or highlight the remarkable job she had done. Instead, she explained – in the calm, methodical, low-key style that came naturally to her – why the project had run into difficulty and what progress had been made. She then moved on to what the remaining problems were, how long it would take to solve them, and how much it would cost.

Robert was not impressed. All he heard was 'a number of problems remain' and 'it'll take two years and an additional budget of 5 million a year to solve them'. As far as he was concerned, Connie had failed to reach the targets she had been given; the problems had to be solved by the end of the current year; and he was going to put in a new team to make sure that they were. Connie didn't try to argue with him. She simply applied for a job in a different department and left the new team to take responsibility for the project. By the end of the year, they seemed to have created more problems than they had solved. The project continued for a further two years and went way over the budget Connie had projected. The Swiss were all convinced that if Robert had left Connie to handle the project her way, it would have been completed much faster and cheaper.

So why didn't Robert accept Connie's proposal? Well, we can't read his mind. But Connie, who had worked with Americans before, was convinced that it was because he had been unable to bridge the gap between American and Swiss culture. 'In my experience,' she told us, 'Robert's reaction was typically American. They always take the short- term view. They never want to hear about problems; just quick solutions. And they expect you to tell them everything is wonderful, even if it isn't. Well, I'm sorry, but that's not the way we do things in Switzerland.'

As everyone knows, of course, the USA is a relatively young country. It was only in 1620 that the Pilgrim Fathers settled in Plymouth, Massachusetts – the first permanent colony in New England. There have been many waves of other immigrants since then, most of them trying to escape the religious persecution, political unrest or extreme poverty of the old world; and all of them attracted by the freedom and opportunities that were on offer. Between the 1840s and the early 1920s, for example, some 30 million people immigrated to the USA. These immigrants were determined to build a new and better life for themselves. They were convinced that, with hard work and a little luck, there would be no limit to what they could achieve. Naturally enough, their attitudes and expectations have had a strong influence on American cultural values. According to *The Stuff Americans are Made Of* (Hammond and Morrison, 1996), there are seven cultural forces that define Americans:

- they insist on choice;
- they pursue *impossible* dreams;
- they are obsessed with *big* and *more;*
- they are impatient with time;
- they accept mistakes;
- they have an urge to improvise;
- they have a fixation with what is new.

The above seven forces link together like this:

Our freedom of *choice* allows us to tackle an *'impossible' dream* that is *bigger* than anything we've done before; we want to achieve it *now;* but *fail* in our initial attempts; we try again and through some sort of improvisation succeed, only to wonder *what's new* so that we can start all over and make another *choice*. It's hardly surprising, then, that Robert was unimpressed by Connie's *low-key* presentation, rejected her *two-year* schedule, and decided to put a *new* team in.

But, as we've seen, this was the wrong decision. There are plenty of people in the world – from countries as diverse as Japan, Switzerland and the UK – whose culture has taught them to take a longer- term view; who instinctively express themselves in a low-key way; and who would be embarrassed to talk openly about their own achievements. That doesn't mean they're incompetent, pessimistic or lacking in dynamism.

But Connie was the presenter, you may say. *So surely it was up to her to adapt her style to suit Robert's expectations.* Well, yes, you're quite right. She should have tried to sound more positive and even, perhaps, to emphasize the remarkable progress that had been made during the first half of the year.

But, she was a Swiss woman, working at the Swiss headquarters of a Swiss company. She knew, of course, that Robert spoke no German. And she was perfectly happy to make her presentation in English. But it didn't occur to her that she needed to adapt her style too. In any case, she knew she had done a first rate job; and she knew her Swiss bosses valued her highly. As far as her career and reputation were concerned, Robert's opinion was irrelevant. For most presenters, though, choosing the right style to suit their audience is vital:

George, a senior fund manager with a British asset management firm (let's call them BAM), came to Canning to polish up a presentation he was going to make to his firm's largest American client. His aim was to persuade the Americans to renew BAM's mandate. The trouble was, the performance figures for the previous and current year looked very bad, and the Americans were threatening to take their business elsewhere. George would have just half an hour to change their minds.

He was planning to spend most of that time looking back over the previous 18 months, and justifying the way in which BAM had managed the fund. His trainer persuaded him to take a much more upbeat approach. Instead of looking at what had gone wrong in the past, George tried to focus on the good results BAM could achieve in future: 'Stay with BAM and we'll beat the target you have set us' was his new central message. This new approach made his presentation much shorter. George practised it again and again, paying particular attention to his tone of voice. By the end of the two-day coaching session, he knew the introduction and conclusion off by heart. And he really *sounded* positive and optimistic.

The following week, George phoned his trainer in triumph: 'They've renewed the mandate,' he said. 'Thank God you made me change my central message! When I arrived, their consultant told me I only had 5 minutes, not 30. So I just went in and presented the introduction and conclusion. According to their consultant, the trustees were very impressed that I had been able to adapt so flexibly to the time constraint. And they had confidence in me because I sounded so positive and didn't give them any of the "usual British bullshit".'

On the strength of this five-minute presentation, over a hundred million dollars of pension fund money were allocated. All of us carry around very fixed images of other cultures. These stereo- types are often negative, and nearly always the result of measuring what foreigners do or say against our own cultural norms. When George's client referred to *the usual British bullshit*, we knew exactly what he meant. On our cross-cultural workshops, we always ask the participants how they perceive other nationalities. And we have discovered that the image the Americans and British have of one another is remarkably consistent. For example, on one course we ran for the European head office of a major American company, the expatriate American managers said that, in their view, the British were:

- Always talking about problems, not solutions;
- Always focusing on what has happened, and not on what will happen;

- *Gloomy* (pessimistic) and depressing, even when they are giving good news;
- Rude and disrespectful;
- Badly prepared.

The trouble is, taking the kind of upbeat, positive attitude that impresses the Americans doesn't come naturally to the British. Our culture values understatement, irony and self-deprecation. Maybe that's why the British managers on the course told us that, in their view, the Americans were:

- Always over-optimistic;
- Not prepared to analyse a problem properly in order to reach workable solutions;
- Boastful and superficial;
- Not prepared to disagree with superiors, even when they are wrong;
- Badly prepared.

A few years ago, Canning was considering the possibility of offering an e-learning service. We invited a number of software consultancies to present their proposals for a tailored solution. One of the consultancies was American and they flew two of their vice-presidents over to the UK to do some research and make their proposal. The presenters were friendly, dynamic and enthusiastic. They started their presentation something like this: *It's a real privilege for us to be here. And we're very excited about the prospect of handling this project for you.*

They then spent what seemed like 20 minutes telling us, in glowing terms, about their personal experience and many successes. As they spoke, they showed us slide after slide, and animated graphic after animated graphic, taken from the e-learning programmes they had developed for other clients – few of whom seemed to be in the same business as Canning. When they finally started talking about us, it was immediately clear that they had little understanding of our training style or our clients' needs. During the question and answer session at the end, we raised many objections to their proposals. Instead of trying to answering these objections, they simply said things like: We've got a lot of experience in this field. We'll be able to work through that kind of issue when the project's under way.

The audience were all international communication trainers who were more prepared than most to make an effort to bridge the culture gap. And if these presenters had been able to show us that they really understood our business, we would have forgiven them for the emphasis they had placed on their own achievements and successes. But because they weren't prepared to engage with the problems we raised, we left the presentation feeling mildly angry that they had wasted so much of our time. And even we allowed ourselves to think, for a few moments, that their performance had been *typically American*. In other words, that it had conformed to most of the negative images in the list above.

Clearly, when you're presenting internationally, you have to make a conscious effort to avoid reinforcing negative stereotypes such as these. If not, there's a danger you will alienate the audience almost as soon as you open your mouth. That's not to say you should try to change your natural style so radically that you feel uncomfortable. No one could have expected the American software consultants to stop sounding enthusiastic and positive. Indeed, we believe that putting your message across persuasively and positively is something that all presenters should aim to do. But there has to be something behind the positive noises you're making. You've got to show the audience that you understand their needs and expectations. And you've got to make sure that everything you say is relevant and interesting to them. The American consultants seemed to have made little effort to understand us. And the many successes and achievements that they presented were simply not relevant. That was why we found them superficial and boastful. If they had put us first, we would probably have been very favourably impressed by their upbeat and dynamic style.

Similarly, when Canning was helping George from BAM to prepare his presentation, we did not, for one moment, expect him to say anything that made him feel uncomfortable. We didn't, for example, ask him to tell his clients how excited he was about the prospect of managing the fund next year. We simply suggested that, to suit the expectations of his American audience, he should try to look forward rather than back. And once he did that, he was able to find a central message: *Stay with BAM and we'll beat the target you have set us,* that his clients could relate to. His whole presentation was structured around this upbeat, forward-looking message. So when he only had time to deliver the introduction and conclusion, it came across loud and clear to his clients. All the more so because he tried very hard to *sound* positive and optimistic.

It would be wrong to assume, from the examples we've looked at, that the British and Americans are at opposite ends of every scale. The two cultures actually have a lot of views and values in common. Both nations would, for example, probably fall to the left of the following scales:

> Of course, there are plenty of American and British presenters who include a lot of detail and talk at considerable length. The American software consultants spent 20 minutes telling us about their successes and achievements; and George originally planned to talk to his clients for half an hour. But the American presentation didn't succeed; and George's original structure and style would have lost him the mandate.

In general, American and British audiences respond best to presentations that are short and selective. As you might expect, not every culture shares their expectations:

> An English manager was at a meeting in Milan. The Italian participants belonged to a network of professional service companies who wanted to pool their skills. Each of the delegates had been asked to prepare a *brief* presentation of their company. The Englishman was annoyed to find that his fellow delegates ignored the request to keep their presentations *brief* and in some cases spoke for as long as 20 minutes. When it was his turn to speak, he delivered a two-minute presentation. It had a clear message, was well structured and gave the key information relevant to his listeners. As he sat down, there was an awkward silence; and then polite applause. After the meeting, which finished two hours late, an Italian friend came up to the Englishman. 'Why,' he asked, 'didn't you explain in much greater detail the many things I know your company

can offer the group?' Where you would place yourself on the short–long and selective–comprehensive scales will be heavily influenced by the educational norms in your country. At school and university in Italy, the examinations are often oral. So, throughout their education, Italian students are taught all the rhetorical skills; and they learn to give long, impressive speeches that will show their examiners how much they have learnt and thought about the subject. Naturally enough, when they come to make a business presentation, they take the same approach. They aim to be eloquent and positive; and, of course, to speak for as long as it takes to show the audience that they have thought of all the points.

The British education system, on the other hand, encourages a crisper, more concise style. When your writers were at school, we had lessons and exams where we had to précis texts – in other words, reduce several pages of complicated prose into one short, simple paragraph. As we mentioned above, we were also conditioned, from a very early age, to understate our abilities and give our messages indirectly. When the Englishman made his short, low-key presentation, he was really sending the signal 'less is more'. This would have been fine for a British audience, but the message was completely *lost on* (misunderstood by) his Italian listeners. The structure he chose came across to them as over-simplistic and far too low-key. They expected him to illustrate the facts with relevant examples and opinions, to argue his case with eloquence, and to project a positive and upbeat attitude.

To most Brits, the word *rhetoric* describes a speech that sounds impressive, but isn't actually sincere or useful. For the Italians, however, it's the art of speaking eloquently, impressively and persuasively. *Rhetorik* is also an important part of the academic and business school syllabus in Germany. But the Germans seem to interpret the word in a different way again. In his comparative study of German and British culture (*Crossroads and Roundabouts*, 1997), Thomas Kielinger suggests that his fellow Germans most value people who are *konsequent* (logical, consistent, uncompromising) and *grundlich* (thorough). So, for them, *Rhetorik* is the art of presenting a logical and detailed sequence of arguments – as reflected in the dialectical methods of Hegel and Marx. For

German students to pass their oral exams, there's no need for them to put forward a lot of new or original ideas. They simply have to learn all the facts and present them in a logical and thorough way.

The French enjoy debate, value eloquence and, above all, expect the presenter to give them a logically consistent argument that can't be demolished. In French schools, pupils are taught to present their arguments in a very Cartesian way: *thèse, anti-thèse, synthèse* (thesis, antithesis, synthesis). As we mentioned earlier, many of the techniques that are taught on international presentation skills courses originate in the USA. And the Americans tend to state their central message at the beginning of their presentation. But this technique does not come naturally to the French. That's because a good central message is effectively a synthesis or conclusion. And the French are taught from an early age to lead up to the conclusion step by step – not state it upfront at the beginning.

It's quite possible that, at this point, your head is starting to spin. Don't worry! There may be over 200 countries in the world, but we aren't going to try to talk about all of them. The cultures we have looked at, and the scales we have shown you, cover the main style differences you will come across. Before you can adapt to your audience's expectations, you need to do two things: first, analyse your own style and preferences as objectively as possible; and second, resist the temptation to believe that you are right and the rest of the world is wrong. If you know yourself, keep an open mind and make every effort to know your audience, you can always find a way to bridge even the widest culture gap.

Finding a Concrete Context

In a typical year, many of the international business people we work with have to attend at least 25 presentations. But when we ask them how many of these presentations they would describe as really impressive or memorable, their answer is nearly always the same: No more than 20 per cent. So what do the presenters who belong to this elite minority do that sets them apart from everyone else? Well, part of the answer is in the quotation at the head of this chapter: they realize that people only see something when they have the right metaphor to perceive it.

Imagine for a moment that you work for a large pharmaceutical company which is about to launch an anti-fungal cream. As product manager, it's your job to present the new cream and ways of selling it to each of the four regional sales teams in your country. So what do you think you should do: deliver exactly the same presentation to each of the four teams; or try to adapt it each time?

In our experience, most people would see nothing wrong with delivering exactly the same presentation to each of the teams. And many would also assume that, in this situation, it would be perfectly acceptable to let the facts speak for themselves. After all, they argue, there's no need to agonize over what might appeal to these audiences. They all work for the same company and they're all salespeople. So they're bound to be interested in the product and how to sell it.

Well, yes, that may be true. But it doesn't mean they will necessarily be fascinated by what you have to say. What if they already know a lot of the information you're planning to present? What if they've already decided that some of your new sales policies are wrong or unsuitable for their region? What if the members of one team are at war with their colleagues in one of the other teams?

It doesn't matter how relevant you think the subject matter is, you've still got to try to put it in a context that the audience can relate to. And, as every audience is different, you're going to have to change the context to suit each one. We don't believe you can create a universal presentation that will be equally relevant and memorable to a series of different listeners. What interests and appeals to one group may well bore or irritate another.

The situation we asked you to imagine – like all the situations in this book – was a real one. After some research and careful thought, the product manager concerned came up with a neat way of making his message relevant to each of the teams. He had discovered that nearly all the sales representatives were keen football fans. So he worked out a way of describing the new sales strategy in footballing terms: the sales team was to be divided into strikers who would go out and find new customers, defenders who would concentrate on cultivating existing customers, sweepers who would be sent out to solve problems, and so on. He was sure that this metaphor would be equally attractive to each of the four sales teams. But he knew it would have even greater impact if he could show them a picture.

That was when he realized how he could tailor his presentation to each region. He got his graphics department to prepare four different visuals. Each one showed football players wearing the colours of the top local team. When he showed the visual, the sales reps immediately identified with the players and started teasing one another. On a couple of occasions, their jokes gave the product manager a clearer under- standing of their needs. And he was able to adapt his presentation accordingly.

But what can I do, our clients often ask us, *if I don't know the people I'm presenting to?* Well, if you don't know the members of your audience personally, ask yourself what you know about them as a group: are they, for example, all engineers; do they all come from India; are they all in their twenties? You have to keep asking questions about them until you find some common denominator.

But what if the audience do different jobs, come from different countries, and are all different ages? you may ask. Surely the only common denominator then is the information I'm going to present. Well, no. You're forgetting the most important thing they have in common. They're all human beings. And no matter where they come from or what they do, all human beings have certain needs and aims in common. It's just a question of finding which of their needs and aims you could most effectively appeal to in this particular presentation. Often, the answers won't come to you straight away. But if you want your audience to really take notice of what you're saying, you need to persevere.

Finding a context and developing a concrete image your audience can relate to takes time, patience, effort, and a bit of imagination. But it isn't rocket science. In fact, as the example below shows, it's often the simplest ideas that work best:

Our colleague Richard was running a presentations course for a group of six Finns. They worked for a large industrial conglomerate whose core business was paper production. On the first day, Richard invited each of them to make a short presentation about their company. The first five presentations were almost identical:

> 'Our company employs thousands of people in many different countries. We have factories in this town, that town and the other town. We produce paper, paper-making machinery, drilling platforms, power plants. . . .'

They're both Europeans; they're both from developed, stable democracies; they're both widely travelled. So it was relatively easy for Matti to put himself in Richard's shoes. Finding the right context for an audience whose cultural values and expectations are very different from yours can be more challenging. That's because many of your perceptions are so instinctive that it doesn't even occur to you that there's another way of looking at the world. This was certainly the case for Al – a young American Peace Corps volunteer – whom Richard worked with in Africa in the 1970s:

> Al was in his early twenties when he arrived at the junior high school in a large village in southern Africa to teach mathematics. The village consisted of traditional mud huts where the 40,000 inhabitants lived, the school (eight large rectangular buildings), a church and a hospital (both built by Scottish missionaries). At first, Al was very impressed with the pupils' enthusiasm and aptitude for his subject. But when he moved on to geometry – starting with squares, rectangles and triangles as he did in the States – they seemed to lose interest. They simply couldn't see the point of the exercises their teacher was asking them to do. After a particularly frustrating lesson, Al went for a walk to clear his head. He climbed a nearby hill, stood at the top, and looked down at the village. 'But of course!', he thought. 'Most of the buildings in the village are circular. No wonder they're not interested in right angles. Why didn't I see that before?'

Next day, he started the maths class by saying: 'I want you to imagine you're an eagle. You're looking down on the village. What do you see?' The children immediately drew a lot of circular huts and walls. 'OK,' said the teacher. 'So how much space do you have in each hut? And how far is it from the edge of the hut to the edge of the wall?' From that moment on, the children were hooked. They eagerly learned about 'pi', and were soon working out circumferences and areas. And they were just as interested when the teacher moved from circles to tangents and from tangents to angles. From a Western perspective, it makes no sense to start with circles and end with squares. In fact, that's doing things *the wrong way round*. But for these young Africans, it was *the right way round*. And the American teacher only realized that when he started to see the world through his pupils' eyes. Making a conscious effort to step outside your own cultural preconceptions is the key to finding the right context for your international audiences.

Sooner or later, you will make or attend a presentation where one of the visuals is a map. When you learnt geography at school, you probably assumed that the maps your teachers gave you were universal. After all, everyone lives in the same world and countries are a fixed shape and size. And it probably never occurred to you that different cultures see the world, literally, through different eyes:

A Swedish professor was presenting the results of some clinical trials at an international pharmaceutical symposium in Florence. A high proportion of the delegates were from the Middle East and Asia. To show where the people who had taken part in the trial came from, the professor had a slide with a map of the world on it. Instead of illustrating his point, however, the slide seemed to be confusing the audience. Some of them frowned, others exchanged glances, and one or two of them raised their eyebrows. From that point on, the professor sensed that he had lost the audience's attention. 'I can't understand what the problem was,' he confided to a friend several days later. 'I mean, this is the slide I used. Can you see anything wrong with it?' His friend looked at the slide for a moment, smiled and asked: 'Where did you get this map from?' The professor replied: 'I don't know. The people in our graphics department produced all the slides. Why?' His friend said: 'Well, they shouldn't have put Sweden right at the centre of the map, should they?' The professor looked puzzled: 'But that's where most of the clinical trials took place.' His friend shook his head and pointed to the tiny landmass that represented the Indian sub-continent: 'Yes, but most of your audience came from this part of the world. I expect they were pretty shocked to see that you thought Sweden was three times the size of India.'

The world map that many Americans and Europeans are used to seeing is based on Mercator's projection. And according to Mercator's projection, North America is bigger than Africa, Scandinavia is bigger than India, and Europe is bigger than South America. But, in fact, this is a gross distortion of the world. A map using an equal area projection (e.g. Arno Peters') reveals that North America is far smaller than Africa; India is three times the size of Scandinavia; and South America is twice the size of Europe. When we show a Peters' world map on our presentation courses, some of the participants react quite negatively. They declare that it's *wrong;* that the continents are *shaped wrongly*. Maybe they expect the industrialized countries to look bigger than the developing ones because they're richer. Or maybe they've simply never realized that the world maps they've always used give an inaccurate impression of each country's size and are, therefore, not universally accepted.

That was certainly the case with the Swedish professor. The last thing he wanted to do was offend or alienate his audience. If only he had asked someone from India or the Middle East for their advice while he was preparing his presentation. It's such a simple and obvious thing to do. And yet, in our experience, it's something that far too many presenters forget – particularly when the presentation they're preparing involves a lot of creative work:

A large European company were trying to sell their high-tech systems to clients around the world. They tailored each presentation to the individual client's interests, but there was one key metaphor and visual that they always used: 'Your problems,' they told their clients, 'are like lions – wild, unpredictable, and hard to control. But with our systems, you can be a lion tamer. You can subdue the lions and keep them under control.' This worked very well until they went to a country in Africa. As soon as they showed the visual, the audience looked horrified. The lion was a symbol of their country, and the image that came across to them was of a colonial power subduing their State. The Europeans lost the contract to a competitor.

The trouble was, these Europeans had invested a lot of time, money and effort in developing the lion-tamer image. In any case, it had already been tried out on a number of audiences and worked very well. So they didn't see any reason why it shouldn't succeed with their prospective African clients too. For the international presenter, this is a dangerous position to be in. It's only human nature to believe that an idea you've worked hard to create is sure to succeed. But before you get too attached to it, you need to check it out with a local expert, and act on the advice they give you. And you should never assume that, just because an image has already succeeded with one audience, it will necessarily have the right impression on another. Remember, every audience is different. What engages and amuses one group of people may mystify or offend another.

Speaking with Impact

There's one thing, however, that every audience in the world has in common. If a presenter uses language that is unclear, or speaks in an over- complicated or monotonous way, they will fall asleep.

Try reading the sentence below out loud:

> With the installation of our new manufacturing software platform, and the implementation of the seven-step quality initiative which, as some of you are probably aware, represent a substantial investment of some 15 million, our ultimate objective, once these two projects have been implemented at the end of next year, is the achievement of optimal production performance, a reduction in lead times, and an overall improvement to customer service. . . .

It sounds horrible, doesn't it? If you speak like this, you'll lose your audience's attention before you even get to the end of your first sentence. So what's going wrong here? Well, more or less everything, to be honest.

For a start, there are far too many nouns: installation, implementation, investment, objective, achievement, performance, reduction, improvement. And look at them. They're all very long – three syllables or more; and most of them are very abstract. Can you actually visualize *implementation, achievement*, or *performance*? You certainly couldn't draw a picture to explain what these abstractions mean. And listen to the rhythm: instalLATion, implemenTATion, inVESTment, and so on. In every case, the stress falls on the next to last syllable. That kind of rhythm is guaranteed to send an audience to sleep – as your writers know from long experience of listening to the first presentations our clients make when they come on one of our courses. So why do people use these long abstract nouns? Well, for the native speaker of English, they're the kind of words you find in very formal, written documents – economic reports, academic theses and contracts, for example. So they probably think that using them in their presentation will make them sound more intellectual or impressive. And, of course, a lot of non-native speakers use these words all the time – particularly the Germans and the Italians – because that's the way they speak in their own language.

But English is a language that loves verbs. If you want your audience to be able to visualize what you're saying, you need to talk about people doing things. For example:

We're going to install some new production software.

We're going to set up a better quality control system.

We're investing more than 15 million in these projects.

What we're aiming to do is boost output, cut lead times, and improve customer satisfaction.All these verbs are short – no more than two syllables. And the minute you start using them, you can help your audience understand what you're saying by stressing the parts of the sentence that you think are important, for example:

We're going to install some NEW production SOFTware and SET UP a BETter quality conTROL system.

You see, in natural spoken English, every sentence is a combination of long beats and short beats, rather like the drum rhythm in a pop song. As soon as you stress the important parts of the sentence, you adopt this natural rhythm. And you start sounding like a real person talking to other real people – rather than someone who is reading from a script, or delivering a pedantic lecture.

So the sentence we asked you to read out loud has far too many long, abstract nouns. But that's not the only thing that's wrong with it. The sentence itself is much too long. Successful international presenters keep their sentences short and simple. If you try to put too many ideas into one sentence, you'll be forced to use subordinate clauses: which, as some of you are probably aware, represent a substantial investment of some 15 million; and once these two projects have been implemented at the end of next year. And subordinate clauses make it very difficult for your listeners to remember how the sentence began. If you want to speak with impact, aim for one idea per sentence. And, where possible, keep your sentences active:

Instead of: once these two projects have been implemented (passive verb construction)

Say: once we've implemented these two projects (active verb construction)

Instead of: The new machines were checked by us.

Say: We checked the new machines.

Of course, there will be occasions when you need to use a passive construction. You may well prefer, for example, to say a lot of mistakes were made rather than the sales director made a lot of mistakes. But when you're not worried about saying who did what, active sentences generally have far greater impact.

So if you follow all the advice above, and also try to add some 'you- appeal' – in other words, make sure that what you're saying is relevant to the audience – this speech might sound something like this:

What can we do to boost our output? How can we cut lead times? How can we improve customer service? These are questions you've been asking for some time. And today, I've got some answers for you. We've decided to spend 15 million updating our systems. First, we're going to install the latest production software. And, second, we're going to set up a much tighter quality control system. Both projects should be up and running by the end of next year…

OK. Are you ready for a short exercise? If so, look at the sentence below, and work out how you would replace the nouns with verbs:

It is necessary to have a detailed examination of the specification before the installation of the new line.

If you are a non-native speaker of English, you will probably instinctively say something like this:

We need to examine the specification very carefully before we install the new line.

If you are a native English speaker, your proposal may be more like this:

We need to go through the spec with a fine-tooth comb before we put the new line in.

English has an enormous vocabulary – twice as big, for example, as French. Words are derived from two main language streams: Germanic (German and Scandinavian) and Romance (Latin-based). Native speakers tend automatically to choose short Germanic verbs (for example: *get, go through, put in, tell*) in preference to their Latin-based equivalents (*obtain, examine, install, inform*). That's because, to their ear, Latin-based verbs sound too formal for speaking, and are more appropriate for writing – rather like the long, abstract nouns we looked at above.

But non-native speakers have most probably learnt *written* rather than *spoken* English. This means that they are likely to feel far more comfortable with words that are derived from Latin. Even people, like the Japanese, whose own language has no connection with Latin, tend to feel this way. And, somewhat paradoxically, many Germans prefer Latin- based words too. That's because they sound more formal and, therefore, more similar to High German. We still have Germans on our language courses who believe that *get* isn't correct English. And, of course, to speakers of Romance languages – French, Spanish, Italian, Portuguese, Romanian – Latin-based words are much easier to understand.

The fact that English has become the common language of international business should be very good news for the monolingual American, Australian, New Zealander or Brit. All too often, however, the native English speaker is at a disadvantage. Some years ago, an East Asian airline chose to buy flight simulators from a French firm rather than a British one: as their pilots would have to be trained in English to use the simulators, the airline preferred to buy them from the people who spoke the clearer English – in other words, the French. And one of Italy's top companies refuses to have American or British consultants running their courses; they prefer Swiss or Dutch people who can speak English in a way that will be understood by all their staff.

If you're a native English speaker and you're presenting to an audience for whom English is a second or foreign language, you need to choose the kind of verbs they're likely to understand. That means, for example, saying *examine* rather than *go through;* and *install* instead of *put in*. And rather than use idiomatic expressions like *with a fine-tooth comb* and abbreviations like *spec,* you should say *very carefully* and *specification* instead.

And try to control your tone and tempo. Many presenters, particularly native speakers, make the mistake of speaking too *fast*. But, of course, if you speak too *slowly*, you could sound artificial and patronizing. The secret is to keep your natural tone, enunciate clearly, and pause at the end of a phrase or sentence – *not* after each word. When you're rehearsing your presentation, record part of your speech and listen to yourself critically. Do you sound natural? Are the pauses long enough? Whoever you're presenting to, you'll need to pause more frequently and for longer than you do in normal conversation.

Even if you're a native speaker presenting to a native-speaking audience, you can't assume that they will immediately understand what your main points are and how they link together. Listening to a presentation isn't like reading a book. Your audience can't *see* when you are 'starting a new paragraph'. If they miss a step in your argument, they can't go back and 'read' it again. It's your job, as presenter, to guide your audience through your speech. At every step, you need to tell them where they are, where they've been, and where they're going. So try to create plenty of beginnings, where you summarize your argument so far, and tell them what the next step is.

9

Organizational Communication Management

Organizational communication is a subfield of the larger discipline of communication studies. Organizational communication, as a field, is the consideration, analysis, and criticism of the role of communication in organizational contexts.

History of Organizational Communication

The field traces its lineage through business information, business communication, and early mass communication studies published in the 1930s through the 1950s. Until then, organizational communication as a discipline consisted of a few professors within speech departments who had a particular interest in speaking and writing in business settings. The current field is well established with its own theories and empirical concerns distinct from other communication subfields and other approaches to organizations.

Several seminal publications stand out as works broadening the scope and recognizing the importance of communication in the organizing process, and in using the term "organizational communication". Nobel Laureate Herbert Simon wrote in 1947 about "organization communications systems", saying communication is "absolutely essential to organizations". In the 1950s, organizational communication focused largely on the role of communication in improving organizational life and organizational output. In the 1980s, the field turned away from a business-oriented approach to communication and became concerned more with the constitutive role of communication in organizing. In the 1990s, critical theory influence on the field was felt as organizational communication scholars focused more on communication's possibilities to oppress and liberate organizational members.

Assumptions underlying early Organizational Communication

Some of the main assumptions underlying much of the early organizational communication research were:

- Humans act rationally. Sane people behave in rational ways, they generally have access to all of the information needed to make rational decisions they could articulate, and therefore will make rational decisions, unless there is some breakdown in the communication process.
- Formal logic and empirically verifiable data ought to be the foundation upon which any theory should rest. All we really need to understand communication in organizations is (a) observable and replicable behaviors that can be transformed into variables by some form of measurement, and (b) formally replicable syllogisms that can extend theory from observed data to other groups and settings
- Communication is primarily a mechanical process, in which a message is constructed and encoded by a sender, transmitted through some channel, then received and decoded by a receiver. Distortion, represented as any differences between the original and the received messages, can and ought to be identified and reduced or eliminated.
- Organizations are mechanical things, in which the parts (including employees functioning in defined roles) are interchangeable. What works in one organization will work in another similar organization. Individual differences can be minimized or even eliminated with careful management techniques.
- Organizations function as a container within which communication takes place. Any differences in form or function of communication between that occurring in an

organization and in another setting can be identified and studied as factors affecting the communicative activity.

Herbert Simon introduced the concept of bounded rationality which challenged assumptions about the perfect rationality of communication participants. He maintained that people making decisions in organizations seldom had complete information, and that even if more information was available, they tended to pick the first acceptable option, rather than exploring further to pick the optimal solution.

Through the 1960s, 1970s and 1980s the field expanded greatly in parallel with several other academic disciplines, looking at communication as more than an intentional act designed to transfer an idea. Research expanded beyond the issue of "how to make people understand what I am saying" to tackle questions such as "how does the act of communicating change, or even define, who I am?", "why do organizations that seem to be saying similar things achieve very different results?" and "to what extent are my relationships with others affected by our various organizational contexts?"

In the early 1990s Peter Senge developed a new theories on Organizational Communication. This theories were learning organization and systems thinking. These have been well received and are now a mainstay in current beliefs toward organizational communications.

Communications Networks

Networks are another aspect of direction and flow of communication. Bavelas has shown that communication patterns, or networks, influence groups in several important ways. Communication networks may affect the group's completion of the assigned task on time, the position of the de facto leader in the group, or they may affect the group members' satisfaction from occupying certain positions in the network. Although these findings are based on laboratory experiments, they have important implications for the dynamics of communication in formal organizations.

There are several patterns of communication:

- "Chain",
- "Wheel",
- "Star",
- "All-Channel" network,
- "Circle".

The Chain can readily be seen to represent the hierarchical pattern that characterizes strictly formal information flow, "from the top down," in military and some types of business organizations. The Wheel can be compared with a typical autocratic organization, meaning one-man rule and limited employee participation. The Star is similar to the basic formal structure of many organizations. The All-Channel network, which is an elaboration of Bavelas's Circle used by Guetzkow, is analogous to the free-flow of communication in a group that encourages all of its members to become involved in group decision processes. The All-Channel network may also be compared to some of the informal communication networks.

If it's assumed that messages may move in both directions between stations in the networks, it is easy to see that some individuals occupy key positions with regard to the number of messages they handle and the degree to which they exercise control over the flow of information. For example, the person represented by the central dot in the "Star" handles all messages in the group. In contrast, individuals who occupy stations at the edges of the pattern handle fewer messages and have little or no control over the flow of information.These "peripheral" individuals can communicate with only one or two other persons and must depend entirely on others to relay their messages if they wish to extend their range.

In reporting the results of experiments involving the Circle, Wheel, and Star configurations, Bavelas came to the following tentative conclusions. In patterns with positions located centrally, such as the Wheel and the Star, an organization quickly develops around the people occupying these central positions. In such patterns, the organization is more stable and errors in performance are lower than in patterns having a lower degree of centrality, such as the Circle. However, he also found that the morale of members in high centrality patterns is relatively low. Bavelas speculated that this lower morale could, in the long run, lower the accuracy and speed of such networks.

In problem solving requiring the pooling of data and judgments, or "insight," Bavelas suggested that the ability to evaluate partial results, to look at alternatives, and to restructure problems fell off rapidly when one person was able to assume a more central (that is, more controlling) position in the information flow. For example, insight into a problem requiring change would be less in the Wheel and the Star than in the Circle or the Chain because of the "bottlenecking" effect of data control by central members. It may be concluded from these laboratory results that the structure of communications within an organization will have a significant influence on the accuracy of decisions, the speed with which they can be reached, and the satisfaction of the people involved. Consequently, in networks in which the responsibility for initiating and passing along messages is shared more evenly among the members, the better the group's morale in the long run.

Direction of Communication

If it's considered formal communications as they occur in traditional military organizations, messages have a "one-way" directional characteristic. In the military organization, the formal communication proceeds from superior to subordinate, and its content is presumably clear because it originates at a higher level of expertise and experience. Military communications also carry the additional assumption that the superior is responsible for making his communication clear and understandable to his subordinates. This type of organization assumes that there is little need for two-way exchanges between organizational levels except as they are initiated by a higher level. Because messages from superiors are considered to be more important than those from subordinates, the implicit rule is that communication channels, except for prescribed information flows, should not be cluttered by messages from subordinates but should remain open and free for messages moving down the chain of command. "Juniors should be seen and not heard," is still an unwritten, if not explicit, law of military protocol.

Vestiges of one-way flows of communication still exist in many formal organizations outside the military, and for many of the same reasons as described above.Although management recognizes that prescribed information must flow both downward and upward, managers may not always be convinced that two-wayness should be encouraged. For example, to what extent is a subordinate free to communicate to his superior that he understands or does not understand a message? Is it possible for him to question the superior, ask for clarification, suggest modifications to instructions he has received, or transmit unsolicited messages to his superior, which are not prescribed by the rules? To what extent does the one-way rule of direction affect the efficiency of communication in the organization, in addition to the morale and motivation of subordinates?

These are not merely procedural matters but include questions about the organizational climate, pr psychological atmosphere in which communication takes place. Harold Leavitt has suggested a simple experiment that helps answer some of these questions. À group is assigned the task of re-creating on paper à set of rectangular figures, first as they are described by the leader under one-way conditions, and second as they are described by the leader under two-way conditions. (A different configuration of rectangles is used in the second trial.) In the one-way trial, the leader's back is turned to the group. He describes the rectangles as he sees them. No one in the group is allowed to ask questions and no one may indicate by any audible or visible sign his understanding or his frustration as he attempts to follow the leader's directions. In the two-way trial, the leader faces the group. In this case, the group may ask for clarifications on his description of the rectangles and he can not only see but also can feel and respond to the emotional reactions of group members as they try to re-create his instructions on paper.

On the basis of a number of experimental trials similar to the one described above, Leavitt formed these conclusions:

1. One-way communication is faster than two-way communication.
2. Two-way communication is more accurate than one-way communication.

3. Receivers are more sure of themselves and make more correct judgments of how right or wrong they are in the two-way system.
4. The sender feels psychologically under attack in the two-way system, because his receivers pick up his mistakes and oversights and point them out to him.
5. The two-way method is relatively noisier and looks more disorderly. The one-way method, on the other hand, appears neat and efficient to an outside observer.

Thus, if speed is necessary, if a businesslike appearance is important, if a manager does not want his mistakes recognized, and if he wants to protect his power, then one-way communication seems preferable. In contrast, if the manager wants to get his message across, or if he is concerned about his receivers' feeling that they are participating and are making a contribution, the two-way system is better.

Interpersonal Communication

Another facet of communication in the organization is the process of face-to-face, interpersonal communication, between individuals. Such communication may take several forms. Messages may be verbal (that is, expressed in words), or they may not involve words at all but consist of gestures, facial expressions, and certain postures ("body language"). Nonverbal messages may even stem from silence.

Managers do not need answers to operate a successful business; they need questions. Answers can come from anyone, anytime, anywhere in the world thanks to the benefits of all the electronic communication tools at our disposal. This has turned the real job of management into determining what it is the business needs to know, along with the who/what/where/when and how of learning it. To effectively solve problems, seize opportunities, and achieve objectives, questions need to be asked by managers—these are the people responsible for the operation of the enterprise as a whole.

Ideally, the meanings sent are the meanings received. This is most often the case when the messages concern something that can be verified objectively. For example, "This piece of pipe fits the threads on the coupling." In this case, the receiver of the message can check the sender's words by actual trial, if necessary. However, when the sender's words describe a feeling or an opinion about something that cannot be checked objectively, meanings can be very unclear. "This work is too hard" or "Watergate was politically justified" are examples of opinions or feelings that cannot be verified. Thus they are subject to interpretation and hence to distorted meanings. The receiver's background of experience and learning may differ enough from that of the sender to cause significantly different perceptions and evaluations of the topic under discussion. As we shall see later, such differences form a basic barrier to communication.

Nonverbal content always accompanies the verbal content of messages. This is reasonably clear in the case of face-to-face communication. As Virginia Satir has pointed out, people cannot help but communicate symbolically (for example, through their clothing or possessions) or through some form of body language. In messages that are conveyed by the telephone, a messenger, or a letter, the situation or context in which the message is sent becomes part of its non-verbal content. For example, if the company has been losing money, and in a letter to the production division, the front office orders a reorganization of the shipping and receiving departments, this could be construed to mean that some people were going to lose their jobs — unless it were made explicitly clear that this would not occur.

A number of variables influence the effectiveness of communication. Some are found in the environment in which communication takes place, some in the personalities of the sender and the receiver, and some in the relationship that exists between sender and receiver. These different variables suggest some of the difficulties of communicating with understanding between two people. The sender wants to formulate an idea and communicate it to the receiver. This desire to communicate may arise from his thoughts or feelings or it may have been triggered by something in the environment. The communication may also be influenced or distorted by the relationship between the sender and the receiver, such as status differences, a staff-line relationship, or a learner-teacher relationship.

Whatever its origin, information travels through a series of filters, both in the sender and in the receiver, before the idea can be transmitted and re-created in the receiver's mind. Physical capacities to see, hear, smell, taste, and touch vary between people, so that the image of reality may be distorted even before the mind goes to work. In addition to physical or sense filters, cognitive filters, or the way in which an individual's mind interprets the world around him, will influence his assumptions and feelings. These filters will determine what the sender of a message says, how he says it, and with what purpose. Filters are present also in the receiver, creating a double complexity that once led Robert Louis Stevenson to say that human communication is "doubly relative". It takes one person to say something and another to decide what he said.

Physical and cognitive, including semantic filters (which decide the meaning of words) combine to form a part of our memory system that helps us respond to reality. In this sense, March and Simon compare a person to a data processing system. Behaviour results from an interaction between a person's internal state and environmental stimuli. What we have learned through past experience becomes an inventory, or data bank, consisting of values or goals, sets of expectations and preconceptions about the consequences of acting one way or another, and a variety of possible ways of responding to the situation. This memory system determines what things we will notice and respond to in the environment. At the same time, stimuli in the environment help to determine what parts of the memory system will be activated. Hence, the memory and the environment form an interactive system that causes our behaviour. As this interactive system responds to new experiences, new learnings occur which feed back into memory and gradually change its content. This process is how people adapt to a changing world.

Communication Approaches

Informal and Formal Communication are used in an organization. Informal communication: Informal communication, generally associated with interpersonal, horizontal communication, was primarily seen as a potential hindrance to effective organizational performance. This is no longer the case. Informal communication has become more important to ensuring the effective conduct of work in modern organizations.

Top-down approach: This is also known as downward communication. This approach is used by the Top Level Management to communicate to the lower levels. This is used to implement policies, gudelines, etc. In this type of organizational communication, distortion of the actual information occurs. This could be made effective by feedbacks.

Organizational Communication

Historically, organizational communication was driven primarily by quantitative research methodologies. Included in functional organizational communication research are statistical analyses (such as surveys, text indexing, network mapping and behaviour modeling). In the early 1980s, the interpretive revolution took place in organizational communication. For opening up methodological space for qualitative approaches such as narrative analyses, participant-observation, interviewing, rhetoric and textual approaches readings) and philosophic inquiries. During the 1980s and 1990s critical organizational scholarship began to gain prominence with a focus on issues of gender, race, class, and power/knowledge. In its current state, the study of organizational communication is open methodologically, with research from post-positive, interpretive, critical, postmodern, and discursive paradigms being published regularly.

Organizational communication scholarship appears in a number of communication journals including but not limited to *Management Communication Quarterly, Journal of Applied Communication Research, Communication Monographs, Academy of Management Journal, Communication Studies*, and *Southern Communication Journal*.

The field of organizational communication has moved from acceptance of mechanistic models (e.g., information moving from a sender to a receiver) to a study of the persistent, hegemonic and taken-for-granted ways in which we not only use communication to accomplish certain tasks within organizational settings (e.g., public speaking) but also how the organizations in which we participate affect us. These approaches include "postmodern", "critical", "participatory", "feminist", "power/political", "organic", etc. and adds to disciplines as wide-ranging as sociology, philosophy, theology, psychology, business, business administration, institutional management, medicine (health communication), neurology (neural nets), semiotics, anthropology, international relations, and music.

Currently, some topics of research and theory in the field are:

Constitution, e.g.,

- how communicative behaviors construct or modify organizing processes or products
- how the organizations within which we interact affect our communicative behaviours, and through these, our own identities
- structures other than organizations which might be constituted through our communicative activity (e.g., markets, cooperatives, tribes, political parties, social movements)
- when does something "become" an organization? When does an organization become (an)other thing(s)? Can one organization "house" another? Is the organization still a useful entity/thing/concept, or has the social/political environment changed so much that what we now call "organization" is so different from the organization of even a few decades ago that it cannot be usefully tagged with the same word—"organization"?

Narrative, e.g.,

- how do group members employ narrative to acculturate/initiate/indoctrinate new members?
- do organizational stories act on different levels? Are different narratives purposively invoked to achieve specific outcomes, or are there specific roles of "organizational storyteller"? If so, are stories told by the storyteller received differently than those told by others in the organization?
- in what ways does the organization attempt to influence storytelling about the organization? under what conditions

does the organization appear to be more or less effective in obtaining a desired outcome?

- when these stories conflict with one another or with official rules/policies, how are the conflicts worked out? in situations in which alternative accounts are available, who or how or why are some accepted and others rejected?

Identity, e.g.,

- who do we see ourselves to be, in terms of our organizational affiliations?
- do communicative behaviours or occurrences in one or more of the organizations in which we participate effect changes in us? To what extent do whe consist of the organizations to which we belong?
- is it possible for individuals to successfully resist organizational identity? what would that look like?
- do people who define themselves by their work-organizational membership communicate differently within the organizational setting than people who define themselves more by an avocational (non-vocational) set of relationships?

Interrelatedness of organizational experiences, e.g.,

- how do our communicative interactions in one organizational setting affect our communicative actions in other organizational settings?
- how do the phenomenological experiences of participants in a particular organizational setting effect changes in other areas of their lives?
- when the organizational status of a member is significantly changed (e.g., by promotion or expulsion) how are their other organizational memberships affected?
- what kind of future relationship between business and society does organizational communication seem to predict?

Power e.g.,

- how does the use of particular communicative practices within an organizational setting reinforce or alter the various interrelated power relationships within the setting? Are the potential responses of those within or around these organizational settings constrained by factors or processes either within or outside of the organization—(assuming there is an "outside"?

- do taken-for-granted organizational practices work to fortify the dominant hegemonic narrative? Do individuals resist/confront these practices, through what actions/agencies, and to what effects?
- do status changes in an organization (e.g., promotions, demotions, restructuring, financial/social strata changes) change communicative behaviour? Are there criteria employed by organizational members to differentiate between "legitimate" (i.e., endorsed by the formal organizational structure) and "illegitimate" (i.e., opposed by or unknown to the formal power structure)? Are behaviours? When are they successful, and what do we even there "pretenders" or "usurpers" who employ these communicativemean by "successful?"

Smart Production Organization

Smart is one of the first car manufacturers worldwide that adopts not only a continuously justintime production without any stockkeeping but also maintains a customized production on demand approach. The Smart car itself and the production system are necessarily highly flexible and differ fundamentally from traditional vehicles and assembling operations. The production process combines innovative concepts with respect to the following:

- the contractual, technical and spatial organization of OEMsupplier relations;
- the organization of the supplychain logistics and assembling process;
- the flexible adaptation of the process organization to the ondemand development with regard to modular production and supplychain reorganization in the automotive sector.

Given these concepts, the following issues are addressed:

- the idea of a communicationbased and logisticsoriented production organization adopted by Smart;
- the concept of the modular Smart car and of modular production which is conducted by integrated system partners located 'onsite' at 'Smartville';
- the process organization 'smartPlus' and the underlying ideas of the 'Continuous Improvement Process' and 'Fractal Organization';
- the image of the 'Breathing Factory', allowing the adaptation to environmental change.

Logisticsoriented Production Organization

The idea of customized ondemand production (within a delay of only a few weeks without any stockkeeping) necessitated the development and organization, not only of a modular product, but also of a modular production process. This process itself is part of an integrated supply chain which is based upon an overall information system and logistics concept. In a highly sophisticated way, this system links together the (external) parts and modules suppliers, the car manufacturer, the car dealers, and the clients. Originally, even the development and management of this information system were to be the responsibility of an external service provider. But after tremendous technical problems faced by the service provider in introducing and running this system, MCC (later Smart France S.A.S.) itself took over this key element of the Smart production process. With the exception of special small product series, Smart assembles cars only on demand. The dealers are booking the cars according to the specifications given by their clients in the Smart booking and information system.

In order to stabilize the daily production programme and to optimize the level of utilization of the plant equipment, the orders which have been accumulated to a weekly production volume are ordered sequentially according to product specifications and are distributed among the days of one production week. After this step, the date of car delivery can be confirmed to the client. Three days before the scheduled production, the systems and part suppliers are informed about the definite sequence of the respective car varieties in order to produce and supply the components and parts just in sequence to the production line. Over the entire period, from the order to the delivery, the status and process of the orders can be controlled online on both sides of the supply chain. This realtime control of the supply chain allows a fairly precise anticipation of the workload for several weeks, and the finetuning of the production cadence which is called the 'breathing factory' in the Smart terminology.

Smart and Smartville

Realtime customization without large stock formation is feasible only under the following conditions:

- *Modular product design.* With regard to the specifications made by the client, the modular car is easily convertible by the combination of a limited number of different modules. Various design and equipment features can be added, removed or changed, only by a few hand grips (e.g. different colored door panels in the case of the Smart car). That means that through smart product development, perceived customization can be achieved, while at the same time, product variation and production complexity is limited. Modular product design allows for both customization and modularization of the production process.
- *Onside modular production.* Modular production can be optimized logistically by the spatial concentration of the module production and by an assembling process linking these production steps onsite.

Following these conceptions, MCC did not develop a modular product and production design by itself, but invited potential module suppliers at the very beginning of the product development process to send in competitive bids for a product concept. The potential suppliers were intensively integrated in the development process with respect to the definition of modules in terms of "function, materials, layout, design etc. . . . to production technologies, processes, logistic systems, target costs. . . ." At the same time, MCC developed a modular and fractal factory which is called Smartville.

Smartville is not only a 68 hectares greenfield but is also a new type of modular and fractal factory. It integrates the central crossshaped assembly plant which is operated by Smart France S.A.S. with the systems suppliers which are called 'System partners'. The plant itself is surrounded by about 20 buildings that house the main firsttier system partners. MCC/Smart GmbH has invested approximately a358 million (assembly plant, including machinery) in Smartville, whereas the system suppliers at Smartville have invested around a197 million, the suppliers in the vicinity around Smartville another a150 million. Thus, prior to launching production, total investment was approximately a1.2 billion including the development of the car, the establishment of a distribution and dealer network in several European countries (a280 million), subsidies paid by the European Union and the public French development agency SOFIREM, assisting the restructuring of old French mining regions.

When production began in 1998, seven system partners were located in Smartville who were responsible for the production and justinsequence delivery of the basic modules making up the Smart car. Not only were they responsible for the assembly of the safety body cell (socalled 'Tridion' cell), but also the dashboard and cockpit, the front module including the front axle and lighting system, the rear module driveline including the engine, the doors and the body panels. The innovative and 'environmentally friendly' powder coat paint and body protection was completed by a specialized system partner who was also integrated into the modular production process at Smartville. By 2005, the paint and body protection had been taken over by Smart itself, due to the fact that they are core competences of each car manufacturer. However, this reinternalization seems to be an exception rather than a general trend; although similar decisions could recently be observed in other automotive corporations.

External partners even provide human resource management, background information systems management, the continuous data processing of the justinsequence assembling process, and the logistics of the internal and external material flows along the entire production and value chain. However, the management of the central information system and the control of the material flows have been taken over and reinternalized by Smart very early, whereas the management of the transportation facilities, the logistics and operation of the small part transports within Smartville is still under the responsibility and control of an external service partner located in Smartville. The vertical integration of the Smart assembly plant is therefore only 7 percent; around 30–40 percent of the value is generated by the system partners located in Smartville.

Smartville is called a 'logisticfocused' factory, i.e. the OEM has the responsibility for, and the control over, the final assembling of the car. All other upstream and downstream steps of the value chain are completed by external partners and are logistically coordinated with, and controlled by an integrated information system that is now run by the central assembling plant. With respect to the material flows to the assembly line of the Smart plant, we can distinguish among four different types of delivery:

- *Module Delivery (MD)*. This type of delivery, guaranteed by the system partners, comprises approximately 80 per cent of the total volume of material flows. The module suppliers which receive the needed parts and submodules by second tier suppliers deliver the assembling plant justinsequence and provide for a continuous assembling process.
- *Small Parts Distribution (SPD)*. Logistic service providers are transporting and distributing small parts directly to the assembly line as needed by using the *Kanban* system from a central warehouse located in Smartville. The warehouse is operated by the logistic partner and functions as a buffer.
- *Direct Delivery (DD)*. Bulky parts (e.g. seats) are shipped justintime by external suppliers. The suppliers who are not located in Smartville are using docking stations which are located no further than ten meters away from the assembly line.
- *Assembly Service Providers (ASP)*. Assembly service providers located in Smartville or in the vicinity assemble parts to submodules and modules (e.g. wheels) and deliver them directly to the assembly line, also by using docking stations.

With respect to the level of integration and the position within the production process, we can distinguish between integrated and nonintegrated suppliers. Among the nonintegrated suppliers we can differentiate those who are supplying mostly bulky parts on demand, usually justintime from those who deliver (mostly) small parts which can be stored on the shelf. Conforming with the modular design and the customization approach adopted by Smart, there are a wide range of supplementary parts which can be added after sale on demand.

Semiconductor Industry

In order to understand the organization of the semiconductor industry it is first necessary to understand the different activities which take place within the industry. The different activities in the semiconductor industry can be compared more or less directly with the different activities which take place in the book publishing industry.

The first stage of the production process is the silicon chip design stage, in which the functional logic of the microchip, and threedimensional circuit layout of transistors and capacitors within the silicon wafer is determined. This activity is carried out primarily using computer aided design (CAD) systems. This stage of the process can be compared with the planning, editing and layout stages of the book publishing process. The result of this stage is the production of masks, which are the threedimensional templates of the chip. These Integrated Circuit (IC) design activities are undertaken both by the large number of small specialized IC design firms, and by large verticallyintegrated semiconductor producing firms. The activities are provided for by specialist CAD vendor firms which provide customized design software for the designers. At the same time, there has also emerged recently a subsector of the industry which is concerned only with the construction of intellectual property rights relating to IC designs.

These firms design only logic functions without circuit layouts, and act in consultation with both small and large IC design firms in order to ensure that patents are granted for the new chip protocol designs. The number of firms involved in this stage of the production process has grown enormously during the last two decades, with small designoriented firms tending to be clustered in locations such as Silicon Valley. It is this part of the industry which has received so much academic attention. Yet there are still very many IC design activities which take place within verticallyintegrated semiconductor producers, both inside and outside of Silicon Valley, with locations in other parts of the US, as well as in both Europe and Asia. These are the types of firms which we will investigate in this paper, with our examples being Intel, Texas Instruments, Philips, and Toshiba. Other such firms are NEC, Mitsubishi, Sanyo, OKI, Motorola, Sony, Sharp, Rohm, Fujitsu, Matsushita and Hitachi.

The second stage of the process is the wafer process, the technology of which is determined by materials science. At this stage of the production process the circular silicon wafers, produced by specialist chemicals firms, are subjected to lithography. This is a process whereby ultraviolet light is used to illuminate certain parts of the wafer, according to the mask design, in order to bring about chemical changes within certain parts of the wafer. The wafers are then etched and treated, thereby removing the parts of the wafer subjected to the lithography. After as many as fifteen stages of lithography and treating, the result is a threedimensional silicon structure. This stage of the semiconductor production process can be compared to the platemaking and phototypesetting process which takes place in the book printing industry.

The third stage of the wafer production process is that of the wafer assembly process. Here, the circular wafers which have been subjected to lithography and treating are extracted and dissected into many small square chips, each of which is then framed in plastic or ceramics for insulation and protection. This stage of the chip production process is the equivalent of the book binding process within the book publishing industry. The level of technology of the second and third stages of the wafer and assembly process is defined in terms of the minimum processing rule and the wafer size. The minimum processing rule is the definition of the level of miniaturization of the technology, and the wafer size is the size of the individual silicon wafers which can be produced and then dissected to produce chips. The smaller is the minimum processing rule and the greater is the wafer size, the more advanced is the technological generation. In terms of technology, the second and third stages of the semiconductor production process are just as important to the semiconductor industry as the first stage, and the product lifecycles are just as short. Different minimum processing rules and wafer sizes represent completely different generations of technology.

The majority of these second and third stage activities tend to be carried out by two groups of firms in more geographically dispersed locations outside of the US, and this may explain why these sectors have received relatively little academic interest. The first group of firms undertaking the wafer and assembly processes are the verticallyintegrated semiconductor producers such as Intel and NEC, which undertake all of their own chip design and manufacturing activities. Firms such as Nippon Electronics Company (NEC), Philips, Fujitsu, and Motorola, which also manufacture finished goods, produce for internal demand as well as for other consumer firms, whereas firms such as Intel produce entirely for external customers. The common feature of the production of these firms is high volumes.

The second group of firms undertaking the wafer and assembly processes are the specialist East Asian subcontracting IC manufacturing firms. These are primarily Taiwanese (*Business Week* 2005), Korean, and Japanese firms. They are comprised of a small number of specialist large firms, such as the Taiwan Semiconductor Manufacturing Company, which have both the capacity to produce ICs in large numbers, and also the technology to allow both the high degree production specificity and flexibility required to manufacture customdesigned ICs. The second and third stages of the semiconductor manufacturing process are at least as technologically advanced as the first stage, requiring enormous physical, financial and human capital inputs. Therefore, simple observations based primarily on contrasts between Silicon Valley and other parts of the semiconductor industry (Saxenian 1994) are of very limited analytical use for more general industryorganization discussions.

Having discussed the nature of the semiconductor industry, in the next section we will look at the relationship between technological change and spatial industrial organization in the case of the semiconductor manufacturers who are located in the USA and Europe. In particular we will focus on those firms which carry out the second and thirdstage wafer process and assembly activities. The object of this exercise is to assess the extent to which orthodox product lifecycle approaches can broadly account for the technology–space relationship.

Organisation Management

"Management"-the act, manner, or practice of managing, handling, or controlling something. Certainly a dictionary's basic definition of this word helps us understand why so many blunders can occur in this area of business. An American executive's mishandling of a presentation prepared for a small Caribbean country serves as a simple example of a management blunder. The meeting was held in the Prime Minister's conference room, and the executive began his presentation with, "Honorable Mr. Tollis and esteemed members of the cabinet." The Prime Minister interrupted him several times, asking him to start over. Eventually, someone advised the bewildered and then embarrassed businessman that Mr. Tollis had been deposed six months earlier!

Unfortunately, people sometimes get careless. Thoughtless conversations, however, can prove costly. When in a foreign-speaking country, it is easy to forget that some people may understand many languages. All too often, speakers learn too late that others understand what they are saying. In fact, visitors to the United States often assume no one understands their native tongue and then promptly say something they quickly regret. An Italian businessman, for example, reportedly flew to Los Angeles to talk with a potential American investor. The driver of the American picked up the Italian at the airport. Believing that the driver did not understand Italian, the visitor, speaking in Italian, apparently made some very negative remarks about the potential investor to his accompanying business associate. These remarks were reported by the driver, who did indeed understand what was being said, and the business deal collapsed.

There are many facets of management. Consider Renault, which, like many firms, has tried to use various barter plans but has experienced mixed success. Trading cars for other products can be profitable but only if the traded products are correctly marketed. In order to sell its cars in South America, Renault agreed to accept coffee beans in payment. The plan seemed safe, as coffee beans are easily traded on world commodity markets. Renault's problems began when the company decided to use the beans to produce instant coffee rather than simply sell the coffee beans wholesale. Without carefully checking the credentials of a fast-talking businessman, Renault agreed to build two plants employing his "miracle new process" for the production of instant coffee. Renault later learned that its new associate had earlier run into legal problems with some of his other international business schemes, but not before it discovered that the "miracle process" failed to work properly and that its new associate had disappeared. Renault lost about $120 million but learned a valuable lesson.

Imperial-Eastman Corporation encountered numerous problems in the operations of its various overseas enterprises. In at least one instance, the company experienced unexpected difficulties when it failed to retain its overseas U.S. personnel for a long enough period of time. Before the operation's critical start-up period was completely over, the company relieved its U.S. personnel and relied solely on its locally hired staff to continue running the operation. However, as critical problems developed, Imperial-Eastman discovered that the local staff was not sufficiently experienced to handle the difficult problems resulting from the new operation. In other ventures, the company suffered from poor estimates of initial inventory needs that created production/delivery disruptions. Losses were incurred when the firm did not allow for delayed delivery and subcontractors failed to deliver on time. A precarious balance seems to exist between the number of foreign managers and the number of U.S. managers needed for a successful operation. Imperial-Eastman experienced problems by relying too heavily on inexperienced local managers, but General Electric encountered troubles by its placement and retention of U.S. employees in most managerial positions. In some cases, because the U.S. employees were unfamiliar with the local business practices, they unknowingly nullified the firm's ability to compete with local business people.

General Electric encountered more culturally oriented management problems in France. Its French employees were upset when they were ordered to wear GE T-shirts to a function (too American), post English-language posters, and in general behave as if the subsidiary was an extension of the United States. Eventually, compromises were made on both sides, but morale already had been badly damaged.

The cases cited above are typical of the types of management blunders that have plagued multinational corporations. Management problems are most often caused by cultural differences that outside managers do not understand and by labour practices with which they are unfamiliar.

Cultural Differences

A Korean firm, Kunja Industrial Company, which owns the Kunja Knitting Mills plant in South Carolina, made the news when an American employee innocently "crooked" his "pointing finger" trying to catch the attention of his Korean boss and bring him closer. The employee succeeded in getting attention all right. However, he certainly didn't succeed in getting his boss physically or emotionally any closer. In fact, he was almost fired. The U.S. finger-moving gesture for asking someone to come closer is considered a vulgar gesture in Korea! A similar blunder was made by former President George Bush. The President was visiting Australia. As he walked up the stairs to his plane, he turned and gave a thumbs up signal, thinking he was indicating that things had gone well. Perhaps they had-at least to that point -but the thumbs-up gesture in Australia is essentially the equivalent of the raised middle finger in the United States. Unknowingly, he had correctly indicated that things ended badly.

Culture includes how different people dress and what is considered acceptable business attire. A notable blunder occurred when Spanish businessmen arrived in Saudi Arabia with a full delegation, confident that they had prepared to encourage the Saudis to spend some of their oil money on Spanish products. The entourage included a number of young, intelligent, bilingual (Spanish/English) women dressed in the height of current style. The blunder occurred when the Saudi police took one look at the miniskirts of the female delegates and immediately shipped the entire group home on the next plane to Spain. Traditionally, women do not show their bare legs in Saudi Arabian culture. When doing business in another country, it is often easy to assume that things there are the same as in your country. Sometimes they are, but sometimes they are different. One U.S. firm with a subsidiary in a small island state learned this the hard way when it hired a local manager to run the subsidiary. One person was highly recommended by local contacts, was intelligent, well spoken, and related well to the local workers. She was interviewed by a representative from headquarters and seemed to be the best choice for the position. Initially, operations seemed to go quite well, but it soon became evident that there was a problem. Major discrepancies surfaced in terms of inventory levels and in the reports of parts shipped. The cause of these problems was finally uncovered. The manager could not do the basic arithmetic of adding or subtracting-skills critical to the job. No one had thought to ask about these skills because they were simply assumed.

It is also wise to know the proper way to dismiss an employee when working with other cultures. This is a difficult task to perform in familiar territory but it is especially tricky when one is in a foreign country and does not always fully understand the local culture. An American manager stationed in Indonesia reportedly discovered this when he tried to fire an oilrig employee. Rather than notifying the employee privately of his dismissal, the manager publicly told the timekeeper to send the man "packing." In Indonesia, this public dismissal was considered an unacceptable "loss of face" which offended both the dismissed man and his friends. So, rather than leave quietly, the man grabbed fire axes and ran after the American manager. Reportedly, the American was barely rescued in time. Obviously, it is dangerous to ignore local management practices and customs!

In an attempt to offer U.S. Southern hospitality, an American businessman was saying goodbye to a Saudi Arabian businessman at the airport after a successful meeting and finished with, "Y'all come and visit." Apparently the Saudi businessman was mortally offended because it was inconceivable to the Saudi that he and his chauffeur should be invited to the United States.

Another American manager was sent to Malaysia to close a major deal. While there he was introduced to someone he thought was named Roger so he pro-ceeded to call him "Rog" several times during the negotiations. Unfortunately, this important potential client was a "rajah," which is an important Malaysian title of nobility. The U.S. tendency to use first names, and even more familiar abbreviated names, was the cause of a serious error in this case. Rather than showing respect, the American appeared disrespectful and insensitive. When the error was discovered, the damage had been done. It is always best to know whom you are dealing with in advance and how that person prefers to be addressed.

A Brazilian executive created major problems for his firm when he treated his secretaries in the United States as personal servants. Not only did he ask them to do his personal shopping, he even asked them to mend his clothes!

The acquisition of the Firestone tire company by Japan's Bridgestone did not proceed as smoothly as hoped. In fact, John Nevin, a crusty former chairman of Firestone, admitted that his style appeared abrupt and abrasive at times to the Japanese, whose manner is much more subtle. He needed to be less direct and forceful with them and they had to become more aware of American-style directness. Both sides tried to adjust, but it did not work out, so new managers had to be brought in.

Milwaukee-based Manpower chairman, Mitchell From-stein, reports that Blue Arrow, a British employment firm, took over Manpower in 1987 but put little effort into understanding how the U.S. labour market differed from the British market. Even the company newsletter directed to the U.S. market ignored U.S. interests. American managers began to openly rebel. Eventually, the Americans wound up in control of the combined company.

In Las Vegas, the Japanese owners of the casinos reportedly ran into problems when they tried to use Japanese management techniques. Among other things, they tried to make decisions the typical Japanese way- by consensus. The approach works well in Japan for many firms but was deemed as too slow and cumbersome in the fast-moving casino environment.

An American company went to a great deal of expense to carefully plan a massive layoff of employees in one of its European subsidiaries. Just before the plan was implemented, however, the firm learned that such layoffs were illegal. Time and money could easily have been saved had managers known of the local labour laws. In a wave of ethnocentrism the new American owners of a Spanish company changed the firm's previous prestigious Spanish name to that of the U.S. parent, flew the American flag from the company flagpole, and widely announced the sophisticated and superb technology being introduced. The company even suggested that those who had managed the company prior to the takeover by the Americans were incompetent. Then, in a special interview with a prominent U.S. business publication, the new management elaborated on its revamping of the whole Spanish company, boasting that its efforts had succeeded in rejuvenating the floundering Spanish operation. Naturally, the article found its way back to the Spanish public and greatly angered the Spanish who were associated with the company. In fact, the blunder was so serious that it resulted in a general slowdown of work. (Strikes were then officially banned.)

The Spanish press released an extremely damaging attack, and local authorities made the conduct of the company's business very difficult. The result: the newly acquired subsidiary lost a great deal of its previous business.

Personnel Choices

Just as in any domestic employment position, if a firm places an inappropriate person in an international job, the results can prove disastrous. Several companies have blundered by placing culturally insensitive individuals in sensitive management and sales positions overseas.

A friend of mine reports that he was involved in negotiations with Saudis to sell them material to clean up oil spills. As the deal was about to be closed, a U.S. bank was invited to send some of its people to a closing meeting in Switzerland. The senior banker attending the meeting was well informed of the details of the proposed deal, but it became painfully obvious that at least one of his assistants needed more careful briefing and training when the subject of financing the deal came up. The assistant was asked how he wanted it done and he replied, "It does not matter unless the buyers are Arabs. You can't trust those Arabs."

Interestingly enough, the Saudis were mature enough to realize that one person does not necessarily represent the attitude of the entire bank. When the senior banker immediately apologized, the Saudis simply said they needed time to think things over. They then privately told the senior banker that they would still use his bank and could work with him, but would not under any circumstances work with his anti-Arab assistant. The point was not lost on anyone-including the assistant (who is no longer working for that bank).

In one case, a firm introduced a technical product into a market relatively free of competition. Believing that market entry would pose no problem, the company did not pay enough attention to the personal characteristics of the man it chose as its European sales manager. This was unfortunate. The individual chosen disliked the French and made no effort to ingratiate himself or learn their culture or language. His dislike even spilled over to his abrupt treatment of the sales force. A competitor soon came along and was able to take over much of the market and most of the man's original sales force.

Similarly, an executive from Lucerne, Switzerland, negotiating a business venture with a Japanese firm failed to recognize the importance of personal sentiment to the Japanese and he paid the price. The president of the Japanese company sponsored a party in Tokyo and exclaimed, "I will not do business with a man who does not like us!" The Lucerne executive believed he had concealed his dislike for the Japanese during his stay, but the president of the Japanese company had seen through his mask. The Japanese executive, therefore, refused to proceed with the business deal even though the partnership would undoubtedly have proven mutually profitable.

An employee's attitude, however, is not the only variable of importance. A person may be well intended but simply not be qualified for the job. Several such cases can be cited. A major U.S. appliance manufacturer, for instance, experiencing difficulties in Spain, sent three troubleshooters to investigate. The company overlooked one important fact: the individuals could not speak Spanish. After repeated efforts to communicate failed, the Spaniards eventually lost respect for the three specialists. The problems worsened until a Spanish-speaking manager was sent to help. A similar situation occurred in Germany. A U.S. manager who understood only a little German was sent to Germany to discuss marketing plans with the local subsidiary managers. The local managers, however, spoke little English. Both sides tried to understand each other, but neither nationality did very well. Eventually they parted, thinking that they were in agreement. It was later discovered that during the meeting many important points were overlooked, and the company subsequently lost numerous sales opportunities.

Even though a manager maintains the right attitude and speaks the language, a successful performance is not assured. Raytheon hired Italian-Americans to manage operations in Sicily but found that the strategy was not as effective as hoped. In this case the trouble lay in the origins of the managers. Because their family ties were with the mainland and not Sicilian, these men were not trusted or accepted.

An effective expatriate manager must possess special abilities and traits if he or she is to avoid blundering. Among the most important characteristics are:

- An ability to get along well with people.
- An awareness of cultural differences.
- Open-mindedness.
- Tolerance of foreign cultures.
- Adaptability to new cultures, ideas, and challenges.
- The ability to adjust quickly to new conditions.
- An interest in facts, not blind assumptions.
- Previous business experience.

- Previous experience with foreign cultures.
- The ability to learn foreign languages.

This list is by no means complete. With so many necessary characteristics, it is no wonder that business people sometimes make mistakes.

Labour Relations

Many non-American companies have experienced difficulties adjusting to U.S. labour practices when they acquire U.S. firms. The Japanese have received the most attention concerning this, but Europeans have also run up against their share of troubles. Britain's Grand Met, for example, angered Pillsbury's minority employees when, as the new owner, it fired several black middle managers (including the head of its affirmative action programme). In another case, a European firm lost a talented employee when it purchased a company and expected a female executive to start serving coffee at the board meetings.

Because of cultural similarities, a Japanese company doing business in Indonesia consistently hired Bataks, members of an ethnic group with characteristics similar to the Japanese. Other Indonesians, however, resented this hiring practice, viewed it as discriminatory, and forced the company to change its policy. A U.S. tin mining firm had problems retaining employees in Bolivia even though it paid the employees more than the local competition did. It seems that the problem lay with the method of payment. The U.S. company paid on time every week, but the Bolivians preferred to be paid by the hour. Thus, they could take a few hours off from time to time and not risk the loss of an entire week's wages.

Americans ran into trouble in Iran long before the Iranian revolution. One problem encountered by business people was the widespread belief that foreigners discriminated against Iranians. A U.S. company cemented this belief when it promised local employees that U.S. workers would not be treated preferentially but then provided better health benefits for the U.S. employees.

Verbal promises are taken very seriously in Iran, so the firm's failure to keep its promise was viewed as a major breach of trust and further evidence that foreigners discriminate against Iranians. Many companies have faced labour troubles in Europe, where governments tend to protect employees and often make layoffs difficult. Some of the most sensationalized cases have occurred in France. Shortly after World War II ended, many U.S. companies rushed into France, hired people, and enjoyed the ensuing business boom. However, the good times didn't last for ever and more than a few firms made the mistake of trying to reduce employment levels. General Motors, Remington Rand, General Electric, and other firms soon found themselves in trouble and were forced to reverse layoff decisions. Italy has also been the scene of many unpleasant labour disputes with U.S. firms. Raytheon's layoff attempts eventually forced it to close its plant in Sicily at a loss of many millions of dollars.

Another U.S. firm experienced a different kind of problem. The company had a tradition of holding picnics where management and workers mingled with ease in a comfortable environment, so the firm tried to export its company picnic to Spain. To highlight management's "democratic" beliefs, the U.S. executives even dressed as chefs and served the food. However, the picnic failed to help develop the desired rapport between the U.S. managers and the Spanish workers. In fact, it was a very awkward event, as the lower-level staff clung together and did not want to be served by their superiors. When an executive approached the picnic table, everyone stood up. The company quickly learned that Spanish attitudes of class distinction and social groups make casual mixing and socializing of workers with executives very difficult.

The United Kingdom has been the home for some of the best-known labour problems of U.S. companies. Ford Motor Company, for example, ran into hard times in England because the British managers and laborers felt that the U.S. managers there were treated better and were given more power. Many employees openly resented this apparent favoritism. Several key British executives even quit. The company lowered the number of Americans there and this reduced the problem, but decisions from headquarters were still resented. At one point, British newspapers ran such headlines as "Local Ford plants can't even build a bathroom without permission from Detroit." Actually, this was not far from the truth at the time.

Now, much more power is delegated to the local managers (who are more likely now to be British) and Ford's labour relations are much better. The Roberts Arundel textile machinery plant in Stockport, England had to close down after managers tried to impose U.S. labour practices. Mr. Arundel later admitted that it was a mistake to try to change worker habits, but they had thought that production line work would go better if those famous tea breaks were dropped. Employees thought otherwise! It is usually easier to change management practices than radically alter local work habits.

Mass communication

Mass communication is the term used to describe the academic study of the various means by which individuals and entities relay information through mass media to large segments of the population at the same time. It is usually understood to relate to newspaper and magazine publishing, radio, television and film, as these are used both for disseminating news and for advertising.

Field of Study

Mass communication research includes media institutions and processes such as diffusion of information, and media effects such as persuasion or manipulation of public opinion. In the United States, for instance, several university journalism departments degraded into schools or colleges of mass communication or "journalism and mass communication". In addition to studying practical skills of journalism, public relations or advertising, they offer programmes on "mass communication" or "mass communication research." The latter is often the title given to doctoral studies in such schools, whether the focus of the student's research is journalism practice, history, law or media effects. Departmental structures within such colleges may separate research and instruction in professional or technical aspects of mass communication.

With the increased role of the Internet in delivering news and information, mass communication studies and media organizations tend to focus on the convergence of publishing, broadcasting and digital communication.

The academic mass communication discipline historically differs from media studies and communication studies programmes with roots in departments of theatre, film or speech, and with more interest in "qualitative," interpretive theory, critical or cultural approaches to communication study. In contrast, many mass communication programmes historically lean toward empirical analysis and quantitative research—from statistical content analysis of media messages to survey research, public opinion polling, and experimental research. Interest in "New Media" and "Computer Mediated Communication" is growing much faster than educational institutions can assimilate it. So far, traditional classes and degree programmes have not been able to accommodate new shifts of the paradigm in communication technologies. Although national standards for the study of interactive media have been present in the U.K. since the mid-nineties, course work in these areas tends to vary significantly from university to university.

Graduates of Mass Communication programmes work in a variety of fields in traditional news media and publishing, advertising, public relations and research institutes.

Such programmes are accredited by the Accrediting Council on Education in Journalism and Mass Communication. The Association for Education in Journalism and Mass Communication is the major membership organization for academics in the field, offering regional and national conferences and refereed publications. The International Communication Association and National Communication Association (formerly the Speech Communication Association) include divisions and publications that overlap with those of AEJMC, but AEJMC historically has stronger ties to the mass communication professions in the United States.

The terms 'Mass' and 'Communication'

The term 'mass' denotes great volume, range or extent (of people or production) and reception of messages. The important point about 'mass' is not that a given number of individuals receives the products, but rather that the products are available in principle to a plurality of recipients.

The term 'mass' suggests that the recipients of media products constitute a vast sea of passive, undifferentiated individuals. This is an image associated with some earlier critiques of 'mass culture' and Mass society which generally assumed that the development of mass communication has had a largely negative impact on modern social life, creating a kind of bland and homogeneous culture which entertains individuals without challenging them. However, with the advancement in Media Technology, people are no longer receiving gratification without questioning the grounds on which it is based. Instead, people are engaging themselves more with media products such as computers, cell phones and Internet. These have gradually became vital tools for communications in society today.

The aspect of 'communication' refers to the giving and taking of meaning, the transmission and reception of messages. The word 'communication' is really equated with 'transmission', as viewed by the sender, rather than in the fuller meaning, which includes the notions of response, sharing and interaction. Messages are produced by one set of individuals and transmitted to others who are typically situated in settings that are spatially and temporally remote from the original context of production. Therefore, the term 'communication' in this context masks the social and industrial nature of the media, promoting a tendency to think of them as interpersonal communication. Furthermore, it is known that recipients today do have some capacity to intervene in and contribute to the course and content of the communicative process. They are being both active and creative towards the messages that they are conveyed of. With the complement of the cyberspace supported by the Internet, not only that recipients are participants in a structured process of symbolic transmission, constraints such as time and space are reordered and eliminated.

'Mass communication' can be seen as institutionalized production and generalized diffusion of symbolic goods via the fixation and transmission of information or symbolic content. It is known that the systems of information codification has shifted from analog to digital. This has indeed advanced the communication between individuals. With the existence of Infrared, Bluetooth and Wi-Fi, cell phones are no longer solely a tool for audio transmission. We can transfer photos, music documents or even games and email at any time and anywhere. The development of media technology has indeed advanced the transmission rate and stability of information exchange.

Characteristics of Mass Communication Five characteristics of mass communication have been identified by Cambridge University's John Thompson. Firstly, it "comprises both technical and institutional methods of production and distribution". This is evident throughout the history of the media, from print to the Internet, each suitable for commercial utility.

Secondly, it involves the "commodification of symbolic forms", as the production of materials relies on its ability to manufacture and sell large quantities of the work. Just as radio stations rely on its time sold to advertisements, newspapers rely for the same reasons on its space.

Mass communication's third characteristic is the "separate contexts between the production and reception of information",[15] while the fourth is in its "reach to those 'far removed' in time and space, in comparison to the producers".

Mass communication, which involves "information distribution". This is a "one to many" form of communication, whereby products are mass produced and disseminated to a great quantity of audiences.

10

Challenges of Science, Technology and Internet Communication

Introduction

For the past two decades or so, science communication activities have gained momentum in India. Efforts have been made from both governmental and non-governmental platforms to enhance the public understanding of science. The idea is to help science and a scientific culture penetrate India's socio-culturally diverse society, and to transform it into a nation of scientifically thinking and scientifically aware people.

Historical Backdrop

India has an impressive scientific heritage. Scientific research-in fields such as mathematics, astronomy, medicine and material science-has been carried out in the Indian sub-continent since ancient times. However, a remarkable gap has persisted between this scientific knowledge and the 'common' man and woman and, until recently, almost no effort has been made to bridge this gap. Throughout history, there have been attempts to take science to the common people. For example, *Vigyan* (Science) - a monthly popular science magazine in Hindi - has been published by Vigyan Parishad (a learned society of scientists and academics) since 1915.

Following Independence in 1947, the first Prime Minister of India, Pandit Jawaharlal Nehru, introduced the concept of modern 'scientific temper' - a phrase taken to mean an enquiring attitude and analytical approach that leads to rational thinking and the pursuit of truth without prejudice. Accordingly, the constitution of India has a special provision "to develop the scientific temper, humanism and spirit of enquiry".

Science Communication Movement in India

After Independence, a number of government agencies and non-governmental organisations (NGOs) took their cue from the constitution and became involved in science popularisation. In this way, science communication was taken up at various levels, institutional as well as individual. Nehru was a major force behind this advancement of science in independent India. The National Institute of Science Communication (NISCOM) - previously the Publications and Information Directorate - began publishing of the Hindi popular science journal *Vigyan Pragati* (Progress in Science) in 1952. *The Science Reporter* (an English monthly) and *Science Ki Dunia* (an Urdu quarterly) followed soon after. Today, NISCOM also brings out 11 professional scientific journals and publishes various popular science books (often in Indian languages).

In 1980, science communication was given prominence in India's sixth Five-year Plan, and two years later the National Council for Science and Technology Communication (NCSTC) was established. The Council has a mandate to integrate, coordinate, catalyse and support science communication and popularisation, at the micro as well as macro level. NCSTC's programmes include training in science and technology communication, software development, research, field-based projects, and creating information networks and databases.

Other Indian government initiatives include Vigyan Prasar - an autonomous organisation of the Department of Science and Technology set up in 1989 - which plays an important role in coordinating efforts among various scientific institutions, educational and academic bodies, laboratories, museums, industry and other organisations for the effective exchange and dissemination of scientific information. Vigyan Prasar also develops and disseminates software materials and organises popular science events including workshops, debates and lectures. The National Council of Science Museums, based in Calcutta, is the coordinating body of 26 science museums and science centres across the country. Science City in Calcutta has more than 1,000 exhibits and attracts around 500,000 visitors a year. Based on the experiences and popularity of Science City, other such projects are being developed across the country.

Several NGOs have also pursued science communication programmes. The Indian Science Writers' Association (ISWA), for example, was founded in 1985 with a view to developing and nurturing the science writing profession in India. The association has around 200 members and undertakes a broad spectrum of activities including training courses, lectures and fellowships. ISWA also works with government agencies and NGOs in promoting science communication activities.

Science Communication Media

India's science communicators have used various modes of communication to reach out to the masses. As a result, a lot of infrastructure, software and human resources are available in the country. Each has its own significance and utility, given the vast diversities that exist in the country.

Print Media

In addition to the scientific journals (both popular and technical) published by the government, several national and regional daily newspapers have now started producing weekly science pages. In a unique initiative, Vigyan Prasar provides a weekly ready-to-print science page, in both Hindi and English, which some 21 newspapers use at a nominal cost. Sadly, however, there are signs that interest in science communication is waning in the print media. For example, the Indian science magazines Science Today and Bulletin of Sciences have been discontinued, as have Indian editions of certain foreign magazines, such as La Recherche and Scientific American.

Audio-visual Media

A variety of science-based programmes are now available on All India Radio (AIR), such as Radioscope, Science Today, Science

Magazine and Science News. In the early 1990s a landmark 144-part radio serial *Manav Ka Vikas* (Human Evolution) was jointly produced by NCSTC and AIR. The programme was broadcast simultaneously from more than 80 radio stations in 18 Indian languages with 100,000 children and 10,000 schools registered as dedicated listeners.

A number of television channels have also been broadcasting science programmes for many years. For example, a 13-part film serial on the history of science and technology in the Indian sub-continent and its impact on the world, entitled *Bharat Ki Chhaap,* was produced by NCSTC and broadcast on the state-run Doordarshan channel in 1989.

Folk Media

It is a common observation that folk media - such as puppet shows, street plays, stage performances, and folk songs and dances-successfully reach segments of society where other forms of media have limitations. These traditional means of communication have all been exploited as alternative media for science communication. They are not only entertaining, but also offer two-way communication and are cost effective.

Several voluntary agencies, such as Kerala's Shastra Sahitya Parishad (People's Science Movement), are actively involved in taking science to the people, especially through folk forms. Where print and electronic media have limits rooted in literacy levels and accessibility, folk media can play a crucial role.

'Interactive' Media

Science exhibitions, science fairs, demonstrations, seminars, workshops, lectures, scientific tours, conferences and, more recently, digital software, have the advantage of being interactive forms of science communication.

Perhaps the most impressive example is the *Vigyan Jatha.* During this massive event, science communicators march in groups from village to village, interacting with local people and spreading information about science relevant to their day-to-day lives.

Catalysed by NCSTC, Vigyan Jatha could be considered the biggest science communication experiment anywhere in the world. Held in 1987 and 1992, themes have included health, water, environment, appropriate technology, superstitions, scientific thinking and literacy. Some 2,500 government agencies and NGOs have been actively involved, and the Jatha have covered nearly 40,000 locations in about 400 districts, touching almost a third of the country's population.

The annual Children's Science Congress - started in 1993 by the NCSTC Network - has become a highlight in the science communication calendar. The congress aims to extend classroom science teaching by providing 10-to 17-year old with an open 'laboratory' for enjoyable hands-on learning.

Another very popular and important programme in India has been the 'scientific explanation of miracles'. This programme uses trained science 'activists' to demonstrate and explain so-called miracles. In 1995, for example, the author investigated and demonstrated the phenomenon of deities drinking milk on television, and exposed it as a hoax.

Most recently, information technology has given birth to a comparatively new form of interactive science communication-digital media-which includes the Internet and CD-ROMs. This is proving to be an effective way to illustrate difficult scientific concepts. It has also made science communication more accessible both to handicapped and less educated people. Though the reach of the technology is still a limiting factor, the government is working to extend this and reduce the costs of connectivity.

Present Challenges and Visions

Although much has been achieved in India, there is still an urgent need to make science communication activities more effective, both in terms of quality and quantity. We have yet to make a dent in wiping out superstitions that have prevailed throughout the ages, particularly in tribal areas where literacy levels are low and superstition is a way of life. Also, the general public is still largely ignorant about common scientific principles, such as the fact that the Earth orbits the Sun.

Mass Media

Science is not succeeding in attracting mass media interest. It rarely appears as a lead story, as editors and reporters do not consider science to be 'news' in the normal sense. On average, science only accounts for around three per cent of coverage by India's mass media. Additionally, readership of popular science magazines has declined-people no longer rely on print material as their only source of information.

For this reason, the Indian Science Writers' Association aims to encourage the editors of newspapers and magazines to regularly feature a science column. It also hopes to increase the readership of popular science magazines, for example by making them available through digital media. In addition, publications must cater to India's many languages. It is encouraging that radio, which is extremely popular in rural areas, has an increasing amount of scientific content. Television is following a similar pattern, with a few special channels on science and technology, and other channels featuring scientific discussions and interviews of scientists about their research. But it hasn't yet reached a satisfactory level as far as science communication is concerned.

Mass Education

There is no doubt that scientific information is becoming an essential and integral part of people's daily lives. Present and future science communication efforts have great potential in shaping the lives of the people and making their decisions more informative and rational. However, illiteracy and ignorance are major challenges. While literacy levels are increasing (currently estimated at 52 per cent of the population), scientific literacy is still drastically low. Given India's large population, limited resources and multitude of languages, mass science education faces particularly great challenges. There have been efforts to popularise science through our 18 regional languages, for example by producing some scientific publications in vernaculars and translating certain television and radio programmes. But without more attention on local languages, much of the population will miss out on science communication efforts.

In an ideal world science communication activities would be widespread right down to the village level. In order to create awareness among illiterates or the newly literate-and to maintain the knowledge they acquire-folk forms must be used more frequently. In this way, superstitious beliefs could be wiped from society and a scientific environment created even at the grassroots level.

Training of Science Communicators

Science writing still tends to be dry and boring, making it unsurprising that few science articles interest newspapers and magazines. The number of capable science communicators and voluntary scientific organisations is alarmingly low and hardly sufficient to cater to the country's large and diverse population.

That said, a number of science communicators are being trained through postgraduate degree and diploma courses in science communication, and short-term science writing and journalism workshops. Indeed, four Indian science communicators have won UNESCO's Kalinga Prize for their outstanding contributions to science communication and popularisation. The way that scientific information is presented in the media needs to undergo a metamorphosis, with a new generation of the science writers and journalists presenting useful science in an interesting and innovative manner. For example, a science and technology news and features pool could be formed to allow writers and journalists to exchange information on scientific research and developments.

Networking

Most importantly, science communication activities must be conducted and governed in a systematically planned manner, under one umbrella organisation, and according to a properly defined national policy. To an extent this issue is already being addressed. An All India People's Science Network was created in the late 1980s, with 27 constituent voluntary organisations. The NCSTC Network started in 1991 with the objective of taking science popularisation activities to all the corners of the country. Presently it has around 100 members, including NGOs and government organisations. NCSTC has also started a countrywide project to compile information on science communication software, hardware, 'humanware' and agencies to facilitate further networking. But the formation of networks of organisations alone is not sufficient. A suitable mechanism must be evolved to ensure we work together in a more cohesive manner. I would also argue that we need a formal Science Media Network. In fact, moves have already been made towards a national database of science editors, writers, journalists, columnists, translators, 'scientoonists', illustrators, media-persons, producers, and media organisations interested in science coverage.

Following the industrial revolution in western countries, the level of science communication activities increased dramatically. In some ways, India is presently passing through a similar stage. As technology advances, the need for scientific information will also increase. Accordingly, an industrial India should soon witness a similar increase in science communication and popularisation. Indeed, the success of the information technology industry is proof of a growing scientific awareness in India. India has undertaken a large number of science communication initiatives, and has sometimes led the way in innovative approaches. However, we should also be open to new ideas, methodologies and programmes available in other parts of the world, and similarly share with others the successful strategies we have employed.

As far as science writing and journalism are concerned, there is ample scope for furthering such efforts in developing countries. India could take the initiative in mobilising like-minded people in South Asia to form Science Writers' and Journalists' Associations in each country, ideally with help from international organisations. The science communication scenario of our dreams is not unobtainable. Rather, it is based on technologies available today, which can be better utilised to carry scientific messages to the people. I believe that science communication in India has a bright future.

E-mail

Electronic mail, often abbreviated as email, e.mail or e-mail, is a method of exchanging digital messages. E-mail systems are based on a store-and-forward model in which e-mail computer server systems accept, forward, deliver and store messages on behalf of users, who only need to connect to the e-mail infrastructure, typically an e-mail server, with a network-enabled device (e.g., a personal computer) for the duration of message submission or retrieval. Originally, e-mail was always transmitted directly from one user's device to another's; nowadays this is rarely the case. An electronic mail message consists of two components, the message *header*, and the message *body*, which is the email's content. The message header contains control information, including, minimally, an originator's email address and one or more recipient addresses. Usually additional information is added, such as a subject header field.

Originally a text-only communications medium, email was extended to carry multi-media content attachments, which were standardized in with RFC 2045 through RFC 2049, collectively called, Multipurpose Internet Mail Extensions (MIME).

The foundation for today's global Internet e-mail service was created in the early ARPANET and standards for encoding of messages were proposed as early as 1973 (RFC 561). An e-mail sent in the early 1970s looked very similar to one sent on the Internet today. Conversion from the ARPANET to the Internet in the early 1980s produced the core of the current service.

Network-based email was initially exchanged on the ARPANET in extensions to the File Transfer Protocol (FTP), but is today carried by the Simple Mail Transfer Protocol (SMTP), first published as Internet standard 10 (RFC 821) in 1982. In the process of transporting email messages between systems, SMTP communicates delivery parameters using a message *envelope* separately from the message (headers and body) itself.

Spelling

There are several spelling variations that are occasionally the cause of vehement disagreement. email is the form officially required by IETF Request for Comments and working groups and is also recognized in most dictionaries. e-mail is a form still recommended by some prominent journalistic and technical style guides.

Less common forms include *eMail* and simply *mail*. mail was the form used in the original RFC. The service is referred to as *mail* and a single piece of electronic mail is called a *message*. eMail, capitalizing only the letter *M*, was common among ARPANET users and early developers from Unix, CMS, AppleLink, eWorld, AOL, GEnie, and Hotmail. EMail is a traditional form that has been used in RFCs for the "Author's Address", and is expressly required "*. . . for historical reasons . . .*".

Origin

Electronic mail predates the inception of the Internet, and was in fact a crucial tool in creating the Internet. MIT first demonstrated the Compatible Time-Sharing System (CTSS) in 1961. It allowed multiple users to log into the IBM 7094 from remote dial-up terminals, and to store files online on disk. This new ability encouraged users to share information in new ways. E-mail started in 1965 as a way for multiple users of a time-sharing mainframe computer to communicate. Although the exact history is murky, among the first systems to have such a facility were SDC's Q32 and MIT's CTSS.

Host-based Mailsystems

The original email systems allowed communication only between users who logged into the one host or "mainframe", but this could be hundreds or thousands of users within a company or university. By 1966 (or earlier, it is possible that the SAGE system had something similar some time before), such systems allowed email between different companies as long as they ran compatible operating systems, but not to other dissimilar systems. Examples include BITNET, IBM PROFS, Digital All-in-1 and the original Unix mail.

LAN-based Mailsystems

From the early 1980s networked personal computers on LANs became increasingly important - and server-based systems similar to the earlier mainframe systems developed, and again initially allowed communication only between users logged into the one server, but these also could generally be linked between different companies as long as they ran the same email system and (proprietary) protocol. Examples include cc:Mail, WordPerfect Office, Microsoft Mail, Banyan VINES and Lotus Notes - with various vendors supplying gateway software to link these incompatible systems.

Attempts at Interoperability

- Novell briefly championed the open MHS protocol
- uucp was used as an open "glue" between differing mail systems
- The Coloured Book protocols on UK academic networks until 1992
- X.400 in the early 1990s was mandated for government use under GOSIP but almost immediately abandoned by all but a few — in favour of Internet SMTP

The Rise of ARPANET-based Mail

The ARPANET computer network made a large contribution to the development of e-mail. There is one report that indicates experimental inter-system e-mail transfers began shortly after its creation in 1969. Ray Tomlinson is credited by some as having sent the first email, initiating the use of the "@" sign to separate the names of the user and the user's machine in 1971, when he sent a message from one Digital Equipment Corporation DEC-10 computer to another DEC-10. The two machines were placed next to each other. The ARPANET significantly increased the popularity of e-mail, and it became the killer app of the ARPANET.

Most other networks had their own email protocols and address formats; as the influence of the ARPANET and later the Internet grew, central sites often hosted email gateways that passed mail between the Internet and these other networks. Internet email addressing is still complicated by the need to handle mail destined for these older networks.

Some well-known examples of these were UUCP (mostly Unix computers), BITNET (mostly IBM and VAX mainframes at universities), FidoNet (personal computers), DECNET (various networks) and CSNet a forerunner of NSFNet.

This was necessary because in early years UUCP computers did not maintain (or consult servers for) information about the location of all hosts they exchanged mail with, but rather only knew how to communicate with a few network neighbors; email messages (and other data such as Usenet News) were passed along in a chain among hosts who had explicitly agreed to share data with each other.

Operation Overview

The diagram to the right shows a typical sequence of events that takes place when Alice composes a message using her mail user agent (MUA). She enters the e-mail address of her correspondent, and hits the "send" button.

1. Here MUA formats the message in e-mail format and uses the Simple Mail Transfer Protocol (SMTP) to send the message to the local mail transfer agent (MTA), in this case smtp.a.org, run by Alice's Internet Service Provider (ISP).
2. The MTA looks at the destination address provided in the SMTP protocol (not from the message header), in this case bob@b.org. An Internet e-mail address is a string of the form localpart@exampledomain. The part before the @ sign is the local part of the address, often the username of the recipient, and the part after the @ sign is a domain name or a fully qualified domain name. The MTA resolves a domain name to determine the fully qualified domain name of the mail exchange server in the Domain Name System.
3. The DNS server for the b.org domain, ns.b.org, responds with any MX records listing the mail exchange servers for that domain, in this case mx.b.org, a server run by Bob's ISP.
4. smtp.a.org sends the message to mx.b.org using SMTP, which delivers it to the mailbox of the user bob.
5. Bob presses the "get mail" button in his MUA, which picks up the message using the Post Office Protocol (POP3).

That sequence of events applies to the majority of e-mail users. However, there are many alternative possibilities and complications to the e-mail system:

- Alice or Bob may use a client connected to a corporate e-mail system, such as IBM Lotus Notes or Microsoft Exchange. These systems often have their own internal e-mail format and their clients typically communicate with the e-mail server using a vendor-specific, proprietary protocol. The server sends or receives e-mail via the Internet through the product's Internet mail gateway which also does any necessary reformatting. If Alice and Bob work for the same company, the entire transaction may happen completely within a single corporate e-mail system.
- Alice may not have a MUA on her computer but instead may connect to a webmail service.
- Alice's computer may run its own MTA, so avoiding the transfer at step 1.
- Bob may pick up his e-mail in many ways, for example using the Internet Message Access Protocol, by logging into mx.b.org and reading it directly, or by using a webmail service.
- Domains usually have several mail exchange servers so that they can continue to accept mail when the main mail exchange server is not available.
- E-mail messages are not secure if e-mail encryption is not used correctly.

Many MTAs used to accept messages for any recipient on the Internet and do their best to deliver them. Such MTAs are called *open mail relays*. This was very important in the early days of the Internet when network connections were unreliable. If an MTA couldn't reach the destination, it could at least deliver it to a relay closer to the destination. The relay stood a better chance of delivering the message at a later time. However, this mechanism proved to be exploitable by people sending unsolicited bulk e-mail and as a consequence very few modern MTAs are open mail relays, and many MTAs don't accept messages from open mail relays because such messages are very likely to be spam.

Message Format

The Internet e-mail message format is defined in RFC 5322

and a series of RFCs, RFC 2045 through RFC 2049, collectively called, *Multipurpose Internet Mail Extensions*, or *MIME*. Although as of July 13, 2005, RFC 2822 is technically a proposed IETF standard and the MIME RFCs are draft IETF standards, these documents are the standards for the format of Internet e-mail. Prior to the introduction of RFC 2822 in 2001, the format described by RFC 822 was the standard for Internet e-mail for nearly 20 years; it is still the official IETF standard. The IETF reserved the numbers 5321 and 5322 for the updated versions of RFC 2821 (SMTP) and RFC 2822, as it previously did with RFC 821 and RFC 822, honoring the extreme importance of these two RFCs. RFC 822 was published in 1982 and based on the earlier RFC 733. Internet e-mail messages consist of two major sections:

- *Header* — Structured into fields such as summary, sender, receiver, and other information about the e-mail.
- *Body* — The message itself as unstructured text; sometimes containing a signature block at the end. This is exactly the same as the body of a regular letter.

The header is separated from the body by a blank line.

Message Header

Each message has exactly one header, which is structured into fields. Each field has a name and a value. RFC 5322 specifies the precise syntax.

Informally, each line of text in the header that begins with a printable character begins a separate field. The field name starts in the first character of the line and ends before the separator character ":". The separator is then followed by the field value (the "body" of the field). The value is continued onto subsequent lines if those lines have a space or tab as their first character. Field names and values are restricted to 7-bit ASCII characters. Non-ASCII values may be represented using MIME encoded words.

Header Fields

The message header should include at least the following fields:

- *From*: The e-mail address, and optionally the name of the author(s). In many e-mail clients not changeable except through changing account settings.

- *To*: The e-mail address(es), and optionally name(s) of the message's recipient(s). Indicates primary recipients (multiple allowed), for secondary recipients see Cc: and Bcc.
- *Subject*: A brief summary of the topic of the message.
- *Date*: The local time and date when the message was written. Like the *From:* field, many email clients fill this in automatically when sending. The recipient's client may then display the time in the format and time zone local to her.
- *Message-ID*: Also an automatically generated field; used to prevent multiple delivery and for reference in In-Reply-To:.

Note that the "To:" field is not necessarily related to the addresses to which the message is delivered. The actual delivery list is supplied separately to the transport protocol, SMTP, which may or may not originally have been extracted from the header content. The "To:" field is similar to the addressing at the top of a conventional letter which is delivered according to the address on the outer envelope. Also note that the "From:" field does not have to be the real sender of the e-mail message. One reason is that it is very easy to fake the "From:" field and let a message seem to be from any mail address. It is possible to digitally sign e-mail, which is much harder to fake, but such signatures require extra programming and often external programmes to verify. Some Internet service providers do not relay e-mail claiming to come from a domain not hosted by them, but very few (if any) check to make sure that the person or even e-mail address named in the "From:" field is the one associated with the connection. Some Internet service providers apply e-mail authentication systems to e-mail being sent through their MTA to allow other MTAs to detect forged spam that might appear to come from them.

RFC 3864 describes registration procedures for message header fields at the IANA; it provides for permanent and provisional message header field names, including also fields defined for MIME, netnews, and http, and referencing relevant RFCs. Common header fields for email include:

- *Bcc*: Blind Carbon Copy; addresses added to the SMTP delivery list but not (usually) listed in the message data, remaining invisible to other recipients.
- *Cc*: Carbon copy; Many e-mail clients will mark e-mail in your inbox differently depending on whether you are in the To: or Cc: list.
- *Content-Type*: Information about how the message is to be displayed, usually a MIME type.
- *In-Reply-To: Message-ID* of the message that this is a reply to. Used to link related messages together.
- *Precedence*: commonly with values "bulk", "junk", or "list"; used to indicate that automated "vacation" or "out of office" responses should not be returned for this mail, eg. to prevent vacation notices from being sent to all other subscribers of a mailinglist.
- *Received*: Tracking information generated by mail servers that have previously handled a message, in reverse order (last handler first).
- *References*: Message-ID of the message that this is a reply to, and the message-id of the message the previous was reply a reply to, etc.
- *Reply-To*: Address that should be used to reply to the message.
- *Sender*: Address of the actual sender acting on behalf of the author listed in the From: field (secretary, list manager, etc.).
- *X-Face*: Small icon.

Message body

E-mail was originally designed for 7-bit ASCII. Much e-mail software is 8-bit clean but must assume it will communicate with 8-bit servers and mail readers. The MIME standard introduced character set specifiers and two content transfer encodings to enable transmission of non-ASCII data: quoted printable for mostly 7 bit content with a few characters outside that range and base64 for arbitrary binary data. The 8BITMIME extension was introduced to allow transmission of mail without the need for these encodings but many mail transport agents still do not support it fully. In some countries, several encoding schemes coexist; as the result, by default, the message in a non-Latin alphabet language appears in non-readable form (the only exception is coincidence, when the sender and receiver use the same encoding scheme). Therefore, for international character sets, Unicode is growing in popularity.

Plain text and HTML

Most modern graphic e-mail clients allow the use of either plain text or HTML for the message body at the option of the user. HTML e-mail messages often include an automatically-generated plain text copy as well, for compatibility reasons. Advantages of HTML include the ability to include inline links and images, set apart previous messages in block quotes, wrap naturally on any display, use emphasis such as underlines and italics, and change font styles. Disadvantages include the increased size of the email, privacy concerns about web bugs, abuse of HTML email as a vector for phishing attacks and the spread of malicious software.

Mailing lists commonly insist that all posts to be made in plain-text for all the above reasons, but also because they have a significant number of readers using text-based e-mail clients such as Mutt. Some Microsoft e-mail clients have allowed richer formatting by using RTF rather than HTML, but unless the recipient is guaranteed to have a compatible e-mail client this should be avoided.

Servers and Client Applications

Messages are exchanged between hosts using the Simple Mail Transfer Protocol with software programmes called mail transfer agents. Users can retrieve their messages from servers using standard protocols such as POP or IMAP, or, as is more likely in a large corporate environment, with a proprietary protocol specific to Lotus Notes or Microsoft Exchange Servers. Webmail interfaces allow users to access their mail with any standard web browser, from any computer, rather than relying on an e-mail client. Mail can be stored on the client, on the server side, or in both places.

Standard formats for mailboxes include Maildir and mbox. Several prominent e-mail clients use their own proprietary format and require conversion software to transfer e-mail between them.

Accepting a message obliges an MTA to deliver it, and when a message cannot be delivered, that MTA must send a bounce message back to the sender, indicating the problem.

Filename Extensions

Upon reception of e-mail messages, e-mail client applications save message in operating system files in the filesystem. Some clients save individual messages as separate files, while others use various database formats, often proprietary, for collective storage. A historical standard of storage is the *mbox* format. The specific format used is often indicated by special filename extensions:

.eml

Used by many e-mail clients including Microsoft Outlook Express, Windows Mail and Mozilla Thunderbird. The files are plain text in MIME format, containing the e-mail header as well as the message contents and attachments in one or more of several formats.

.emlx

Used by Apple Mail.

.msg

Used by Microsoft Office Outlook.

.mbx

Used by Opera Mail, KMail, and Apple Mail based on the mbox format.

Some applications (like Apple Mail) also encode attachments into messages for searching while also producing a physical copy of the files on a disk. Others separate attachments from messages by depositing them into designated folders on disk.

URI scheme *mailto*

The URI scheme, as registered with the IANA, defines the mailto: scheme for SMTP email addresses. Though its use is not strictly defined, URLs of this form are intended to be used to open the new message window of the user's mail client when the URL is activated, with the address as defined by the URL in the "To:" field.

In Society

There are numerous ways in which people have changed the way they communicate in the last 50 years; e-mail is certainly one of them. Traditionally, social interaction in the local community was the basis for communication – face to face. Yet, today face-to-face meetings are no longer the primary way to communicate as one can use a landline telephone, mobile phones or any number of the computer mediated communications such as e-mail. Research has shown that people actively use e-mail to maintain core social networks, particularly when others live at a distance. However, contradictory to previous research, the results suggest that increases in Internet usage are associated with decreases in other modes of communication, with proficiency of Internet and e-mail use serving as a mediating factor in this relationship. With the introduction of chat messengers and video conference there are more ways to communicate.

Flaming

Flaming occurs when a person sends a message with angry or antagonistic content. Flaming is assumed to be more common today because of the ease and impersonality of e-mail communications: confrontations in person or via telephone require direct interaction, where social norms encourage civility, whereas typing a message to another person is an indirect interaction, so civility may be forgotten. Flaming is generally looked down upon by Internet communities as it is considered rude and non-productive.

E-mail Bankruptcy

Also known as "e-mail fatigue", e-mail bankruptcy is when a user ignores a large number of e-mail messages after falling behind in reading and answering them. The reason for falling behind is often due to information overload and a general sense there is so much information that it is not possible to read it all. As a solution, people occasionally send a boilerplate message explaining that the e-mail inbox is being cleared out. Stanford University law professor Lawrence Lessig is credited with coining this term, but he may only have popularized it.

In Business

E-mail was widely accepted by the business community as the first broad electronic communication medium and was the first 'e-revolution' in business communication. E-mail is very simple to understand and like postal mail, e-mail solves two basic problems of communication: logistics and synchronization. LAN based email is also an emerging form of usage for business. It not only allows the business user to download mail when *offline*, it also provides the small business user to have multiple users e-mail ID's with just *one e-mail connection*.

Pros

- *The problem of logistics*: Much of the business world relies upon communications between people who are not physically in the same building, area or even country; setting up and attending an in-person meeting, telephone call, or conference call can be inconvenient, time-consuming, and costly. E-mail provides a way to exchange information between two or more people with no set-up costs and that is generally far less expensive than physical meetings or phone calls.
- *The problem of synchronization*: With real time communication by meetings or phone calls, participants have to work on the same schedule, and each participant must spend the same amount of time in the meeting or call. E-mail allows asynchrony: each participant may control their schedule independently.

Cons

Most business workers today spend from one to two hours of their working day on e-mail: reading, ordering, sorting, 're-contextualizing' fragmented information, and writing e-mail. The use of e-mail is increasing due to increasing levels of globalization—labour division and outsourcing amongst other things. E-mail can lead to some well-known problems:

- Loss of Context: which means that the context is lost forever; there is no way to get the text back. Information in context (as in a newspaper) is much easier and faster to understand than unedited and sometimes unrelated fragments of information. Communicating in context can only be achieved when both parties have a full understanding of the context and issue in question.
- Information overload: E-mail is a push technology—the sender controls who receives the information. Convenient availability of mailing lists and use of "copy all" can lead to people receiving unwanted or irrelevant information of no use to them.
- Inconsistency: E-mail can duplicate information. This can be a problem when a large team is working on documents and information while not in constant contact with the other members of their team.

Despite these disadvantages, e-mail has become the most widely used medium of communication within the business world.

Information Overload

A December 2007 New York Times blog post described E-mail as "a $650 Billion Drag on the Economy", and the New York Times reported in April 2008 that "E-MAIL has become the bane of some people's professional lives" due to information overload, yet "none of the current wave of high-profile Internet start-ups focused on e-mail really eliminates the problem of e-mail overload because none helps us prepare replies". Technology investors reflect similar concerns.

Spamming and Computer Viruses

The usefulness of e-mail is being threatened by four phenomena: e-mail bombardment, spamming, phishing, and e-mail worms. Spamming is unsolicited commercial (or bulk) e-mail. Because of the very low cost of sending e-mail, spammers can send hundreds of millions of e-mail messages each day over an inexpensive Internet connection. Hundreds of active spammers sending this volume of mail results in information overload for many computer users who receive voluminous unsolicited e-mail each day. E-mail worms use e-mail as a way of replicating themselves into vulnerable computers. Although the first e-mail worm affected UNIX computers, the problem is most common today on the more popular Microsoft Windows operating system. The combination of spam and worm programmes results in users receiving a constant drizzle of junk e-mail, which reduces the usefulness of e-mail as a practical tool.

A number of anti-spam techniques mitigate the impact of spam. In the United States, U.S. Congress has also passed a law, the Can Spam Act of 2003, attempting to regulate such e-mail. Australia also has very strict spam laws restricting the sending of spam from an Australian ISP, but its impact has been minimal since most spam comes from regimes that seem reluctant to regulate the sending of spam.

E-mail Spoofing

E-mail spoofing occurs when the header information of an email is altered to make the message appear to come from a known or trusted source. It is often used as a ruse to collect personal information.

E-mail Bombing

E-mail bombing is the intentional sending of large volumes of messages to a target address. The overloading of the target email address can render it unusable and can even cause the mail server to crash.

Privacy Concerns

E-mail privacy, without some security precautions, can be compromised because:

- e-mail messages are generally not encrypted;
- e-mail messages have to go through intermediate computers before reaching their destination, meaning it is relatively

easy for others to intercept and read messages;

- many Internet Service Providers (ISP) store copies of e-mail messages on their mail servers before they are delivered. The backups of these can remain for up to several months on their server, despite deletion from the mailbox;
- the Received: fields and other information in the e-mail can often identify the sender, preventing anonymous communication.

There are cryptography applications that can serve as a remedy to one or more of the above. For example, Virtual Private Networks or the Tor anonymity network can be used to encrypt traffic from the user machine to a safer network while GPG, PGP, SMEmail, or S/MIME can be used for end-to-end message encryption, and SMTP STARTTLS or SMTP over Transport Layer Security/Secure Sockets Layer can be used to encrypt communications for a single mail hop between the SMTP client and the SMTP server. Additionally, many mail user agents do not protect logins and passwords, making them easy to intercept by an attacker. Encrypted authentication schemes such as SASL prevent this. Finally, attached files share many of the same hazards as those found in peer-to-peer filesharing. Attached files may contain trojans or viruses.

Tracking of Sent Mail

The original SMTP mail service provides limited mechanisms for tracking a transmitted message, and none for verifying that it has been delivered or read. It requires that each mail server must either deliver it onward or return a failure notice (bounce message), but both software bugs and system failures can cause messages to be lost. To remedy this, the IETF introduced Delivery Status Notifications (delivery receipts) and Message Disposition Notifications (return receipts); however, these are not universally deployed in production.

US Government

The US Government has been involved in e-mail in several different ways. Starting in 1977, the US Postal Service (USPS) recognized that electronic mail and electronic transactions posed a significant threat to First Class mail volumes and revenue. Therefore, the USPS initiated an experimental e-mail service known as E-COM. Electronic messages were transmitted to a post office, printed out, and delivered as hard copy. To take advantage of the service, an individual had to transmit at least 200 messages. The delivery time of the messages was the same as First Class mail and cost 26 cents. Both the Postal Regulatory Commission and the Federal Communications Commission opposed E-COM. The FCC concluded that E-COM constituted common carriage under its jurisdiction and the USPS would have to file a tariff. Three years after initiating the service, USPS canceled E-COM and attempted to sell it off.

The early ARPANET dealt with multiple e-mail clients that had various, and at times incompatible, formats. For example, in the system Multics, the "@" sign meant "kill line" and anything after the "@" sign was ignored. The Department of Defence DARPA desired to have uniformity and interoperability for e-mail and therefore funded efforts to drive towards unified interoperable standards. This led to David Crocker, John Vittal, Kenneth Pogran, and Austin Henderson publishing RFC 733, "Standard for the Format of ARPA Network Text Message" (November 21, 1977), which was apparently not effective. In 1979, a meeting was held at BBN to resolve incompatibility issues. Jon Postel recounted the meeting in RFC 808, "Summary of Computer Mail Services Meeting Held at BBN on 10 January 1979" (March 1, 1982), which includes an appendix listing the varying e-mail systems at the time. This, in turn, lead to the release of David Crocker's RFC 822, "Standard for the Format of ARPA Internet Text Messages" (August 13, 1982).

The National Science Foundation took over operations of the ARPANET and Internet from the Department of Defence, and initiated NSFNet, a new backbone for the network. A part of the NSFNet AUP forbade commercial traffic. In 1988, Vint Cerf arranged for an interconnection of MCI Mail with NSFNET on an experimental basis. The following year Compuserve e-mail interconnected with NSFNET. Within a few years the commercial traffic restriction was removed from NSFNETs AUP, and NSFNET was privatized. In the late 1990s, the Federal Trade Commission grew concerned with fraud transpiring in e-mail, and initiated a series of procedures on spam, fraud, and phishing. In 2004, FTC jurisdiction over spam was codified into law in the form of the CAN SPAM Act. Several other US Federal Agencies have also exercised jurisdiction including the Department of Justice and the Secret Service.

Electronic Commerce - Tools

Electronic Commerce is about improving business communications. There is no single solution to implementing Electronic Commerce. Selecting the most effective tool and the best communications channels for your type of business is the key to successful Electronic Commerce.

Types of Electronic Commerce

There are four principal types of Electronic Commerce, although the fourth is only beginning to take shape now. This is happening because of new approaches to marketing on the Internet. The main types are:

- *organisation to consumers* (e.g. a book or video store displaying titles on a website and taking orders for sales; or a travel agent providing information on fares, accommodation and car hire online and providing the facility for clients to make bookings and even pay for them)
- *organisation to organisation* (e.g. order/delivery/payment in a supply chain, such as between BHP and its suppliers). Businesses can now also interact with government agencies more efficiently, through initiatives such as the Business Entry Point, allowing for a reduction in the burden created by regulation.
- *within an organisation* (e.g. Ford and GMH between their divisions and the suppliers of car components, using an Intranet)
- *customer to customer* - variations on the Internet 'news groups' are being created by online services groups (eg Ozemail through online interest groups). These groups may include people with common interests (e.g. golf), a

common need (e.g. hearing impairment) or a common activity (e.g. drive a particular make of car). These customers, or potential customers, will exchange product information and reviews, recommend products and sources of supply, and even assist each other in solving problems.

Communication Channels

Like the four types of Electronic Commerce, there are four communications channels for the delivery of Electronic Commerce services:

- *person to person* (e-mail, phone, fax) contact between organisations and customers or between individuals
- *person to computer* (e-forms, ATM machines, phone banking) used by individuals or individuals in organisations
- *computer to person* (automated e-mail, fax back, and automated invoices) used by organisations to reach individuals
- *computer to computer* (EDI, barcode scanning etc) used between organisations.

Business Processes

Every business uses a similar set of business skills and processes for both buying and selling:

- *identity* – contact with suppliers or customers and marketing products
- *quantity* – demand from customers and supply from related businesses
- *delivery* – delivery and receipt of goods and services, after sales service
- *payment* – obtain payment from customers and pay suppliers

Developing the skills and understanding of what is the best tool and the most effective communications channel for the type of business is the key to the success for any organisation getting started with Electronic Commerce.

Each of the four identified processes may use a different set of tools to best perform the process electronically. For example, new product information may be sent via e-mail, and this may be satisfactory if you have a small group of regular customers. However, if your customer base is limited by their ability to find out about you, presenting the same information on a website will give you far greater marketing 'reach'. To start with you may want to use Electronic Commerce to assist you in marketing, quoting and negotiation, and after sales service, but retain more traditional means of collecting payments.

Electronic Communications

The world of a typical knowledge worker is changing once again. Over the past two decades the technology revolution has broadened access to authoring tools, e-mail and other forms of electronic communication.

While the truly paperless office still has not arrived, business decisions, research and number-crunching activities have all moved into a predominantly online form. Records managers and other information professionals have been playing catch-up over the last decade to ensure that appropriate lifecycle management practices cover electronic as well as paper documents. The next wave of technology change is upon us: the proliferation of new communication methods and the ubiquitous presence of e-mail on a variety of portable devices. This paper will review the technology trends that are accelerating an increasingly decentralized and distributed workforce, and highlight the areas that records managers need to watch most closely.

Mainstream content and document management vendors recognize electronic records management (ERM) as the cornerstone to an enterprise approach to an information management strategy. Larger enterprise content management (ECM) vendors have acquired standalone ERM vendors over the last few years, and this industry consolidation is expected to continue.

The culture of compliance that is permeating information management programmes in corporate and public-sector enterprises has pushed records management practices onto the front burner for the first time. The recent string of financial scandals provoked a wave of legislation aimed at providing more guidance on information handling practices and forced additional accountability onto corporate executives. Records managers have been in the thick of this debate, and industry organizations such as ARMA (www.arma.org) and AIIM (www.aiim.org) have helped move their members into these leadership roles.

While many organizations have begun to review enterprise-wide information management practices, technology continues to move at an accelerating pace.

Organizations with traditionally strong paper record management programmes have begun to apply these principles and lifecycle rules to the electronic documents captured and controlled within their environments. Integrated ERM systems working synchronously with mainstream office applications and electronic document management (EDM) systems are becoming standard applications in law firms, government organizations and many regulated industries. Records managers and information professionals in IT need to continually look forward, and understand where the next source of corporate records will come from.

The E-Mail Problem

E-mail continues to be an area of weakness for many organizations. E-mail is not a new communication platform, but the compliance culture (and recognition that e-mails can have legal standing as records) has put increased pressure on IT and records staffs to ensure that appropriate capture, control and disposal rules are reviewed. Even where a firm has a structured approach to the management of electronic office documents, e-mail often is ignored or left exclusively to the realm of IT control. Organizations can face legal exposure, embarrassment and other forms of risk if e-mail is not managed according to context and content. Many IT departments, when left without guidance, will formulate disposition policies based purely on storage capacity or age of the message.

The sheer volume of incoming and outgoing e-mail is often overwhelming for the records manager to consider. This dilemma will continue to escalate as the proliferation of e-mail-enabled devices grows exponentially. According to research analysts IDC, in the year 2000, e-mail volume reached 9.7 billion per day worldwide, and has been increasing at a rate of approximately 19%, reaching a volume of 16.2 billion e-mail messages in 2002. At that rate, IDC predicts that e-mail volumes reached nearly 21 billion messages per day or about 7.6 trillion e-mail messages for 2003—and that e-mail volume will continue to increase to 60 billion per day in 2006.

Wireless cards in laptops, Blackberry devices, smart phones and other PDAs are moving into the hands of mobile knowledge workers at an accelerating pace and are being used to keep on top of business issues 24/7 while away from the office. The sight of an attorney checking e-mails between appointments at the courthouse, the home office worker with a wireless hub catching up on e-mail from the patio, the field inspector filing reports and photos from the job site: this is the work environment becoming commonplace today. The more easily accessible e-mail becomes, the more consistently it is being used as the dominant form of business communication. But e-mail is only the first wave in facilitating business in a distributed environment. New communication platforms are being adopted across public and private-sector organizations at an increasing rate. Instant messaging, on-line collaboration and threaded discussions, access to corporate portals and intranets from mobile devices: this is the technology shift we see today.

IM: The "New E-Mail"

Instant Messaging (IM) has been called "the new e-mail." What started as a predominantly casual and unmonitored communication tool has evolved into a new and legitimate forum for business communications.

The market is evolving as the technology finds its home within the enterprise. Organizations are beginning to recognize the value of real-time communication and discussion and knowing when key employees are present online and available for queries. Business decisions are now being made in these one-to-one or group chats. More enterprise applications are incorporating IM capabilities into their offerings as a complement to other collaborative and information management offerings. IM is moving into the context of business applications.

What about the corporate records? Since IM has now become an authoring platform for business decisions, records managers need to understand the implications when IT introduces new forums for communication and ensure that key messages and discussions can be captured according to approved record-keeping principles. Records professionals need to be aware of the technology choices facing IT and ensure that systems selected are open to monitoring and easy capture into a managed environment.

Organizations are also investing in secure systems through which to share information and communicate with external stakeholders. Collaborative applications permitting discussion, document authoring and other project-related work allow enterprises to open up selected elements of its information repository to external contractors, suppliers, constituents, customers and other outside contacts. Security is a key requirement when corporate data is selectively shared with external parties and the ability to capture works-in-progress and discussions on shared initiatives also falls under record-keeping requirements. Moving this collaborative...

Voice over Internet Protocol

Voice over Internet Protocol (VoIP) is a general term for a family of transmission technologies for delivery of voice communications over IP networks such as the Internet or other packet-switched networks. Other terms frequently encountered and synonymous with VoIP are IP telephony, Internet telephony, voice over broadband (VoBB), broadband telephony, and broadband phone.

Internet telephony refers to communications services—voice, facsimile, and/or voice-messaging applications—that are transported via the Internet, rather than the public switched telephone network (PSTN). The basic steps involved in originating an Internet telephone call are conversion of the analog voice signal to digital format and compression/translation of the signal into Internet protocol (IP) packets for transmission over the Internet; the process is reversed at the receiving end.

VoIP systems employ session control protocols to control the set-up and tear-down of calls as well as audio codecs which encode speech allowing transmission over an IP network as digital audio via an audio stream. Codec use is varied between different implementations of VoIP (and often a range of codecs are used); some implementations rely on narrowband and compressed speech, while others support high fidelity stereo codecs.

History

- 1974 — The Institute of Electrical and Electronic Engineers (IEEE) published a paper titled "A Protocol for Packet Network Interconnection."
- 1981 — IPv4 is described in RFC 791.
- 1985 — The National Science Foundation commissions the creation of NSFNET.
- 1995 — VocalTec releases the first commercial Internet phone software.
- 1996 —
  - ITU-T begins development of standards for the transmission and signaling of voice communications over Internet Protocol networks with the H.323 standard.
  - US telecommunication companies petition the US Congress to ban Internet phone technology.
- 1997 — Level 3 began development of its first softswitch, a term they coined in 1998.
- 1999 —
  - The Session Initiation Protocol (SIP) specification RFC 2543 is released.
  - Mark Spencer of Digium develops the first open source Private branch exchange (PBX) software (Asterisk).
- 2004 — Commercial VoIP service providers proliferate.
- 2005 — OpenSER (later Kamailio and OpenSIPS) SIP proxy server is forked from the SIP Express Router.
- 2006 — FreeSWITCH open source software is released.

VoIP Technologies and Implementations

Voice-over-IP has been implemented in various ways using both proprietary and open protocols and standards. Examples of technologies used to implement Voice over Internet Protocol include:

- H.323
- IP Multimedia Subsystem (IMS)
- Media Gateway Control Protocol (MGCP)
- Session Initiation Protocol (SIP)
- Real-time Transport Protocol (RTP).

The Session Initiation Protocol has gained wide-spread VoIP market penetration, while H.323 deployments are increasingly limited to carrying existing long-haul network traffic. A notable proprietary implementation is the Skype network. Other examples of specific implementations and a comparison between them are available in Comparison of VoIP software.

Consumer Market

A major development starting in 2004 has been the introduction of mass-market VoIP services over broadband Internet access services, in which subscribers make and receive calls as they would over the PSTN. Full phone service VoIP phone companies provide inbound and outbound calling with Direct Inbound Dialing. Many offer unlimited domestic calling, and some to other countries as well, for a flat monthly fee as well as free calling between subscribers using the same provider. These services have a wide variety of features which can be more or less similar to traditional POTS.

There are three common methods of connecting to VoIP service providers:

- An Analog Telephone Adapter (ATA) may be connected between an IP network (such as a broadband connection) and an existing telephone jack in order to provide service nearly indistinguishable from PSTN providers on all the other telephone jacks in the residence. This type of service, which is fixed to one location, is generally offered by broadband Internet providers such as cable companies and telephone companies as a cheaper flat-rate traditional phone service.

- Dedicated VoIP phones are phones that allow VoIP calls without the use of a computer. Instead they connect directly to the IP network (using technologies such as Wi-Fi or Ethernet). In order to connect to the PSTN they usually require service from a VoIP service provider; most people therefore will use them in conjunction with a paid service plan.
- A softphone (also known as an Internet phone or Digital phone) is a piece of software that can be installed on a computer that allows VoIP calling without dedicated hardware.

Mobile Network Providers

It is becoming increasingly common for telecommunications providers to use VoIP telephony over dedicated and public IP networks to connect switching stations and to interconnect with other telephony network providers; this is often referred to as "IP backhaul". Many telecommunications companies are looking at the IP Multimedia Subsystem (IMS) which will merge Internet technologies with the mobile world, using a pure VoIP infrastructure. It will enable them to upgrade their existing systems while embracing Internet technologies such as the Web, email, instant messaging, presence, and video conferencing. It will also allow existing VoIP systems to interface with the conventional PSTN and mobile phone networks.

"Dual mode" telephone sets, which allow for the seamless handover between a cellular network and a Wi-Fi network, are expected to help VoIP become more popular. Phones such as the NEC N900iL, many of the Nokia Eseries and several other Wi-Fi enabled mobile phones have SIP clients built into the firmware. Such clients operate independently of the mobile phone network (however some operators choose to remove the client from subsidised handsets). Some operators such as Vodafone actively try to block VoIP traffic from their network. Others, like T-Mobile, have refused to interconnect with VoIP-enabled networks as was seen in the legal case between T-Mobile and Truphone, which ultimately was settled in the UK High Court in favour of the VoIP carrier.

Corporate Use

Because of the bandwidth efficiency and low costs that VoIP technology can provide, businesses are gradually beginning to migrate from traditional copper-wire telephone systems to VoIP systems to reduce their monthly phone costs.

VoIP solutions aimed at businesses have evolved into "unified communications" services that treat all communications—phone calls, faxes, voice mail, e-mail, Web conferences and more—as discrete units that can all be delivered via any means and to any handset, including cellphones. Two kinds of competitors are competing in this space: one set is focused on VoIP for medium to large enterprises, while another is targeting the small-to-medium business (SMB) market. VoIP runs both voice and data communications over a single network, which can significantly reduce infrastructure costs.

The prices of extensions on VoIP are lower than for PBXs and key systems. VoIP switches run on commodity hardware, such as PCs or Linux systems. Rather than closed architectures, these devices rely on standard interfaces. VoIP devices have simple, intuitive user interfaces, so users can often make simple system configuration changes. Dual-mode cellphones enable users to continue their conversations as they move between an outside cellular service and an internal Wi-Fi network, so that it is no longer necessary to carry both a desktop phone and a cellphone. Maintenance becomes simpler as there are fewer devices to oversee.

Skype, which originally marketed itself as a service among friends, has begun to cater to businesses, providing free-of-charge connection between any users on the Skype network and connecting to and from ordinary PSTN telephones for a charge. In the United States the Social Security Administration (SSA) is converting its field offices of 63,000 workers from traditional phone installations to a VoIP infrastructure carried over its existing data network.

Operational Cost

VoIP can be a benefit for reducing communication and infrastructure costs. Examples include:

- Routing phone calls over existing data networks to avoid the need for separate voice and data networks.
- Conference calling, IVR, call forwarding, automatic redial, and caller ID features that traditional telecommunication companies (telcos) normally charge extra for are available free of charge from open source VoIP implementations such as Asterisk or FreeSWITCH or TrixBox.
- Costs are lower, mainly because of the way Internet access is billed compared to regular telephone calls. While regular telephone calls are billed by the minute or second, VoIP calls are billed per megabyte (MB). In other words, VoIP calls are billed per amount of *information* (data) sent over the *Internet* and not according to the *time* connected to the telephone network. In practice the amount charged for the data transferred in a given period is far less than that charged for the amount of time connected on a regular telephone line.

Flexibility

VoIP can facilitate tasks and provide services that may be more difficult to implement using the PSTN. Examples include:

- The ability to transmit more than one telephone call over a single broadband connection without the need to add extra lines.
- Secure calls using standardized protocols (such as Secure Real-time Transport Protocol.) Most of the difficulties of creating a secure telephone connection over traditional phone lines, such as digitizing and digital transmission, are already in place with VoIP. It is only necessary to encrypt and authenticate the existing data stream.
- Location independence. Only a sufficiently fast and stable Internet connection is needed to get a connection from anywhere to a VoIP provider.

- Integration with other services available over the Internet, including video conversation, message or data file exchange during the conversation, audio conferencing, managing address books, and passing information about whether other people are available to interested parties.

Quality of Service

Because the underlying IP network is inherently less reliable, in contrast to the circuit-switched public telephone network, and does not provide a mechanism to ensure that data packets are delivered in sequential order, or provide Quality of Service (QoS) guarantees, VoIP implementations may face problems mitigating latency and jitter. Voice, and all other data, travel in packets over IP networks with fixed maximum capacity. This system is more prone to congestion and DoS attacks than traditional circuit switched systems; a circuit switched system of insufficient capacity will refuse new connections while carrying the remainder without impairment, while the quality of real-time data such as telephone conversations on packet-switched networks degrades dramatically.

Fixed delays cannot be controlled (as they are caused by the physical distance the packets travel), however some delays can be minimized by marking voice packets as being delay-sensitive. Fixed delays are especially problematic when satellite circuits are involved, because of long round-trip propagation delay (400–600 milliseconds for links through geostationary satellites). A cause of packet loss and delay is congestion, which can be avoided by means of teletraffic engineering.

The receiving node must restructure IP packets that may be out of order, delayed or missing, while ensuring that the audio stream maintains a proper time consistency. Variation in delay is called jitter. The effects of jitter can be mitigated by storing voice packets in a jitter buffer upon arrival and before producing analog audio, although this further increases delay. This avoids a condition known as buffer underrun, in which the voice engine is missing audio since the next voice packet has not yet arrived. When IP packets are lost or delayed at any point in the network between VoIP users there will be a momentary dropout of voice if all packet delay and loss mechanisms cannot compensate.

It has been suggested to rely on the packetized nature of media in VoIP communications and transmit the stream of packets from the source phone to the destination phone simultaneously across different routes (multi-path routing). In such a way, temporary failures have less impact on the communication quality. In capillary routing it has been suggested to use at the packet level Fountain codes or particularly raptor codes for transmitting extra redundant packets making the communication more reliable.

A number of protocols have been defined to support the reporting of QoS/QoE for VoIP calls. These include RTCP Extended Report (RFC 3611), SIP RTCP Summary Reports, H.460.9 Annex B (for H.323), H.248.30 and MGCP extensions. The RFC 3611 VoIP Metrics block is generated by an IP phone or gateway during a live call and contains information on packet loss rate, packet discard rate (because of jitter), packet loss/discard burst metrics (burst length/density, gap length/density), network delay, end system delay, signal/noise/echo level, Mean Opinion Scores (MOS) and R factors and configuration information related to the jitter buffer.

RFC 3611 VoIP metrics reports are exchanged between IP endpoints on an occasional basis during a call, and an end of call message sent via SIP RTCP Summary Report or one of the other signaling protocol extensions. RFC 3611 VoIP metrics reports are intended to support real time feedback related to QoS problems, the exchange of information between the endpoints for improved call quality calculation and a variety of other applications.

Layer-2 Quality of Service

A number of protocols that deal with the Data link layer and Physical Layer include Quality of Service mechanisms that can be used to ensure that applications like VoIP work well even in congested scenarios. Some examples include:

- IEEE 802.11e is an approved amendment to the IEEE 802.11 standard that defines a set of Quality of Service enhancements for wireless LAN applications through modifications to the Media Access Control (MAC) layer. The standard is considered of critical importance for delay-sensitive applications, such as Voice over Wireless IP.

- IEEE 802.1p defines 8 different classes of service (including one dedicated to voice) for traffic on layer-2 wired Ethernet.
- The ITU-T G.hn standard, which provides a way to create a high-speed (up to 1 gigabit per second) Local area network using existing home wiring (power lines, phone lines and coaxial cables). G.hn provides QoS by means of "Contention-Free Transmission Opportunities" (CFTXOPs) which are allocated to flows (such as a VoIP call) which require QoS and which have negotiated a "contract" with the network controller.

Power Failure

Telephones for traditional residential analog service are usually connected directly to telephone company phone lines which provide direct current to power most basic analog handsets independently of locally available power. IP Phones and VoIP telephone adapters connect to routers or cable modems which typically depend on the availability of mains electricity or locally generated power.

Some VoIP service providers use customer premise equipment (e.g., cablemodems) with battery-backed power supplies to assure uninterrupted service for up to several hours in case of local power failures. Such battery-backed devices typically are designed for use with analog handsets. The susceptibility of phone service to power failures is a common problem even with traditional analog service in areas where many customers purchase modern handset units that operate wirelessly to a base station, or that have other modern phone features, such as built-in voicemail or phone book features.

Emergency Calls

The nature of IP makes it difficult to locate network users geographically. Emergency calls, therefore, cannot easily be routed to a nearby call center. Sometimes, VoIP systems may route emergency calls to a non-emergency phone line at the intended department. In the United States, at least one major police department has strongly objected to this practice as potentially endangering the public.

A fixed line phone has a direct relationship between a telephone number and a physical location. A telephone number represents one pair of wires that links a location to the telephone company's exchange. Once a line is connected, the telephone company stores the home address that relates to the wires, and this relationship will rarely change. If an emergency call comes from that number, then the physical location is known.

In the IP world, it is not so simple. A broadband provider may know the location where the wires terminate, but this does not necessarily allow the mapping of an IP address to that location. IP addresses are often dynamically assigned, so the ISP may allocate an address for online access, or at the time a broadband router is engaged. The ISP recognizes individual IP addresses, but does not necessarily know what physical location to which it corresponds. The broadband service provider knows the physical location, but is not necessarily tracking the IP addresses in use.

There are more complications, since IP allows a great deal of mobility. For example, a broadband connection can be used to dial a virtual private network that is employer-owned. When this is done, the IP address being used will belong to the range of the employer, rather than the address of the ISP, so this could be many kilometres away or even in another country.

To provide another example: if mobile data is used, *e.g.*, a 3G mobile handset or USB wireless broadband adapter, then the IP address has no relationship with any physical location, since a mobile user could be anywhere that there is network coverage, even roaming via another cellular company. In short, there is no relationship between IP address and physical location, so the address itself reveals no useful information for the emergency services.

At the VoIP level, a phone or gateway may identify itself with a SIP registrar by using a username and password. So in this case, the Internet Telephony Service Provider (ITSP) knows that a particular user is online, and can relate a specific telephone number to the user. However, it does not recognize how that IP traffic was engaged. Since the IP address itself does not necessarily provide location information presently, today a "best efforts" approach is to use an available database to find that user and the physical address the user chose to associate with that telephone number—clearly an imperfect solution. VoIP Enhanced 911 (E911) is another method by which VoIP providers in the United States are able to support emergency services. The VoIP E911 emergency-calling system associates a physical address with the calling party's telephone number as required by the Wireless Communications and Public Safety Act of 1999. All "interconnected" VoIP providers (those that provide access to the PSTN system) are required to have E911 available to their customers. VoIP E911 service generally adds an additional monthly fee to the subscriber's service per line, similar to analog phone service. Participation in E911 is not required and customers can opt-out or disable E911 service on their VoIP lines, if desired. VoIP E911 has been successfully used by many VoIP providers to provide physical address information to emergency service operators.

One shortcoming of VoIP E911 is that the emergency system is based on a static table lookup. Unlike in cellular phones, where the location of an E911 call can be traced using Assisted GPS or other methods, the VoIP E911 information is only accurate so long as subscribers are diligent in keeping their emergency address information up-to-date. In the United States, the Wireless Communications and Public Safety Act of 1999 leaves the burden of responsibility upon the subscribers and not the service providers to keep their emergency information up to date.

Lack of Redundancy

With the current separation of the Internet and the PSTN, a certain amount of redundancy is provided. An Internet outage does not necessarily mean that a voice communication outage will occur simultaneously, allowing individuals to call for emergency services and many businesses to continue to operate normally. In situations where telephone services become completely reliant on the Internet infrastructure, a single-point failure can isolate communities from all communication, including Enhanced 911 and equivalent services in other locales.

Number Portability

Local number portability (LNP) and Mobile number portability (MNP) also impact VoIP business. In November 2007, the Federal Communications Commission in the United States released an order extending number portability obligations to interconnected VoIP providers and carriers that support VoIP providers. Number portability is a service that allows a subscriber to select a new telephone carrier without requiring a new number to be issued. Typically, it is the responsibility of the former carrier to "map" the old number to the undisclosed number assigned by the new carrier. This is achieved by maintaining a database of numbers. A dialed number is initially received by the original carrier and quickly rerouted to the new carrier. Multiple porting references must be maintained even if the subscriber returns to the original carrier. The FCC mandates carrier compliance with these consumer-protection stipulations.

A voice call originating in the VoIP environment also faces challenges to reach its destination if the number is routed to a mobile phone number on a traditional mobile carrier. VoIP has been identified in the past as a Least Cost Routing (LCR) system, which is based on checking the destination of each telephone call as it is made, and then sending the call via the network that will cost the customer the least. This rating is subject to some debate given the complexity of call routing created by number portability. With GSM number portability now in place, LCR providers can no longer rely on using the network root prefix to determine how to route a call. Instead, they must now determine the actual network of every number before routing the call.

Therefore, VoIP solutions also need to handle MNP when routing a voice call. In countries without a central database, like the UK, it might be necessary to query the GSM network about which home network a mobile phone number belongs to. As the popularity of VoIP increases in the enterprise markets because of least cost routing options, it needs to provide a certain level of reliability when handling calls. MNP checks are important to assure that this quality of service is met. By handling MNP lookups before routing a call and by assuring that the voice call will actually work, VoIP service providers are able to offer business subscribers the level of reliability they require. In countries such as Singapore, the most recent Mobile number portability solution is expected to open the doors to new business opportunities for non-traditional telecommunication service providers like wireless broadband providers and voice over IP (VoIP) providers..

PSTN integration

E.164 is a global numbering standard for both the PSTN and PLMN. Most VoIP implementations support E.164 to allow calls to be routed to and from VoIP subscribers and the PSTN/PLMN. VoIP implementations can also allow other identification techniques to be used. For example, Skype allows subscribers to choose "Skype names" (usernames) whereas SIP implementations can use URIs similar to email addresses. Often VoIP implementations employ methods of translating non-E.164 identifiers to E.164 numbers and vice-versa, such as the Skype-In service provided by Skype and the ENUM service in IMS and SIP. Echo can also be an issue for PSTN integration. Common causes of echo include impedance mismatches in analog circuitry and acoustic coupling of the transmit and receive signal at the receiving end.

Security

Voice over Internet Protocol telephone systems (VoIP) are susceptible to attacks as are any internet-connected devices. This means that hackers who know about these vulnerabilities can institute denial-of-service attacks, harvest customer data, record conversations and break into voice mailboxes. Another challenge is routing VoIP traffic through firewalls and network address translators. Private Session Border Controllers are used along with firewalls to enable VoIP calls to and from protected networks. Skype uses a proprietary protocol to route calls through other Skype peers on the network, allowing it to traverse symmetric NATs and firewalls. Other methods to traverse NATs involve using protocols such as STUN or ICE.

Many consumer VoIP solutions do not support encryption, although having a secure phone is much easier to implement with

VoIP than traditional phone lines. As a result, it is relatively easy to eavesdrop on VoIP calls and even change their content. An attacker with a packet sniffer could intercept your VoIP calls if you are not on a secure VLAN. There are open source solutions, such as Wireshark, that facilitate sniffing of VoIP conversations. A modicum of security is afforded by patented audio codecs in proprietary implementations that are not easily available for open source applications, however such security through obscurity has not proven effective in other fields. Some vendors also use compression to make eavesdropping more difficult. However, real security requires encryption and cryptographic authentication which are not widely supported at a consumer level. The existing security standard Secure Real-time Transport Protocol (SRTP) and the new ZRTP protocol are available on Analog Telephone Adapters(ATAs) as well as various softphones. It is possible to use IPsec to secure P2P VoIP by using opportunistic encryption. Skype does not use SRTP, but uses encryption which is transparent to the Skype provider. In 2005, Skype invited a researcher, Dr Tom Berson, to assess the security of the Skype software, and his conclusions are available in a published report. The Voice VPN solution provides secure voice for enterprise VoIP networks by applying IPSec encryption to the digitized voice stream.

Securing VoIP

To prevent the above security concerns the government and military organizations are using; Voice over Secure IP (VoSIP), Secure Voice over IP (SVoIP), and Secure Voice over Secure IP (SVoSIP) to protect confidential, and/or classified VoIP communications. Secure Voice over IP is accomplished by encrypting VoIP with Type 1 encryption. Secure Voice over Secure IP is accomplished by using Type 1 encryption on a classified network, like SIPRNet. Public Secure VoIP is also available with free GNU programmes.

Caller ID

Caller ID support among VoIP providers varies, although the majority of VoIP providers now offer full Caller ID with name on outgoing calls. In a few cases, VoIP providers may allow a caller to spoof the Caller ID information, potentially making calls appear as though they are from a number that does not belong to the caller Business grade VoIP equipment and software often makes it easy to modify caller ID information. Although this can provide many businesses great flexibility, it is also open to abuse.

The "Truth in Caller ID Act" has been in preparation in the US Congress since 2006, but as of January 2009 still has not been enacted. This bill proposes to make it a crime in the United States to "knowingly transmit misleading or inaccurate caller identification information with the intent to defraud, cause harm, or wrongfully obtain anything of value ..."

Compatibility

Some analog telephone adapters do not decode pulse dialing from older phones. The VoIP user may use a pulse-to-tone converter, if needed.

Fax Handling

Support for sending faxes over VoIP implementations is still limited. The existing voice codecs are not designed for fax transmission; they are designed to digitize an analog representation of a human voice efficiently. However, the inefficiency of digitizing an analog representation (modem signal) of a digital representation (a document image) of analog data (an original document) more than negates any bandwidth advantage of VoIP. In other words, the fax "sounds" simply don't fit in the VoIP channel. An alternative IP-based solution for delivering fax-over-IP called T.38 is available.

The T.38 protocol is designed to work like a traditional fax machine and can work using several configurations. The fax machine could be a traditional fax machine connected to the PSTN, or an ATA box (or similar). It could be a fax machine with an RJ-45 connector plugged straight into an IP network, or it could be a computer pretending to be a fax machine. Originally, T.38 was designed to use UDP and TCP transmission methods across an IP network. The main difference between using UDP and TCP methods for a FAX is the real time streaming attributes. TCP is better suited for use between two IP devices. However, older fax machines, connected to an analog system, benefit from UDP near real-time characteristics.

There have been updated versions of T.30 to resolve the fax over IP issues, which is the core fax protocol. Some new fax machines have T.38 built-in capabilities which allow the user to plug right into the network with minimal configuration changes. A unique feature of T.38 is that each packet contains a copy of the main data in the previous packet.

This is an option and most implementations seem to support it. This forward error correction scheme makes T.38 far more tolerant of dropped packets than VoIP. With T.38, two successive lost packets are needed to actually lose any data. The data you lose will only be a small piece, but with the right settings and error correction mode, there is a high probability that you will receive the whole transmission.

Tweaking the settings on the T.30 and T.38 protocols could also turn your unreliable fax into a robust machine. Some fax machines pause at the end of a line to allow the paper feed to catch up. This is good news for packets that were lost or delayed because it gives them a chance to catch up. However, were this to happen on every line, your fax transmittal would take a long time. Another possible solution is to treat the fax system as a message switching system, which does not need a real-time data transmission. The end system can completely buffer the incoming fax data before displaying or printing the fax image.

Telephony Devices

Another challenge for VoIP implementations is the proper handling of outgoing calls from other telephony devices such as DVR boxes, satellite television receivers, alarm systems, conventional modems and other similar devices that depend on access to a PSTN telephone line for some or all of their functionality. These types of calls sometimes complete without any problems, but in other cases they fail. If VoIP and cellular substitution becomes very popular, some ancillary equipment makers may be forced to redesign equipment, because it would no longer be possible to assume a conventional PSTN telephone line would be available in consumer's homes.

Legal Issues

As the popularity of VoIP grows, and PSTN users switch to VoIP in increasing numbers, governments are becoming more interested in regulating VoIP in a manner similar to PSTN services,. Another legal issue that the US Congress is debating concerns changes to the Foreign Intelligence Surveillance Act. The issue in question is calls between Americans and foreigners. The National Security Agency (NSA) isn't authorized to tap Americans' conversations without a warrant—but the Internet, and specifically voice over Internet protocol, or VoIP, doesn't draw as clear a line to the location of a caller or a call's recipient as the traditional phone system does. As VoIP's low cost and flexibility convinces more and more organizations to adopt the technology, the line separating the NSA's ability to snoop on phone calls will only get blurrier. VoIP technology has also increased security concerns because VoIP and similar technologies have made it more difficult for the government to determine where a target is physically located when communications are being intercepted, and that creates a whole set of new legal challenges.

In the US, the Federal Communications Commission now requires all interconnected VoIP service providers to comply with requirements comparable to those for traditional telecommunications service providers. VoIP operators in the US are required to support local number portability; make service accessible to people with disabilities; pay regulatory fees, universal service contributions, and other mandated payments; and enable law enforcement authorities to conduct surveillance pursuant to the Communications Assistance for Law Enforcement Act (CALEA). "Interconnected" VoIP operators also must provide Enhanced 911 service, disclose any limitations on their E-911 functionality to their consumers, and obtain affirmative acknowledgements of these disclosures from all consumers. VoIP operators also receive the benefit of certain US telecommunications regulations, including an entitlement to interconnection and exchange of traffic with incumbent local exchange carriers via wholesale carriers. Providers of "nomadic" VoIP service — those who are unable to determine the location of their users — are exempt from state telecommunications regulation.

Throughout the developing world, countries where regulation is weak or captured by the dominant operator, restrictions on the use of VoIP are imposed, including in Panama where VoIP is taxed, Guyana where VoIP is prohibited and India where its retail commercial sales is allowed but only for long distance service. In Ethiopia, where the government is monopolizing telecommunication service, it is a criminal offense to offer services using VoIP. The country has installed firewalls to prevent international calls being made using VoIP. These measures were taken after a popularity in VoIP reduced the income generated by the state owned telecommunication company.

In the European Union, the treatment of VoIP service providers is a decision for each Member State's national telecoms regulator, which must use competition law to define relevant national markets and then determine whether any service provider on those national markets has "significant market power" (and so should be subject to certain obligations). A general distinction is usually made between VoIP services that function over managed networks (via broadband connections) and VoIP services that function over unmanaged networks (essentially, the Internet).

VoIP services that function over managed networks are often considered to be a viable substitute for PSTN telephone services (despite the problems of power outages and lack of geographical information); as a result, major operators that provide these services (in practice, incumbent operators) may find themselves bound by obligations of price control or accounting separation.

VoIP services that function over unmanaged networks are often considered to be too poor in quality to be a viable substitute for PSTN services; as a result, they may be provided without any specific obligations, even if a service provider has "significant market power".

The relevant EU Directive is not clearly drafted concerning obligations which can exist independently of market power (e.g., the obligation to offer access to emergency calls), and it is impossible to say definitively whether VoIP service providers of either type are bound by them. A review of the EU Directive is under way and should be complete by 2007.

In India, it is legal to use VoIP, but it is illegal to have VoIP gateways inside India. This effectively means that people who have PCs can use them to make a VoIP call to any number, but if the remote side is a normal phone, the gateway that converts the VoIP call to a POTS call should not be inside India.

In the UAE, it is illegal to use any form of VoIP, to the extent that Web sites of Skype and Gizmo5 are blocked.

In the Republic of Korea, only providers registered with the government are authorized to offer VoIP services. Unlike many VoIP providers, most of whom offer flat rates, Korean VoIP services are generally metered and charged at rates similar to terrestrial calling. Foreign VoIP providers such as Vonage encounter high barriers to government registration. This issue came to a head in 2006 when Internet service providers providing personal Internet services by contract to United States Forces Korea members residing on USFK bases threatened to block off access to VoIP services used by USFK members of as an economical way to keep in contact with their families in the United States, on the grounds that the service members' VoIP providers were not registered. A compromise was reached between USFK and Korean telecommunications officials in January 2007, wherein USFK service members arriving in Korea before June 1, 2007 and subscribing to the ISP services provided on base may continue to use their US-based VoIP subscription, but later arrivals must use a Korean-based VoIP provider, which by contract will offer pricing similar to the flat rates offered by US VoIP providers.

International VoIP Implementation

IP Telephony in Japan

In Japan, IP telephony is regarded as a service applied by VoIP technology to the whole or a part of the telephone line. As of 2003, IP telephony services have been assigned telephone numbers. IP telephony services also often include videophone/

video conferencing services. According to the Telecommunication Business Law, the service category for IP telephony also implies the service provided via Internet, which is not assigned any telephone number. IP telephony is basically regulated by Ministry of Internal Affairs and Communications (MIC) as a telecommunication service. The operators have to disclose necessary information on its quality, etc., prior to making contracts with customers, and have an obligation to respond to their complaints cordially. Many Japanese Internet service providers (ISP) are including IP telephony services. An ISP who also provides IP telephony service is known as a "ITSP (Internet Telephony Service Provider)". Recently, the competition among ITSPs has been activated, by option or set sales, in connection with ADSL or FTTH services. The tariff system normally applied to Japanese IP telephony is described below;

- A call between IP telephony subscribers, limited to the same group, is usually free of charge.
- A call from IP telephony subscribers to a fixed line or PHS is usually a uniformly fixed rate all over the country.

Between ITSPs, the interconnection is mostly maintained at VoIP level.

- Where the IP telephony is assigned normal telephone number (0AB-J), the condition for its interconnection is considered same as normal telephony.
- Where the IP telephony is assigned specific telephone number (050), the condition for its interconnection is described below;
    - Interconnection is sometimes charged. (Sometimes, it is free of charge.) In case of free-of-charge, mostly, communication traffic is exchanged via a P2P connection with the same VoIP standard. Otherwise, certain conversions are needed at the point of the VoIP gateway which incurs operating costs.

Since September 2002, the MIC has assigned IP telephony telephone numbers on the condition that the service falls into certain required categories of quality. High-quality IP telephony is assigned a telephone number, normally starting with the digits 050. When VoIP quality is so high that a customer has difficulty telling the difference between it and a normal telephone, and when the provider relates its number with a location and provides the connection with emergency call capabilities, the provider is allowed to assign a normal telephone number, which is a so-called "0AB-J" number.

Bibliography

Borcherding, K., : *Contemporary Issues in Decision Making,* Amsterdam, North-Holland, 1990.

Carey, W.: *Public Opinion and the Communication of Consent,* New York: Guilford Publications, 1995.

Cootner, Paul : *The Random Character of Stock Market Prices,* MIT Press, 1964.

Desmond, Glenn, and John A, Marcell, *Handbook of Small Business Valuation Formulas and Rules of Thumb,* Valuation Press, 1993.

Gitman, Lawrence J.: *Principles of Managerial Finance,* MA: Addison Wesley Longman, 2000.

Gowdy, J., *Coevolution Economics: The Economy, Society and the Environment,* Kluwer, Boston, 1994.

Harrigan, K. R.: *Strategies for Declining Businesses.* Lexington, MA: Heath, 1980

Johnson, Hazel: *Financial Institutions and Markets: A Global Perspective,* NY, McGraw Hill, 1993.

Knapp, C. L.: *Commercial Damages, A Guide to Remedies in Business Litigation,* Matthew Bender, 1993.

Meyer, M. W.: *Theory of Organizational Structure,* Indianapolis, 1977.

Petty, Keown, Scott, and Martin: *Basic Financial Management,* Prentice Hall, 1993.

Primrose, S.B.: *Business Communication Management,* London, Blackwell Scientific Publications, 1989.

Rifkin, Jeremy: *Introduction to Business*, New York, Penguin Putnam, 1998

Schall and Haley: *Introduction to Financial Communication Management*, McGraw-Hill, 1988.

Taylor, F. W.: *The Principles of Scientific Management*, New York, 1917.

Vallette, J.: *A Handbook of Business Communcation*, Washington, Greenpeace, 1989.

Index